Praise for *The Writing R*

"For years, I have recommended *The Writing Revolution* for the following reasons: powerful sequencing from sentence to composition, skills broken down into obtainable chunks, explicit, systematic instruction, writing assignments connected to class content, and focus on planning and revising. Teachers are supported and students emerge as writers. *The Writing Revolution* truly makes a difference, so schools, teachers, and students should follow this road map to excellence."

— **Anita Archer**, author of *Explicit Instruction: Effective and Efficient Teaching*

"The impact of *The Writing Revolution,* which has expanded our understanding of how writing builds knowledge and taught us how to embed great writing lessons into daily instruction across content areas, has been profound. When Judith Hochman, Natalie Wexler, and Kathleen Maloney think there's more to say about how we produce strong writers, educators need to stop and listen. Drawing on thousands of hours of onsite work with teachers, *The Writing Revolution 2.0* is a testament to the authors' belief that good writing instruction is within the grasp of all teachers and that, indeed, it must be their charge."

— **Barbara Davidson**, president of StandardsWork, Inc., and executive director of the Knowledge Matters Campaign

"We've been inspired by the practical approach of the Hochman Method for over three decades and so have the many teachers we've shared it with. We couldn't be happier about this second edition since the practices laid out so clearly in this book will make every student exposed to them a more supple and lucid writer."

— **David and Meredith Liben**, Reading Done Right, authors of *Know Better, Do Better: Comprehension*

"This guide needs to be on every educator's bookshelf! Grounded in *The Writing Revolution*'s research on writing instruction, this supremely practical book provides teachers, administrators, and other practitioners with a robust guide for building students' writing ability and knowledge. This book is the best tool a teacher can keep in their toolkit."

— **Esther Klein Friedman**, PhD, executive director of Literacy and Academic Intervention (retired), New York City Department of Education; literacy learning specialist

"As a principal, it was clear that students in my elementary school needed an organized system of instruction to improve their writing. My team of teachers fully embraced the Hochman Method and enjoyed collaboratively learning and planning writing lessons using the multiple reources provided in *The Writing Revolution*. Every principal and teacher should make it a priority to utilize the latest edition to advance their knowledge and understanding of how to effectively teach writing. Your students will develop a love of writing that will last a lifetime."

— **Gwendolyn Payton**, instructional superintendent, DCPS

"*The Writing Revolution 2.0* provides teachers with powerful strategies to embed explicit writing instruction into the content of the curriculum. These strategies equip children with the tools they need to be confident writers while also developing their comprehension and critical thinking skills."

—**Lori D'Andrea**, literacy specialist, Greenburgh Central School District

"For many Australian teachers, *The Writing Revolution* has, like no other resource, raised their knowledge and provided educators with the tools they need. I observe the impact of this instruction on the quality of writing produced by students in settings ranging from remote communities to large metropolitan areas."

—**Dr. Lorraine Hammond**, AM, professional learning and instructional coach, associate professor at Elizabeth Cowan University, School of Education, Australia

"The first edition of *The Writing Revolution* was a landmark publication. Not only was it packed with brilliant classroom techniques, its focus on sentence-level activities changed the way many people thought about teaching writing. The second edition has even more examples taken from the extensive work the authors have done in so many schools and includes important updates about assessment and comparative judgment. It is a must-read for anyone involved with teaching writing."

—**Daisy Christodoulou**, director of education, No More Marking

"*The Writing Revolution* transformed my thinking about the power of writing and how it can improve outcomes for students in all content areas. As a former STEM teacher and school and system leader, I am grateful that the authors have brought the science of writing so effectively to classrooms."

—**Jean-Claude Brizard**, president and CEO, Digital Promise Global

"Teachers, district leaders, superintendents, and stakeholders—anyone who wishes to witness the transformative power of content-embedded explicit writing instruction—will benefit exponentially from *The Writing Revolution 2.0*. When it's fully embraced and taught campus-wide, even the hardest-to-reach subgroups succeed, prosper, and excel, acquiring the tools and strategies they need to write well!"

—**Serena White**, interim superintendent of Monroe City Schools

"Simple and brilliant. Practical and insightful. *The Writing Revolution 2.0* is canon in how to teach the structures of writing while enabling students to express their individual identities."

—**Anthony Cosentino Jr.**, principal, Public School 21—The Margaret P. Emery Elm Park School

The Writing Revolution 2.0

The Writing Revolution 2.0

A GUIDE TO ADVANCING THINKING THROUGH

WRITING IN ALL SUBJECTS AND GRADES

Judith C Hochman
Natalie Wexler

WITH Kathleen Maloney

FOREWORD BY Doug Lemov

JB JOSSEY-BASS
A Wiley Brand

Jossey-Bass, a Wiley brand
Published by John Wiley & Sons, Inc., Hoboken, New Jersey.
Published simultaneously in Canada.

ISBNs: 9781394182039 (paperback), 9781394359905 (spiral bound), 9781394182046 (ePDF), 9781394182053 (ePub)

For general information on our other products and services or for technical support, please contact our Customer Care Department within the United States at (800) 762-2974, outside the United States at (317) 572-3993 or fax (317) 572-4002.

Wiley also publishes its books in a variety of electronic formats. Some content that appears in print may not be available in electronic formats. For more information about Wiley products, visit our web site at www.wiley.com.

Library of Congress Cataloging-in-Publication Data
Names: Hochman, Judith, author. | Wexler, Natalie, author.
Title: The writing revolution 2.0 : a guide to advancing thinking through writing in all subjects and grades / Judith C. Hochman, Natalie Wexler.
Description: San Francisco : Jossey-Bass, 2024. | Includes bibliographical references and index.
Identifiers: LCCN 2024007513 (print) | LCCN 2024007514 (ebook) | ISBN 9781394182039 (paperback) | ISBN 9781394359905 (spiral bound) | ISBN 9781394182046 (adobe pdf) | ISBN 9781394182053 (epub)
Subjects: LCSH: Report writing—Study and teaching. | Critical thinking—Study and teaching. | Composition (Language arts)—Study and teaching.
Classification: LCC LB1047.3 .H633 2024 (print) | LCC LB1047.3 (ebook) | DDC 808/.0427—dc23/eng/20240314
LC record available at https://lccn.loc.gov/2024007513
LC ebook record available at https://lccn.loc.gov/2024007514

Cover Design: Wiley
Cover Image: © Jeni Iv/Shutterstock; © chrupka/Shutterstock
Author Photos: (Hochman) Photo by Todd France Photography,
(Wexler) Photo by Nina Subin, (Maloney) Photo by Todd France Photography

SKY10098494_021725

Contents

Appendixes

To Toni-Ann Vroom and Dina Zoleo, for their unwavering dedication and outstanding leadership in the dissemination and implementation of the Hochman Method.

Acknowledgments

First and foremost, we want to acknowledge the co–chief executive officers of The Writing Revolution, Dr. Dina Zoleo and Dr. Toni-Ann Vroom. Together with team members Christine Teahan, Alexandria Chalonec, and Tania Hasselwander-Chang, they read the manuscript multiple times, displayed endless patience, and made excellent suggestions based on their experience training teachers in the Hochman Method and working with schools that are using it. We are forever grateful for their cooperation and talent.

The TWR courses and its Resource Library, created by members of the TWR team, supplied us with many of the materials we used to illustrate the strategies and activities in this book.

We also learned a great deal directly from educators who have implemented the Hochman Method. Reviewing assessments, visiting schools, listening to teachers and administrators, and looking at countless activities based on TWR strategies helped inform many of the changes in the second edition. Teachers throughout the United States and beyond shared their work, asked questions, and made suggestions that were invaluable in adding to our knowledge about effective writing instruction.

We owe debts of gratitude to several other individuals. Our editor at Jossey-Bass, Amy Fandrei, was supportive, responsive, and patient throughout the process. Maureen Forys helped us immeasurably with the design of the book, and her guidance and positive attitude inspired us throughout the process. Rachel Monaghan's editing and guidance were indispensable. Djamika Smith, TWR's associate creative director, was an important contributor to the book-designing process. Robyn Travers's experience teaching the Hochman Method for many years made her an excellent resource for editing expertise and feedback.

Last, but not least, we appreciate the support of our families and friends and their recognition that our mission is an important one. In particular, two of us—Judith Hochman and Natalie Wexler—owe a deep debt of thanks to our husbands, Steve Hochman and Jim Feldman, for their support.

About the Authors

Judith C. Hochman is the founder of The Writing Revolution, a not-for-profit organization serving educators both in the United States and internationally. She is the former superintendent of the Greenburgh Graham Union Free School District in Hastings, New York, and the head of The Windward School in White Plains, New York. Dr. Hochman is the founder of the Windward Teacher Training Institute and the author of many articles and books on the topic of writing.

Natalie Wexler is the author of *The Knowledge Gap: The Hidden Cause of America's Broken Education System—and How to Fix It* (Avery 2019). She has a Substack newsletter, *Minding the Gap*, and her writing on education has appeared in the *Atlantic*, the *Washington Post*, the *New York Times*, and other publications. She was the host of the first season of the *Knowledge Matters* podcast, a six-episode series called *Reading Comprehension Revisited*.

Kathleen Maloney is the chief operating officer of The Writing Revolution, where she brings her passion for literacy and experience in education to her role, overseeing the organization's daily operations and strategizing its future direction in collaboration with the co-CEOs. Before joining the team, as an English teacher and literacy coach, she used the Hochman Method in her own classroom and led its schoolwide implementation.

Foreword

Judith Hochman and Natalie Wexler's *The Writing Revolution* is a timeless book that is grounded in practical wisdom, refined by application in thousands of classrooms, and supported by learning science. It meticulously describes how to effectively teach a skill that is, and will always be, profoundly important to students. It's a book that stands the test of time.

Perhaps fittingly, this foreword, originally published in the first edition of the book, remains as relevant to me now as it was when I first wrote it. It is a personal reflection of encountering many of the ideas in *The Writing Revolution* and testing them with my own children. Every application of the principles within the book reaffirms their enduring value.

I am not alone in my high regard for this book. Since its publication, hundreds of thousands of teachers have read and used it with great success. It has, honestly, become something of a sensation.

However, while the book remains timeless, the world—both in society at large and within schools—has been rapidly changing. Recognizing this, and in light of Hochman and Wexler's dedication to updating the entire text, I will add a few new thoughts of my own at the end of the original foreword.

A few years ago our family spent a couple of months in London. My kids were thirteen, eleven, and six at the time, and I had work there, so we decided to take the once-in-a-lifetime opportunity to live in one of the world's great capitals. We paid regular visits to the British Museum, combed through the food stalls at Borough Market, and traced on foot the remains of the city's medieval wall. There were day trips to Bath and Cambridge. We even had a *local*—pub, that is, which really should go without saying.

It was an incredible experience, thanks in no small part to what I learned at a lunch I had with one of the authors of this book before we left. I'd read an article about Judith Hochman's work at New Dorp High School in the *Atlantic* a year or two before, and it had stayed with me. Hochman espoused embedding writing instruction in content. She thought sentences were overlooked and rarely taught. She thought syntax—"syntactic control"—was the link to unlock the connection between better writing and better reading. She believed in the power of deliberate practice to build reading skills. Her work was technical and granular. And the results were hard to ignore. It was the kind of thing I was drawn to.

A friend had connected us and I drove down to meet her—with what soon revealed itself as her typical graciousness, she had invited me to her home near New York City—and the result was one of the most memorable days of my working life. I remember scratching notes furiously on page after page of my notebook, trying to capture everything she observed—about writing, its connection to reading and thinking, and why so many kids struggled to learn it. Over and over Hochman would hit on an idea that had been swirling in my head in inchoate wisps and put it into a clear, logical formulation of practice. Here was the idea you were fumbling with, described perfectly; here was how you'd make it work.

I couldn't write fast enough, but I remember thinking that when I got home, I would read everything she'd written. This, however, turned out to be the only disappointment. There wasn't, until now, any place where the ideas Hochman had talked about were written down in one cohesive place for a reader like me. I was left with the observations in my notebook, the hope that Hochman would someday write the book you are now holding, and her sentence expansion activities.

It was these activities that were the gift that transformed our trip to London. Hochman had spent about twenty minutes riffing on the idea the day we met. The sentence was the building block of writing and thinking, the "complete thought," we agreed, but if you looked at the complete thoughts students produced in their writing, they were too often wooden, repetitive, inflexible. If the task of wrestling ideas into written words was to memorialize thinking, students—at least most of them—did not often have control of a sufficient number of syntactic forms and tools to capture and express complex thoughts. They could not express two ideas happening at once, with one predominating over the other. They could not express a thought interrupted by a sudden alternative thesis. Their ideas were poor on paper because their sentences could not capture, connect, and, ultimately, develop them. That last part was the most damning of all. One way to generate complex ideas is to write them into being—often slowly adding and reworking and refining, as I find myself doing now as I draft and revise this foreword for the tenth or twentieth or one hundredth time. Because students could not say what they meant, and because, as a result, they did not practice capturing and connecting complex ideas with precision in writing, they had fewer complex ideas. Or they had ideas like the sentences they wrote: predictable, neither compound nor complex. What might have been a skein of thought was instead a litter of short broken threads, each with a subject-verb-object construction.

Hochman's solution was regular intentional exercises to expand students' syntactic range. You could ask students to practice expanding their sentences in specific and methodical ways, and they'd get better at it. Crucially, she pointed out, this must be done in a content-rich environment because "the content drives the rigor." Sentences need ideas pressing outward from inside them to stretch and expand their limits. Only rich content gives them a reason to seek and achieve nuance.

One example of a Hochman sentence expansion exercise was called *because-but-so.* The idea was deceptively simple: you gave students a sentence stem and then asked them to expand it three different ways—with the common conjunctions *because, but,* and *so.* This would help them to see each sentence as constantly expandable. And it would, as Hochman writes in this book, "prod them to think critically and deeply about the content they were studying—far more so than if you simply asked them to write a sentence in answer to an open-ended question." It would build their ability to conjoin ideas with fluidity. It would help them to understand, through constant theme and variation, the broader concepts of subordination and coordination.

I want to pause here to digress on the seemingly underwhelming concepts of coordination and subordination. I will ask you to stifle your yawn as I acknowledge that they are easy to dismiss—ancient, faintly risible, uttered once long ago by acolytes of sentence diagramming in the era of chalk dust. They smack of grammar for grammar's sake, and almost nobody cares about that. Teachers instead seek mostly to make sure the sentences work and dispense with the parsing of parts. It is so much simpler to tell kids to go with "sounds right" (an idea that inherently discriminates against those for whom the sounds of language are not happily ingrained by luck or privilege) or to make the odd episodic correction and not worry about the principle at work.

But coordination and subordination are in fact deeply powerful principles worth mastering. They describe the ways that ideas are connected, the nuances that yoke disparate thoughts together. It is the connections as much as the ideas that make meaning. To master conjunctions is to be able to express that two ideas are connected but that one is more important than the other, that one is dependent on the other, that one is contingent on the other, that the two ideas exist in contrast or conflict. Mastering that skill is immensely important not just to writing but to reading. Students who struggle with complex text can usually understand the words and clauses of a sentence; it is the piecing together of the interrelationships among them that most often poses the problem. They understand the first half of the sentence but miss the cue that questions its veracity in the second half. And so without mastery of the syntax of relationships, which is what coordination and subordination are, the sentence devolves—for weak readers—into meaninglessness.

For weeks I reflected on the power of these simple activities for teachers and students, but my reflections were not limited to my role as an educator. As a father I was intrigued as well, and I suppose this is the truest test of an educational idea.

Fast-forward to London some months later, where I found myself for three months essentially homeschooling the Lemov children, those regular and long-suffering subjects of a thousand of their father's teaching ideas. To keep them writing and thinking I had them keep journals, and in those journals I found myself using and adapting Hochman's exercises. They were the perfect tidy-wrap summation to a long day out exploring.

Here are some early *because-but-so* exercises I rediscovered a few weeks ago in my then eleven-year-old daughter's journal.

I gave her the sentence stem: "The Great Fire of London burned 4/5 of the city . . ."

She wrote:

> The Great Fire of London burned 4/5 of the city, because *at the time, citizens didn't have the knowledge or equipment to stop the fire before it spread.*

> The Great Fire of London burned 4/5 of the city, but *London survived and thrived.*

> The Great Fire of London burned 4/5 of the city, so *many people had to live in temporary homes until the city was rebuilt.*

After a visit to the Museum of Natural History, for the sentence stem "The length of T-Rex's arms is surprising . . ." she wrote:

> The length of T-Rex's arms is surprising, but **this may have been a mid-evolutionary stage and had they lived for another million years their arms might have disappeared altogether.**

A few weeks later I gave her this sentence stem: "Farleigh Hungerford Castle is now in ruins . . ."

She wrote:

> Farleigh Hungerford Castle is now in ruins because **of weathering and age.**

> Farleigh Hungerford Castle is now in ruins, but **it is arguably even more interesting now (while in ruins) than ever before.**

> Farleigh Hungerford Castle is now in ruins, so **you are able to use some imagination when envisioning the castle at its peak.**

We made these exercises a part of our daily lives, and as we did so their confidence and the range of syntactical forms my kids used in expanding their sentences grew, as did the ideas they developed and encoded in memory.

Another sentence expansion activity Hochman proposed to me in her living room—and describes at long last in this outstanding book—is deliberate practice using appositives: brief, sometimes parenthetical phrases that, like the phrase you are reading, rename or elaborate on a noun in a sentence, and can be surprisingly complex. Mastering this idea enables students to expand ideas within a sentence, adding detail, specificity, or nuance in a manner that subordinates the additional information to the overall idea of the sentence. With appositives mastered, students can link more things into the dance of interrelationships within a sentence, reducing the redundancy and disconnectedness of multiple repetitive sentences, and the Lemov kids reflected on their travels through the music of appositives as well.

After a visit to Cambridge and its historic university, I asked them to use Hochman's appositive exercise with the sentence: "In Cambridge the 'backs' are in fact the 'fronts.'" You may not understand that sentence at all—it refers to the fact that when you punt down the River Cam, you face what are called the backs of the historic colleges, but this name is ironic because the buildings were mostly built to be seen from the riverside—the backs. My daughter's sentence expansion captures this with a smooth elegance that supersedes the laborious description you just read. She wrote:

> In Cambridge, *a small town with a world-renowned university*, the backs, *the sides of the colleges that face away from the street and therefore onto the river*, are in fact *the elaborate entrances*, the fronts.

I put the appositives she added in italics. Note here a few things that are interesting about this sentence from a teaching and learning perspective:

1. It includes three different appositives, which my daughter used to expand her description of Cambridge, turning it from a sentence whose meaning was locked in code—what the "backs" and "fronts" meant is very specific to Cambridge—and unlocked it for readers less familiar with the subject. This form of explication is common to papers written in academic discourse and is a key academic skill. But even so the three appositives are surprisingly complex.

2. The second appositive, which explains what the phrase "the backs" means, is in fact a compound appositive. First she includes the idea that the backs are the sides of Cambridge's colleges that face away from the street. The phrase stands up as an appositive by itself, but then she adds—via subordination—a second appositive explaining that the backs are also the sides of the buildings that face the river. Necessity is the mother of invention. In her effort to explain what she knows and enrich the sentence sufficiently, she's expanded her range, experimenting with a doubly complex form of appositive.

3. The third example is even more interesting. In it, my daughter has reversed the common order of appositive formation. Usually the noun in a sentence is followed by an appositive phrase that expands on it. But here she has instead put the appositive in front of the noun: the sides of the colleges that face away from the street and therefore onto the river, are in fact *the elaborate entrances, the fronts*. She has flipped the form and is again experimenting with her growing proficiency. No

grammar lesson in the world could socialize her to understand and apply compound appositives and inverted appositives, but there she was within just a few weeks crafting carefully wrought sentences.

As our time in London went on, I began experimenting with new sentence expansion activities, and they became a bit of an adventure for my kids— could they express an idea that mattered and also meet the challenges of construction I set for them?

Could they, after visiting Kew Gardens, write a sentence about medicinal plants, starting with *surprisingly* and another sentence using the word *medicinal* and some form of the word *extract* (i.e., extracting, extraction)? Could they write a one-sentence description of the view from Primrose Hill starting *standing atop* but *not* using the name Primrose Hill?

In this sense our time in London was an exploration of the power of several themes that you will find constantly referred to in this book. Hochman and Wexler's study of these themes will be immensely useful to you as an educator, I believe.

The first theme is the idea that if we want students to be great writers we have to be willing to sometimes teach writing through intentional exercises. Writing responds to deliberate practice, and this concept is demonstrably different from mere repetition of an activity, which, as Hochman explains, is how many schools attempt to teach writing. Let me restate that in the plainest terms: merely repeating an activity is insufficient to get you better at it. This is why you are still as poor a driver today as you were when you were twenty-four. You drive to work every morning without intentional focus on a specific aspect of your craft. You don't get feedback. You don't even know what the skills of driving are, really. And so you never get better. You get worse, in fact.

Research—particularly that of psychologist Anders Ericsson—tells us that for practice to improve skills, it has to have a specific and focused goal and must gradually link together a series of smaller goals to created linked skills. It must also be structured in awareness of cognitive load theory—it has to be difficult, to pose a real challenge but not be so difficult that learners engage in random, nonproductive guessing to solve problems and not so difficult that the brain shuts down. As cognitive scientist Daniel Willingham points out, the brain learns best when it is challenged in a manageable amount. Finally, deliberate practice requires all-in focus, and that is maximized in a short and intense burst. This book's proposal of sequences of adaptable high-quality exercises that can allow for deliberate practice should be adopted immediately by nearly every school.

Second is the idea that writing, thinking, and reading are indelibly linked. They are the three tasks of idea formation and so there is far-reaching power for all of these domains in focusing on the craft of formation. "I write," Joan Didion famously observed, "to know what I think." Related, then, is the idea that revision is not especially separable from writing. This much I know as a professional writer: as soon as this sentence emerges on your laptop screen you are planning its revision, and helping students to master this hidden phase of writing is necessary to ensuring that students develop refined ideas, not just hasty first-blush ones. This book's study of revision's wherefores and whys will be invaluable to schools.

Third is the idea that there is a scope and sequence to all this. The numinous task of writing can in fact be taught step-by-step with a bit of intentionality if you have Hochman's wisdom and knowledge to guide you. Now you don't have to invent it. The tasks and activities are outlined and organized for you here. You can move directly to execution.

Fourth is the idea of *embedded in content*. Writing is a learning activity as much or more than a discrete subject. It operates in synergy with ideas—the need to express them is, after all, the reason for being for what is otherwise an unnatural and artificial activity. This book will help you to make every classroom in your school "writing intensive" and therefore learning intensive. If I could wave a magic wand over America's schools and cause one change that would drive the most demonstrable improvement to learning and achievement, I would almost certainly wave that wand and conjure up small bursts of intense, reflective, high-quality writing in every class period or every hour across America's schools.

Perhaps last is my own lesson from London: that writing, when taught well, is a joy. You build something real and enduring every time, and this is a source of pleasure, as is the unexpected form it takes. Successful writing gives its practitioner the mystery and satisfaction of constant invention and construction. When you look at the page and wonder, "Now where did that idea come from?" you know you are doing it right; you know your mastery of the craft itself is now guiding you. In that sense this is a magical book, one that can help you achieve a sea change in the minds of the students in your classrooms.

I previously mentioned the changing world in which the timeless skill of writing must be taught. One of the most significant changes since the book's first edition relates to technology, particularly the universal adaptation of the smartphone and the looming presence of AI. It's worth considering how these developments impact the relevance of the ideas in *The Writing Revolution*. Spoiler alert: they only underscore their importance.

Smartphones have led to the fracturing of students' attention. Smartphones have fractured everyone's attention, but given that students' brains are still developing, they are especially prone to this. This phenomenon affects in all subjects and content areas but doubly so with writing. As Hochman and Wexler note, writing places significant demands on executive functions and working memory. The costs of giving in to distractions, failing to sustain effort, and veering off topic are especially high. Writing and rewriting require constant self-monitoring persistence and sustained focus over time.

Effective instruction, such as that provided by *The Writing Revolution*, which builds and reinforces these essential skills, becomes even more crucial in combating the distractions posed by smartphones. The book's model can be deliberately adapted to cultivate stamina and persistence, providing a structured approach to developing attention skills.

Moreover, in a world where distractions abound and moments of intro-spection are increasingly scarce thanks to push notifications, the TWR model can be adapted to deliberately focus on building stamina and persistence. The flexible exercises, tools, and framework offered in *The Writing Revolution* can be used to structure longer writing sessions and socialize students to help increase their attention skills. Writing gives students a way to slow down their brains and access deliberate thinking, a skill that we cannot afford to let slip away.

Sustained writing is especially valuable when it ends in a final product students feel proud of. The model of careful, deliberate planning of a longer piece is immensely valuable if we want students to see the value of per-sistence. The planning process in *The Writing Revolution* makes the next step clear and actionable, keeps focus top of mind, and allows students to build executive function skills. Put a star next to that chapter, as I know you will want to revisit it often.

I also recommend you frequently reread the chapter on revision tasks. One of the biggest benefits of shorter, sentence-length writing exercises is the ease with which they can allow for immediate study and revision. The shorter the writing, the more quickly and easily we can model that this is how we take an idea and reflect on it, refine it, and develop it. This allows us to implicitly tell students that their first response may not be complete, which is a useful message in a "hot take" world. Techniques like Show Call can be invaluable in facilitating immediate study and revision, fostering a culture of continuous improvement in student writing.

AI presents another set of challenges for educators, particularly regarding the integrity of work done outside the classroom. This may lead to resurgence in in-class, on-demand writing assessments across various subjects. Bell bottoms and vinyl records made their triumphant return to cultural relevance, and this is your sign to not sleep on the blue book!

This likely rise of in-class, on-demand writing across all subjects as a necessary tool for assessing students' own thinking and knowledge will only put a greater value on writing, and the fact that much of this writing will necessarily be time-bound and done under a bit of pressure will instill the good habits of planning and execution. The executive function skills required to define, pursue, and stay focused on a topic will also be some of the most essential in the next era of schooling.

While writing is a timeless skill, it has never been more relevant or important than today, and so, too, is the ability to teach it well. Enjoy the book. Read it deeply, experiment with it, and take pleasure in how it helps you help your students.

Doug Lemov

Doug Lemov trains educators at Uncommon Schools, the nonprofit school management organization he helped found. He has also authored *Teach Like a Champion* (now in its 3.0 version) and has coauthored the companion *Field Guide*, *Reading Reconsidered*, and *Practice Perfect*.

Letter to Readers: What's Different about *The Writing Revolution 2.0*

In the years since the first edition of *The Writing Revolution* came out in 2017, much has changed. But teachers' need for a clear guide to explicit, carefully sequenced writing instruction is as great as ever—if not greater.

We've seen the emergence of artificial intelligence programs that can spit out an essay in less than a minute—one that is better written than what many high school and even college students can produce, and is hard to detect as a computer's creation. This development has led some educators to conclude that it's no longer possible to assign writing since there's no way of ensuring students will turn in their own work. Others have urged that artificial intelligence be used the way a calculator is for basic operations in a math class: given a bot-created piece of writing, students can edit and refine it, devoting their energies to higher-order elements of writing like voice.

Unfortunately, there's no shortcut to enabling students to become better writers. For one thing, many students lack the basic writing skills that would enable them to be good editors. More fundamentally, the writing process is a learning process. If students are merely trying to revise a piece of writing they haven't produced, they're likely to retain less information and have a shallower understanding of the material. They may even struggle to understand the text they're revising if they're not familiar with complex sentence structure. Explicit writing instruction of the kind described in this book, woven into everyday classroom teaching, is the most effective way to ensure that students acquire the skills and knowledge they'll need to succeed academically and beyond—even if some will inevitably choose to rely on artificial intelligence for help in drafting a piece of writing at some point.

Against the background of these developments—and drawing on the expertise of The Writing Revolution organization's faculty, who have trained thousands of teachers in the method and work with partner schools that are implementing it—we have made a number of changes in this new edition. Although the first edition has reached far more teachers than we ever anticipated and has been met with a gratifyingly positive response, we felt there were aspects of the book that could be improved.

If you're familiar with the original version, the changes you'll see in this version include:

- **The addition of two new outlines, the Pre-Transition Outline (PTO) and the Transition Outline (TO), as possible steps between the Single-Paragraph Outline (SPO) and the Multiple-Paragraph Outline (MPO).** It's become clear to us that many students who have learned to outline and write paragraphs are ready to embark on lengthier writing but not yet equipped for the demands of the MPO, which requires students to compose challenging introductory and concluding paragraphs when converting their outlines into drafts. The TO requires only a thesis statement at the beginning and a concluding statement at the end, along with notes for body paragraphs in between. Students who are not ready for the TO or MPO formats can use the PTO to help them begin thinking about the requirements of MPOs and essays.

- **Changes in the sequence of sentence activities.** Sentence expansion is introduced earlier than in the previous edition. When young students learn to expand a bare-bones sentence into one that is more complex, it helps them learn to provide the kind of information readers need for comprehension.

- **The introduction of transitions as sentence activities**. Previously, transition words weren't introduced until the chapter on revision. Using transition words is an important element of revision, but students benefit from using sentence activities to learn and practice the strategy.

- **More illustrations of all strategies.** We hope these examples will help readers adapt the strategies to whatever content they're teaching.

- **Questions for book discussion groups.** We've become aware that many educators are reading and discussing the book collaboratively, and we hope these questions will serve as a guide. Those who read the book on their own may also benefit from them.

- **More online resources**. Readers will be able to access updated customizable templates as well as examples of activities embedded in frequently used content. They'll also have access to posters, sample pacing guides, and assessment resources.

- **An expanded discussion of assessment.** We've added material on formative and summative assessments, and on how to administer writing prompts at the beginning, middle, and end of the year and evaluate students' responses.

Whether this book is your introduction to The Writing Revolution's method or you've been applying the method from your well-thumbed copy of the first edition for years, we hope you'll find these changes helpful—and that you'll soon be seeing your students grow in confidence and ability.

Throughout the book we've included student writing samples. Some of these samples are from actual students (under pseudonyms or first names only), and others were created by The Writing Revolution staff members. Some educator and student names have been changed, and in other cases, and where noted, we've used real names with the individual's blessing. Some anecdotes and classroom examples, although based on actual experience, incorporate invented characters and events.

The Writing Revolution 2.0

CHAPTER 1

Introduction

Why You Need a Writing Revolution in Your Classroom

At the beginning of the school year, Ms. Cappiello was about to give her ninth graders their first writing assignment. Her expectations were low because in previous years, she'd found that students might have no trouble carrying on a conversation, but it was a different story when it came to writing. Even by the end of a school year, the papers they turned in just didn't make sense.

"It's not like there are good papers and bad papers," she had confided to a colleague the previous spring. "It's like, I can't even understand most of these papers."

According to the curriculum, her students were supposed to write an essay at the end of every unit. They would also be expected to answer essay questions on state tests. But how was she supposed to teach them to do that, Ms. Cappiello wondered, if they couldn't even write a paragraph? In the past, many of her students had still struggled to produce coherent sentences. And Ms. Cappiello's training hadn't included anything about how to teach writing.

To gauge her new students' writing abilities, Ms. Cappiello asked them to compose a paragraph about how a character changes in a novel, story, or play. Most of their paragraphs started with a sentence that sounded like something they would have said if they were answering orally.

A student named Michael wrote:

In Star Wars Theres a character named Anakin skywalker who changed OVerTime in a very Dark way

A girl named Maria wrote:

I have been reading a book about a kid who is in school.

Most of the paragraphs went downhill from there. The sentences were in random order, and some of them weren't actually sentences. Even when they were, they all had the same simple structure. Only one or two students had tried to finish the paragraph with something that resembled a concluding sentence.

Ms. Cappiello sighed. It seemed as though this year would be like all the others. She wanted so much to help her students learn to express themselves in writing, but she had no idea where to begin.

What Teachers Need: A Road Map for Explicit Writing Instruction

Ms. Cappiello's class is not unusual. Across the country, countless students have problems expressing themselves clearly and coherently in writing. On nationwide tests, only about 25 percent of students are able to score at a proficient level in writing.[1]

And yet, **expository writing**—the kind of writing that explains and informs—is essential for success in school and the workplace. Students who can't write at a competent level struggle in secondary school and in college. No matter what path students choose in life, the ability to communicate their thoughts in writing in a way that others can easily understand is crucial.

The problem is not that students are incapable of learning to write well. Rather, the problem is that many schools haven't been teaching students how to write. Teachers may assign writing, but they may not know how to explicitly teach it in a careful sequence of logical steps, beginning at the sentence level.

Just as with Ms. Cappiello, most teachers' training didn't include instruction in how to teach writing. The assumption has been that if students read and write enough, they'll simply pick up writing skills, through a kind of osmosis. Sometimes this is called the "writing is caught" approach. But there's little evidence to support it. A recent two-year study done with young children in Norway, for example, found that just having students write *more* had no effect on the quality of their writing.[2]

There's ample evidence that very few students become good writers on their own. Many students—even at the college level—have difficulty constructing a coherent **sentence**, let alone a fluid, cohesive **essay**. Perhaps at least some of your students, maybe most, fall into that category.

To be effective, writing instruction should start in elementary school. However, when students do get a chance to write in elementary school, they're often encouraged to write at length too soon. They don't learn how to construct interesting and grammatically correct sentences first, and they aren't encouraged to plan or outline before they write longer pieces. The idea is that later on they'll refine their writing, under the teacher's guidance, bringing coherence and—perhaps—correct grammar and punctuation to what they've produced. But after getting feedback, students may be reluctant to rewrite a multi-page essay that they've already worked on for hours. And teachers, confronted by pages of incoherent, error-riddled writing, may not know where to begin.

When students get to middle school or high school, it's assumed that they've already learned the basics of writing. As secondary teachers like Ms. Cappiello know, that assumption has little to do with reality. But rather than beginning with teaching the fundamental skills their students lack—by, for example, guiding students through the process of writing well-crafted sentences—teachers feel pressured to have their students meet grade-level expectations and produce multi-paragraph essays.

High school teachers have long been expected to ask students to write analytically about the content of the courses they're taking. But in years past, many students had written nothing except narratives in elementary and middle school, often about their personal experiences. That kind of writing didn't prepare them for the demands of high school, college, or the workforce.

Many states have revamped their standards. As a result, teachers at almost all grade levels are now expected to have students write not just narratives, but also informative and argumentative essays. The result is that websites abound with worksheets designed to teach these skills—for example, an "opinion essay" worksheet asking first graders to write about which they like better, M&M's® or Skittles®.

It's unlikely those kinds of activities will prepare students to write the analytical and argumentative essays they'll be expected to produce at higher grade levels, but there's been little reliable guidance on what to do instead.[3]

The writing standards tell teachers where their students should end up, but what teachers need is a road map that tells them how to get there.

The Writing Revolution (TWR), a nonprofit organization, offers such a road map by disseminating the Hochman Method to educators around the world. The Hochman Method provides a clear, coherent, evidence-based method of instruction that you can use no matter what subject or grade level you teach. The method has demonstrated, over and over, that it can turn weak writers into strong ones by focusing students' writing practice on specific techniques that match their needs and providing them with prompt and clear feedback. Insurmountable as the writing challenges faced by many students may seem, TWR's method can make a dramatic difference. (We will be using the terms "Hochman Method" and "TWR" interchangeably.)

What Writing Instruction Can Do for You and Your Students

Explicit writing instruction will help you and your students in the following ways:

- **Identifying comprehension gaps.** When you ask your students to write about what they're learning, you may uncover significant gaps in their knowledge that are preventing them from accessing grade-level material.

- **Familiarizing students with complex syntax.** The vocabulary and syntax, or sentence structure, of written language is more complex than that of spoken language, and students who are unfamiliar with it often struggle with comprehension. The problem is widespread: One large-scale, long-term study found that fewer than 10 percent of U.S. eighth graders can "evaluate complex syntax."[4] And, as reading expert Timothy Shanahan has observed, "There is now a slew of rigorous studies revealing that an understanding of syntax is correlated with reading comprehension."[5] When students learn to use more sophisticated syntax and vocabulary in their own writing, they become better able to understand it when they encounter it in their reading.[6]

- **Boosting reading comprehension and learning.** Studies have found that when students at any grade level write about texts they have read and content they have been taught—not just in English, but also in social studies, science, and math—their reading comprehension and learning is enhanced.[7] Writing across the disciplines "can improve reading comprehension, critical thinking, and disciplinary content knowledge," according to a panel of experts convened by the U.S. Department of Education.[8] For example, one study done with students who were English-language learners and had also been diagnosed with math disabilities found that when they were taught to rewrite word problems, they made significant, lasting gains in math ability.[9]

- **Enhancing speaking abilities.** As students begin to use more complex terms and sentence constructions in their written language, many of them begin to incorporate those features into their spoken language as well.

- **Improving organizational and study skills.** TWR activities teach students to paraphrase, take notes, summarize, and make **outlines**. These techniques help them absorb and retain crucial information. In particular, studies of summarizing have found strong effects for struggling readers. After reviewing the research, the National Reading Panel concluded that summarizing helps students integrate ideas, generalize, and retain information.[10]

- **Developing analytical capabilities.** The process of writing requires even young students to organize their ideas and sequence information. As they move through the grades, they have to sift through more material, deciding for themselves what's important, which facts and ideas are connected to one another, and how to organize their thoughts into a logical progression. **When done in a systematic and sequenced way, teaching students to write is equivalent to teaching them how to think.**

Students who have the opportunity to learn TWR strategies and practice them through carefully scaffolded activities become better at understanding what they read, expressing themselves orally, and thinking critically.

A Brief History of
The Writing Revolution

Years ago, like most classroom teachers, I would assign writing activities that focused on my students' experiences, creativity, and feelings: a visit to an imaginary country, a meaningful moment in their lives. My undergraduate and graduate training hadn't included any preparation for teaching writing, nor had I been asked to read any research on effective writing instruction. (*I* refers to Judith Hochman.)

Later, as an administrator, I observed many similar lessons. In the higher grades, when teachers assigned compositions, they assumed that students would intuitively know how to sequence and organize information, relate it to a reader with clarity and coherence, and develop sound introductions and conclusions. The results consistently and dramatically disproved these assumptions.

I was struck by the difference in how our school taught writing as opposed to reading. When I taught reading, I didn't just give my students a book and say, "Read this." I used a well-researched approach to teaching reading based on the Orton-Gillingham method.[11] It provided explicit phonics instruction in decoding and used carefully sequenced activities that scaffolded skills until students read fluently and accurately. But when it came to writing, arguably a far more difficult task, I had no way to give students the tools they needed. If their writing fell short, as it often did, we simply told them things like "you can do better" or "add more details." Clearly, that wasn't enough.

Then as now, academic researchers were paying far more attention to reading than writing. As a result, I began to experiment. First as a director of curriculum, and later as head of the school, I asked teachers to stop teaching the mechanics of writing in isolation. Instead, we asked students to write about the content they were learning. Our feedback might be "put your strongest argument last," "use transitions when presenting your points," or "try starting your thesis statement with a subordinating conjunction." Since we had explicitly taught them how to use these strategies, they were able to respond correctly.

As I saw that these techniques were working for our students, I noticed that researchers who were looking into best practices for teaching writing were finding evidence that supported what we were doing. The techniques we were using weren't just turning our students into better writers. We also saw improvements in their analytical thinking, reading comprehension, and oral communication.

In 2012, an article appeared in the magazine *The Atlantic*[12] about how this method produced dramatic results at a low-performing high school in New York City. As the article describes, before the school adopted the Hochman Method, many students didn't know how to construct sentences using conjunctions such as *but* and *so*—not to mention words such as *although* and *despite*. After the school had implemented these new writing strategies for a couple of years, various measures of achievement there rose sharply.

The article spurred a tremendous amount of interest in the method, and in response, I founded a nonprofit that used the title of the *Atlantic* article: The Writing Revolution.

Educators from around the country—in fact, from around the world— have been learning the method and how to implement it through courses provided by TWR. We've found that teachers are eager for guidance in how to explicitly teach writing—something that still isn't covered in most teacher-prep programs.[13] Many educators who take TWR's courses find that their students benefit from explicit, scaffolded writing instruction. The Hochman Method—and the principles that underlie it—can benefit any student in any grade at any school.

Why Many Students Don't Get the Benefits of Writing

Earlier, we listed many potential benefits of writing, noting that it can boost reading comprehension, oral expression, and learning in general. Unfortunately, though, many if not most students aren't getting those benefits.

A basic reason is that writing is extremely difficult. In fact, it may be the hardest thing we ask students to do. That's because it imposes a heavy burden on **working memory**, the aspect of our consciousness that takes in and tries to make sense of new information.

Working memory can hold only a few new items of information—maybe just four or five—for about 20 seconds before it starts to become overwhelmed. Inexperienced writers are trying to juggle many different things in working memory at the same time—everything from letter formation, if they're young, to word choice, to organizing their thoughts. As a result, they may not have the capacity in working memory to learn how to write well or to analyze the content they're writing about. That's especially true if the content is relatively unfamiliar—and if inexperienced writers are asked to write at length. They miss out on the opportunity to learn to write well and on all those other benefits that writing can offer.

Different individuals have different working memory capacities, but there's no reliable way to expand any individual's working memory. There is, however, a reliable way around its constraints: if you have relevant information stored in **long-term memory**, you don't need to juggle it in working memory. That opens up more capacity in working memory to take in new information.

Long-term memory can store an unlimited amount of information for an indefinite period of time. When it comes to writing, that information includes not only knowledge of the content you're writing about, but also knowledge of various writing strategies: how to vary your sentence structure, how to connect your thoughts, or how to organize a paragraph or essay. Once students have acquired knowledge of those strategies, that knowledge will be stored in long-term memory, ready to be drawn on when needed.

Before you can tap into the power of long-term memory, though, two things need to happen. First, you need to transfer the new information from working memory to long-term memory, generally by attaching meaning to it. A powerful way of doing that is to explain the information to another person in our own words—as we do when we write.

Second, you need to be able to *retrieve* the information from long-term memory when you need it. The more you practice retrieving it, the more accessible the information will be. Studies have shown that **retrieval practice** is a great way to commit new learning to memory for students of all ages, from elementary school through college. And one highly effective form of retrieval practice is writing.[14]

The fact that writing is both a form of transfer and retrieval practice helps explain why it can provide such a powerful boost to learning. But it can only provide that boost if a learner's working memory isn't overwhelmed by the act or writing itself.

Writing is double-edged. It can impose a crippling burden on working memory—and it can provide a way around its limitations. The key to unlocking its potential is to break down the writing process into manageable components—and guide students to practice each one.

Deliberate Practice Makes The Writing Revolution Revolutionary

Unlike most other approaches to writing instruction, TWR is as much a method of teaching content as it is a method of teaching writing. There's no separate writing block and no separate writing curriculum. Instead, teachers of all subjects can and should adapt TWR's strategies and activities to their preexisting curriculum and weave them into their content instruction.

But perhaps what's most revolutionary about TWR's method is that it takes the mystery out of learning to write well. In other approaches, a teacher might give students a description of the elements of a good paragraph or essay, or perhaps present a model piece of writing and have them try to emulate it. For many students, that's not enough. They may be able to read and appreciate writing that flows well and uses varied sentence structures, but that doesn't mean they can figure out how to write that way themselves. For them, the techniques of good writing are a secret code they just can't crack.

TWR's method lets them in on the secret. It breaks the writing process down into manageable chunks and then has students practice the chunks they need, repeatedly, while also learning content. For example, many students don't fully understand what makes a sentence a sentence. Giving them a definition—a group of words that contains a subject and a predicate and expresses a complete thought—is not enough. What they need is lots of practice distinguishing between groups of words that form complete sentences and groups of words that are sentence fragments. If you embed this activity in content students have recently learned and ask them to add the information needed to turn the fragments into sentences, they will not only be learning the basic skill of forming a complete sentence but also reinforcing their knowledge of that content.

This kind of practice—**deliberate practice**, as some cognitive scientists call it[15]—is different from having students practice writing by giving them a half an hour to write and simply turning them loose. Merely doing the same thing over and over is unlikely to improve their performance. To make their writing better, they need a series of exercises that specifically target the skills they haven't yet mastered, while building on the skills they already have, in a gradual, step-by-step process. In addition, they need clear, direct feedback to help them identify their mistakes and monitor their progress.

Although you will be the ultimate judge of exactly what your students need and when they need it, TWR provides activities that will enable them to engage in deliberate writing practice—along with vocabulary that you can use to give them prompt, effective feedback.

The Six TWR Principles

TWR's method rests on six basic principles:

1. Students need explicit instruction in writing, preferably beginning in the early elementary grades.

2. Sentences are the building blocks of all writing.

3. When embedded in the content of the curriculum, writing instruction is a powerful teaching tool.

4. The content of the curriculum drives the rigor of the writing activities.

5. Grammar is best taught in the context of student writing.

6. The two most important phases of the writing process are planning and revising.

Principle 1: Students Need Explicit Instruction in Writing, Preferably Beginning in the Early Elementary Grades

Most students won't pick up writing skills just by reading. Many students who are good readers struggle when it comes to writing. Unlike reading, writing involves deciding what to say, which words to use, how to spell them, perhaps how to form the letters, and what order to place the words in—and that's just at the sentence level. Writing a paragraph or an entire essay requires even more decision-making, planning, and analysis.

Just as good readers aren't necessarily good writers, students who can speak coherently often write incoherently. Far too many students write the way they speak, using simple sentences, rambling ones, or fragments. That kind of communication may work when we're speaking to someone in front of us: the listeners' facial expressions and gestures indicate whether they're following what we're saying, and we may already be aware of how much they know about the subject we're discussing.

However, when we write, we don't have visual cues to draw on, and we often don't know exactly who the audience is. We need to express ourselves with far more precision and clarity, anticipating the facts and details a reader will require to grasp our meaning. We also need to rely on words and punctuation rather than intonation and pauses to indicate nuances in meaning or breaks in the narrative. We have to abide by conventions of spelling and grammar to ensure that mistakes don't distract a reader from the content.

Although good writing should be clear and direct, it almost always involves more complex sentence structures and a more varied and precise vocabulary than spoken language. When we speak, we rarely begin sentences with words such as *despite* or *although*, but they can be extremely useful in written language. And connecting our thoughts with phrases like *as a result* or *specifically*, although unnecessary in most conversational speech, can be vital in creating a fluid piece of writing.

More generally, when we write, our words are preserved on paper or on a screen, making not just grammatical and syntactical errors but also logical flaws far more glaring than in spoken language. And we rarely sustain spoken language for the equivalent length of a paragraph, let alone an essay, unless we're delivering a speech or participating in a formal debate. Shaping a logical, unbroken narrative or argument in writing requires far more thought and planning than having a conversation or making a contribution to class discussion.

The elementary grades are the ideal time to begin writing instruction. If we assign only stories, journal entries, and poems in the early grades—as I did as a young teacher—we're wasting precious time. Although it's certainly possible to introduce expository writing skills at higher grade levels, it's much easier to begin the process in elementary school. Even children in the earliest elementary grades can engage in TWR activities orally, under a teacher's guidance, laying the groundwork for actual writing. Later, elementary students can practice their spelling and vocabulary words by completing thoughtfully focused writing activities related to the content they're learning about. At the same time, they can hone their handwriting skills.

We need to equip children with the tools that will give them confidence as writers and enable them to express themselves in a way that others can understand. And far from feeling that practicing the mechanics of writing is drudgery, students often gain a sense of pride and mastery from learning to craft well-constructed sentences and logically sequenced paragraphs.

Principle 2: Sentences Are the Building Blocks of All Writing

In many schools, the quantity of writing has long been valued over its quality. Teachers often feel pressure to assign essay-length writing well before students are capable of producing coherent text. If students haven't learned how to write an effective sentence, that is where instruction needs to begin—no matter what the student's age or grade level.

Of course, students must learn to write at length, and TWR includes strategies and activities designed to guide them through that process. But a writer who can't compose a decent sentence will never produce a decent essay—or even a decent paragraph. And if students are still struggling to write sentences, they have less brain power available to do the careful planning that writing a good paragraph or composition requires. A sentence-level assignment is manageable for students who are still grappling with grammar, syntax, spelling, and punctuation.

Sentence-level writing shouldn't be dismissed as something that's too basic for older students to engage in. As Bruce Saddler has observed, sentences "are literally miniature compositions."[16] Producing even a single sentence can impose major cognitive demands on students, especially if it requires them to explain, paraphrase, or summarize sophisticated content. Many kinds of sentence-level activities, including most described in this book, develop knowledge and analytical abilities while simultaneously enabling students to learn the mechanics of sentence construction.

Even at the sentence level, students need appropriate guidance if their writing skills are to improve. TWR gives teachers an array of activities that guide students to use complete sentences, vary their structure, and employ complex syntax and new vocabulary—while at the same time ensuring that they master content.

As students begin to acquire basic sentence-level skills, TWR also provides structured support for lengthier writing. But crafting an effective sentence is a useful and important exercise, no matter the skill level of the student, and teachers should continue to assign sentence-level activities even after students have moved on to writing paragraphs and compositions. **TWR's method is meant to be recursive, with students returning to activities that have previously been introduced—and not necessarily waiting for "mastery" of one kind of strategy before moving on to another.**

That means that you don't need to wait until your students have mastered *all* the TWR sentence-level strategies before allowing them to move on to lengthier writing. They can begin to develop simple outlines and compose single paragraphs, depending on their ability level. Ideally, however, you won't ask them to write independently at length until after they have learned some basic skills. Those include distinguishing sentences from fragments; using simple conjunctions like *because, but*, and *so*; and using simple subordinating conjunctions like *before* and *when*. Students should also have learned how to outline a paragraph or an essay before being asked to write one independently.

Principle 3: When Embedded in the Content of the Curriculum, Writing Instruction Is a Powerful Teaching Tool

When schools do focus on expository writing, the assignments are often on topics that draw only on students' personal experiences or opinions rather than on the content of what they are actually studying in English, history, science, math, or other subjects. Students may, for example, practice persuasive writing by taking pro or con positions on school uniforms or they may learn to write a compare-and-contrast essay by weighing the benefits and disadvantages of being famous.

Such general topics can be useful for introducing students to a particular aspect of writing—say, creating topic sentences or learning how to develop outlines. But until students have had quite a bit of systematic and targeted instruction, the writing skills they develop when writing about one subject are unlikely to transfer to another. Even if students learn to write a decent persuasive essay on why they should have a bigger allowance, they probably won't be able to apply those skills to an essay arguing that the Civil War was fundamentally about slavery.

Another frequent practice is to have students write about topics in a separate writing curriculum. Often that curriculum provides students with very little information on the topic they're supposed to write about. There are two fundamental problems with that approach.

One is that having students write about topics unrelated to the core curriculum—whether they're grounded in personal experience or opinion or in a separate writing curriculum—represents a huge wasted opportunity to boost their learning. Writing isn't merely a skill; it's also a powerful teaching tool. When students write, they—and their teachers—figure out what they don't understand and what further information they need. And, as we have observed in many classrooms, when students write about the content they're studying, they learn to synthesize information and produce their own interpretations. If students are learning about Ancient Egypt or about tornadoes and hurricanes, part of the instruction in those subjects should include having students write about them.

The other problem is that writing and content knowledge are intimately related. **You can't write well about something you don't know well.** The more students know about a topic before they begin to write, the better they'll be able to write about it. At the same time, the process of writing will deepen their understanding of a topic and help cement that understanding in their memory.

An even more fundamental problem in many elementary schools, and sometimes middle schools, is that the curriculum doesn't go deeply into *any* content. The school day is devoted almost entirely to reading and math, and the reading block often consists mostly of practice in reading comprehension skills, using texts on a random variety of topics. Not only is this an ineffective way to boost reading comprehension,[17] it can make it difficult if not impossible to teach writing. If students are jumping from one topic to another, because the focus is on comprehension skills rather than content, they may not have enough information about any one topic to write coherently about it. If your school isn't covering topics in any depth, don't despair: you can still use TWR's method to develop your students' abilities to write and to learn in general. But you'll probably need to bring in additional materials to enrich the content of the curriculum.

For students to become proficient readers and writers, all subjects, including English language arts, must include substantial content. And all teachers, no matter their subject area, must be writing teachers. Teachers of history, science, world languages, math, and even music, art, and physical education have learned to incorporate TWR activities into their instruction. Although schools may exercise some flexibility in deciding which classes will adopt TWR, keep in mind that the more teachers who use a common language for writing instruction within a given school, the better the results.

Teachers of subjects other than English may be apprehensive about incorporating the teaching of writing into their curricula. They may feel that they never signed up to be writing teachers. However, in our experience most of them find that rather than detracting from their instruction, implementing TWR actually enhances their ability to teach and boosts their students' grasp of the content they're studying. And although the strategies should be practiced daily, they may take only 5 to 15 minutes of class time. They can be used as quick comprehension checks, **do-now activities**, and **exit tickets**.

Principle 4: The Content of the Curriculum Drives the Rigor of the Writing Activities

If you follow Principle 3 and connect your students' writing activities with the subject matter that you're teaching, you'll find that you can use the same activities for any grade level or content area and still challenge your students. The format of the activity will stay the same, but the content is what makes it more or less rigorous. In addition, when the same kind of activity is embedded in different content, it will help build and deepen different bodies of knowledge.

As an illustration, one of TWR's sentence-level strategies uses the conjunctions *because*, *but*, and *so* to encourage extended responses. The teacher gives students a **sentence stem**, which is an independent clause, and asks them to finish it in three different ways, using each of the three conjunctions.

If you're reading *The Real Story of Stone Soup*[18] with young students, the activity might look like this:

The uncle believes the boys are lazy because *he thinks he does all the work.*

The uncle believes the boys are lazy, but *the boys really do all the work.*

The uncle believes the boys are lazy, so *he calls them mean names and complains about them.*

In math, instead of asking, "Why is the square root of two irrational?" you can give your students the same activity embedded in that content:

The square root of two is irrational because *two is a non-square number.*

The square root of two is irrational, but *the value can be approximated on the number line.*

The square root of two is irrational, so *it cannot be written as a ratio of two integers.*

Here's that same activity adapted to a high-school global history class:

The Mongol Empire collapsed because *it was too large to control.*

The Mongol empire collapsed, but *areas in Russia remained under Mongol control for centuries.*

The Mongol Empire collapsed, so *trade declined between Asia and the Middle East.*

If you're teaching science, the activity might go like this:

Wind energy is a sustainable resource because *it does not require fuel.*

Wind energy is a sustainable resource, but *it can be harmful to some wildlife.*

Wind energy is a sustainable resource, so *more companies are investing in wind turbines.*

In each of these cases, students need to return to the material they have been studying and look carefully for information to complete the stems. The activity can be challenging. If you think sentence-level activities are just for elementary students, try finishing this stem: "Immanuel Kant believed that space and time are subjective forms of human sensibility, but _____."

No matter what content you use with these kinds of activities, the specificity of the prompts makes them far more powerful than an open-ended question such as, "Why did the Mongol Empire collapse?" The conjunction *but,* for example, demands that students hold two contrasting ideas in their minds and find evidence to support one of them. Your students will be deciding how to complete the sentence stems independently, but in a way that gives them the structure they need to engage in focused, rigorous thinking.

Principle 5: Grammar Is Best Taught in the Context of Student Writing

Research has found that students who have a better understanding of grammar are better writers.[19] But it has also consistently found that teaching the rules in isolation doesn't work. That doesn't mean teachers can't, or shouldn't, teach grammar. As we've seen over the years, what does work is to teach writing conventions and grammar in the context of students' own writing.[20]

Just as skills developed in writing about one subject may not transfer to another, many students won't be able to apply rules they've learned in the abstract to their own writing. Although it's useful for students to have a general familiarity with basic concepts such as **noun** and **verb**, that won't necessarily prevent them from writing "sentences" that lack one or the other.

Some people swear by sentence diagramming—often, those who feel that they themselves learned to write by using the technique. And it may work for some students. But for many, and especially those who struggle with language, breaking sentences into their component parts, labeling them as parts of speech, and plotting them on a diagram just adds to the confusion.

TWR's method doesn't teach grammar for the sake of teaching grammar. You won't find, for example, lessons on prepositional phrases and their use—although students will undoubtedly be using such phrases in their writing. Instead, students are taught a select number of grammatical terms and functions that appear frequently in written language but rarely in conversation. Students need to become familiar with these grammatical concepts to become proficient writers—and readers.

That's why TWR strategies focus on teaching students how to do things like use **appositives**, which are phrases used to describe nouns, and use **subordinating conjunctions** to introduce **dependent clauses**. Those grammatical terms are discussed in Chapter 4 and found in the glossary. They can serve as a kind of shorthand when teachers are giving feedback. Instead of vague feedback such as "Vary your sentence structure," teachers can say "Add an appositive"—and be confident that students will understand what to do and how it will improve their writing.

Principle 6: The Two Most Important Phases of the Writing Process Are Planning and Revising

When students are ready to tackle longer pieces of writing—paragraphs and compositions—they'll need to go through four steps before producing a final copy: planning, drafting, revising, and editing. But the critical phases are planning and revising.

All students need to plan before they write. This is especially true of expository writing. Although experienced writers may be able to turn out a well-developed paragraph or essay on the fly, most of the students we work with find it overwhelming to organize their thoughts at the same time that they're choosing words and figuring out the best way to structure their sentences. They may forget what they were planning to say next, or they may need to check to see if they're repeating themselves. Again, this is a matter of having too many things to juggle in working memory.

Partly as a result, beginning or non-expert writers may simply put down whatever comes into their heads about a given topic. Here, for example, is how one sixth grader explained his strategy in writing an essay:

> *I have a whole bunch of ideas and write them down till my supply of ideas is gone. Then I might try to think of more ideas up to the point where you can't get any more ideas that are worth putting down on paper and then I would end it.*[21]

Expert writers, on the other hand, decide on their purpose before they begin to write: who their audience is, what they want a reader to learn, and what ideas they want to introduce. They make a plan, listing the points they want to include and the order in which to present them. They may show an outline or draft to a reader or editor and find that they need to modify it. As they try to make their explanations clearer, they may come up with new insights and make new connections between their ideas.

Even young children can learn how to outline paragraphs with a teacher's guidance, if the activity is done orally and collaboratively. In one first-grade classroom using the Hochman Method, a teacher led the children through outlining a paragraph about how they successfully planted seeds and grew vegetables. That kind of activity fosters logical thinking and analytical abilities in a cognitively manageable way, preparing the groundwork for later independent writing.

For students who are ready to engage in this process in written form, we provide multiple basic outline templates: one for planning paragraphs and several for planning compositions. The lion's share of the work of writing occurs at the planning stage, as students identify the main idea or theme of their writing, the points they will make, and the order they will make them in. As they do this work, students are discovering what further information or clarification they need, making the necessary connections between ideas or claims and relevant details or evidence and ensuring that they don't wander off into irrelevancy or repetition.

Once students have a well-organized outline, it's usually a simple matter to translate it into a rudimentary draft. Then comes the next major phase of writing: revising the draft so that it reads smoothly and coherently. This is where students will draw on the sentence-level skills they've acquired, which include using subordinating conjunctions and appositives to vary their sentence structure and inserting transition words and phrases to make their sentences and paragraphs flow.

Teachers who adhere to these six principles while implementing TWR have found it to be a powerful way not only of teaching writing skills, but also of ensuring their students are grasping content and thinking analytically. They've learned to give students clear, explicit writing instruction and feedback, using sentence-level activities regardless of what grade or subject they're teaching. They ground the TWR strategies in whatever content the class is learning, enabling students to deal with text more effectively and using the complexity of the content to ratchet up the activities' rigor. Teachers provide instruction in the correct use of grammar, punctuation, capitalization, and other conventions by embedding those practices within the assignments they give students. And they break the writing process into manageable steps, with particular attention to planning and revising, so that students don't become overwhelmed by all the factors that writing requires them to juggle.

How to Use This Book

The Writing Revolution 2.0 will guide you through a carefully scaffolded sequence of strategies and accompanying activities that you can adapt to any content area, grade level, or ability level. Whether you're teaching large classes, small groups, or tutorials, you'll be able to find many ways to use them. The activities also easily lend themselves to differentiation, enabling you to modify them for a range of ability levels within your classroom.

This book provides you with numerous examples of how the strategies can be implemented, along with a glossary of key terms at the end and an appendix of resources. As a reminder, you'll also find additional resources, including customizable templates, sample activities, posters, and sample pacing guides, at www.thewritingrevolution.org/resources/book-resources.

SCAN ME

Key Points

Before we describe the organization of the book, we'd like to highlight some points that you should keep in mind as you read it.

- We use the term *strategy* to refer to an overarching technique and the word *activity* to refer to scaffolds that support instruction in the strategy. For example, summarizing is a strategy, whereas giving students an article and having them write a sentence that summarizes it is an activity that supports it.

- Every strategy and many of the supporting activities begin with a bulleted list explaining **WHY** it is important for you to provide explicit instruction for these techniques.

- Although this book presents the strategies one after another in a linear sequence, in practice you'll be using *several different* strategies at the same time. For example, you might first ask students to write a one-sentence summary of a news article. That sentence could become the topic sentence in a Single-Paragraph Outline (SPO), which could become the basis for the draft of a paragraph. Students don't have to master all of the sentence strategies before learning how to develop a Single-Paragraph Outline (SPO).

- Follow the sequence we suggest in introducing new strategies, but *have students practice previously taught strategies recursively*. In particular, the sentence-level activities continue to be important when students move on to revising paragraphs and compositions.

- When introducing a strategy, it's best to *model an activity for the class and then have students practice it orally.* This is certainly true for younger students, but older students also need to have demonstrations and participate in whole-class activities. Once students understand the concept, you can have them try the activity on their own in writing.

- When demonstrating a strategy for the first time, it's also best to ground the activity in a topic that all students are familiar with, so that they're not trying to juggle new content in working memory along with a new writing strategy. You could use a topic that has already been covered in class, or you could use one from outside the curriculum, like "winter."

- When you model an activity for the whole class, make sure that you're displaying your work in a way that enables all students to see what you're doing by using a chalkboard, whiteboard, chart paper, SMART Board, projector, or document camera to do this.

- As you adapt TWR strategies and activities to the content of your curriculum, *always anticipate student responses* to the questions you pose or activities you create. It's surprisingly easy to create an activity that is clear to you but confusing to students. Make sure you are certain about what you want your students to understand about the content the activity is focused on, and plan backward from there.[22]

- When we provide examples of activities, we usually include one version for Level 1 students and another for Level 2. These categories apply to students with more basic and more advanced writing skills, respectively, and to some extent they correspond to grade levels in terms of the subject matter we have used in the examples. Level 1 examples tend to focus on elementary-level material, and Level 2 examples focus on secondary-level material. However, even students in high school often lack basic writing skills, so we have avoided using grade-level designations. You will need to use your knowledge of your students' needs and abilities when adapting TWR activities to the content you're teaching.

- As you progress through the school year, you should be giving students *prompt feedback* on their writing and regularly *assessing their progress* to determine what strategies to focus on, how quickly to move through the sequence, and which students need modifications suited to their individual needs.

- The Hochman Method works best when it is implemented *across the curriculum* in as many subject areas as possible. In secondary schools and elementary schools where different subjects are taught by different teachers, this approach requires coordination among teachers and common planning time. To facilitate collaboration, we have provided key terms that all teachers can use as a common language and to share tips about the best ways to introduce and implement TWR strategies and activities. These terms are boldfaced in the text, and their definitions are found in the glossary.

- When we use the word *differentiate*, it means *adapting* an activity to make it less or more challenging.

How This Book Is Organized and What It Covers

This book is divided into three sections. The first section focuses on sentences and a system of note-taking. The second section addresses longer forms of writing—paragraphs, compositions, revision, and summarizing. The third section covers how to assess students' writing and adapt TWR to your classes.

Sentences

The strategies in this section will help your students understand the purpose and structure of sentences and develop the ability to compose complex sentences that reflect extended thinking.

They include:

- Understand the concept of a sentence by distinguishing between sentences and fragments, and unscrambling words to make a sentence
- Expand a basic **kernel sentence** with details
- Use the four types of sentences (statements, questions, exclamations, and commands)
- Develop questions
- Extend responses using basic conjunctions (*because, but, so*)
- Use subordinating conjunctions to reflect written language structures
- Insert appositives to describe a noun
- Combine two or more short sentences into a longer one
- Use transitions to connect thoughts and sentences

These strategies will encourage students to think analytically, enable them to give more information to a reader, and make their writing more engaging.

In addition, this section will introduce a system of abbreviations and symbols your students can use to take notes on their reading. You'll find activities that give your students practice in converting text they have read into notes, using key words and phrases, which they'll later convert back into text they write themselves. This process ensures that your students will actually process and understand what they read, rather than merely copying it.

Writing at Length

In this section, you'll learn why it's important for students to plan before they tackle longer forms of writing. You'll be introduced to an outlining process that will enable your students to shape coherent paragraphs through the use of topic sentences, supporting sentences that provide key details, and concluding sentences. TWR's revision activities will provide your students with the techniques they need to make their writing flow.

We'll also cover the powerful strategy of summarizing and then move on to the challenges of writing compositions: selecting a topic, developing a thesis statement, crafting introductions and conclusions as well as body paragraphs, and incorporating quotations.

TWR covers four types of paragraphs and, ultimately, compositions: expository, narrative, descriptive, and opinion or argumentative. We have a separate chapter (Chapter 10) devoted to writing argumentative essays, given the complexity of that particular genre and the emphasis that has recently been placed on it in many state standards.

How to Assess Writing and Adapt the Hochman Method to Your Classroom

The final section will guide you through the sometimes tricky process of assessment, which involves collecting writing samples early in the school year in order to set goals for individual students and for the class. (Bear in mind that you'll need to be familiar with the contents of this entire book before you'll be able to set those goals.) It's important to administer similar assessments at the middle and end of the year to see how your students are progressing.

The final two chapters provide suggestions about how to easily "revolutionize" your existing instructional materials so that they support the TWR strategies you are teaching. We also detail the sequence in which the strategies should be taught.

All of the activities in this book, when embedded in content that has been taught, are also highly effective tools for assessing students' comprehension and retention of material in the curriculum.

It turned out Ms. Cappiello was wrong: this year *was* different for her ninth graders. She ended up teaching them a number of TWR strategies, embedded in the content of the curriculum

At the end of the year, she gave her students another writing prompt. This one asked them to produce a paragraph about a person they had learned about and their impact.

Several students created topic sentences that used an appositive. Michael's first sentence, for example, was: "Martin Luther King Jr., a celebrated leader, taught and inspired people to follow him."

Students' sentences weren't perfect, but they were far more complex and detailed than what they had produced at the beginning of the year.

Sentence-level instruction had also dramatically boosted their reading comprehension, helping them understand complex syntax. And it had deepened their understanding of the content in the curriculum.

Over the course of the year, Ms. Cappiello had also taught her students how to construct outlines and use them to write paragraphs. Once they learned how to plan before writing, their paragraphs became more coherent. When they drafted and revised the paragraphs, she saw students drawing on their newly acquired sentence-level skills to vary their sentence structure and connect their thoughts.

That spring, she told her colleague that TWR had been transformative for her and her students. "It was a real game-changer," she said.

To Sum Up

As you introduce the sentence activities in these chapters to your students, you should keep the following points in mind:

- When introducing a new activity, model it for students first.

- Have students practice sentence-level activities orally as well as in writing, even if you're teaching older students.

- Have younger students (K–2) engage in sentence-level and outlining activities orally and as a whole class, for the most part.

- At any grade level, introduce new writing strategies or concepts orally and as a whole class, using familiar content.

- Once students have grasped a new writing concept, embed writing activities in the content you're teaching.

- Adapt activities for students at varying ability levels while covering the same content.

- When planning activities, write out the responses you anticipate getting from students.

- Plan your instruction so that your students will have the content knowledge they need to practice the activity successfully.

- As you progress through the sequence of activities, have students keep practicing TWR activities you've already covered to build on the skills they've acquired. You can use several different sentence activities at the same time, and you can have students move on to outlining and possibly writing paragraphs while they're still working on sentence activities.

1. What kind of preparation did you get to teach writing, if any?

2. What kinds of writing approaches have been used in the school(s) you've taught in and how successful do you think they were?

3. Why do many students struggle to learn to write?

4. What are the benefits of embedding explicit writing instruction in the content of the curriculum?

5. Why should the Hochman Method be implemented beginning in elementary school when possible?

6. What role does working memory play in writing?

7. How do each of the six principles contribute to positive learning outcomes?

Notes

1. National Center for Education Statistics, *The Nation's Report Card: Writing 2011* (Washington, DC: Institute of Education Sciences, US Department of Education, 2012), https://nces.ed.gov/nationsreportcard/pdf/main2011/2012470.pdf.

2. G.B. Skar, S. Graham, A. Huebner, et al., "A Longitudinal Intervention Study of the Effects of Increasing Amount of Meaningful Writing across Grades 1 and 2," *Reading and Writing* (2023), https://doi.org/10.1007/s11145-023-10460-0.

3. J. Gilbert and S. Graham, "Teaching Writing to Elementary Students in Grades 4–6: A National Survey," *The Elementary School Journal* 110(4), https://www.journals.uchicago.edu/doi/10.1086/651193.

   G. Troia and S. Graham, "Common Core Writing and Language Standards and Aligned State Assessments: A National Survey of Teacher Beliefs and Attitudes," *Reading and Writing* (2016), 29, 10.1007/s11145-016-9650-z.

   M. Brindle, S. Graham, K.R. Harris, and M. Hebert, "Third and Fourth Grade Teacher's Classroom Practices in Writing: A National Survey," *Reading and Writing: An Interdisciplinary Journal* (2016), 29(5): 929–954, https://doi.org/10.1007/s11145-015-9604-x.

   J. Myers, R.Q. Scales, D.L. Grisham, T.D. Wolsey, S. Dismuke, L. Smetana, K.K. Yoder, C. Ikpeze, K. Ganske, and S. Martin, "What about Writing? A National Exploratory Study of Writing Instruction in Teacher Preparation Programs," *Literacy Research and Instruction* (2016), 55(4), 309–330, https://doi.org/10.1080/19388071.2016.1198442

4. S.F. Reardon et al., "Patterns of Literacy among U.S. Students," *The Future of Children* (2013), 22: 17–37.

5. T. Shanahan, "Trying Again—What Teachers Need to Know about Sentence Comprehension," (13 August 2022), https://www.shanahanonliteracy.com/blog/trying-again-what-teachers-need-to-know-about-sentence-comprehension.

6. M. Hebert, A. Simpson, and S. Graham, "Comparing Effects of Different Writing Activities on Reading Comprehension: A Meta-Analysis," *Reading and Writing* (2013), 26: 111–138, doi:10.1007/s11145-012-9386-3.

   S. Graham, X. Liu, A. Aitken, C. Ng, B, Bartlett, K.R. Harris, and J. Holzapfel, "Effectiveness of Literacy Programs Balancing Reading and Writing

Instruction: A Meta-Analysis," *Reading Research Quarterly* (2018), 53(3): 279–304, https://doi.org /10.1002/rrq.194.

7. C.M. Scott and C.H. Balthazar, "The Role of Complex Sentence Knowledge in Children with Reading and Writing Difficulties," *Perspectives on Language and Literacy* (2013 Summer) 39(3): 18–30, PMID: 25821532; PMCID: PMC4373700.

   G. Gillon and B. Dodd, "The Effects of Training Phonological, Semantic, and Syntactic Processing Skills in Spoken Language on Reading Ability," *Language, Speech, and Hearing Services in Schools* (1995), 26: 58–68.

   E.A. Stevens, S. Park, and S. Vaughn, "A Review of Summarizing and Main Idea Interventions for Struggling Readers in Grades 3 through 12: 1978–2016," *Remedial and Special Education* (2018), 40(3), https://doi.org/10.1177/0741932517749940

   S. Graham and M.A. Hebert, "Writing to Read: Evidence for How Writing Can Improve Reading [A Carnegie Corporation Time to Act Report]," (Washington, DC: Alliance for Excellent Education, 2010).

   S. Graham, S.A. Kiuhara, and M. MacKay, "The Effects of Writing on Learning in Science, Social Studies, and Mathematics: A Meta-Analysis," *Review of Educational Research* 90(2), https:// journals.sagepub.com/doi/abs/10.3102 /0034654320914744?journalCode=rera].

8. S. Graham, J. Bruch, J. Fitzgerald, L. Friedrich, J. Furgeson, K. Greene, J. Kim, J. Lyskawa, C.B. Olson, and C. Smither Wulsin, "Teaching Secondary Students to Write Effectively (2016), NCEE 2017-4002.

9. M.J. Orosco and D.K. Reed, "Effects of Professional Development on English Learners," *Journal of Learning Disabilities* (2023), 56(4): 324–338, https:// doi.org/10.1177/00222194221099671.

10. National Reading Panel, "Teaching Children to Read: An Evidence-Based Assessment of the Scientific Research Literature on Reading and Its Implications for Reading Instruction," Reports of the Subgroups (2000), https://www.nichd.nih .gov/sites/default/files/publications/pubs/nrp /Documents/report.pdf.

11. *Orton-Gillingham: The Orton-Gillingham Approach.* (2022 May 11). https://www.orton-gillingham .com/approach/.

12. P. Tyre, "The Writing Revolution," *The Atlantic* (October 2012), www.theatlantic.com/magazine /archive/2012/10/the-writing-revolution/309090/.

13. Ibid., p. 3.

14. J. Karpicke and J.R. Blunt, "Retrieval Practice Produces More Learning than Elaborative Studying with Concept Mapping," *Science* (2011), 331: 772–775, https://doi.org/10.1126 /science.1199327.

15. M. Neelen and P.A. Kirschner, "Deliberate Practice: What It Is and What It Isn't," https:// 3starlearningexperiences.wordpress.com /2016/06/21/370/.

   K.A. Ericsson and R. Pool, *Peak: Secrets from the New Science of Expertise* (New York: Houghton Mifflin Harcourt, 2016).

16. B. Saddler, *Teacher's Guide to Effective Sentence Writing* (New York: The Guilford Press, 2012), p. 6.

17. N. Wexler, *The Knowledge Gap: The Hidden Cause of America's Broken Education System—and How to Fix It* (New York, Avery, an imprint of Penguin Random House LLC, 2019).

18. M. Brown, *Stone Soup: An Old Tale* (New York, Charles Scribner's Sons, 1947).

19. J. Marjokorpi, "The Relationship between Grammatical Understanding and Writing Skills in Finnish Secondary L1 Education," *Reading and Writing* (2023), 36: 2605–2625, https://doi .org/10.1007/s11145-022-10405-z.

20. S. Graham and D. Perin, *Writing Next: Effective Strategies to Improve Writing of Adolescents in Middle and High Schools. A Report to Carnegie Corporation of New York* (Washington, DC: Alliance for Excellent Education, 2007).

21. M. Scardamalia and C. Bereiter, "Knowledge Telling and Knowledge Transforming in Written Composition." In S. Rosenberg (ed.), *Advances in Applied Psycholinguistics* (1987), *Vol. 1. Disorders of First-Language Development; Vol. 2. Reading, Writing, and Language Learning* (Cambridge University Press), pp. 142–175, p. 149.

22. For more on this kind of "backward planning" and how it relates to writing instruction, see J. Hawkins, E. Ginty, K. LeClaire Kurzman, D. Leddy, and J. Miller, *Writing for Understanding* (South Strafford, VT: Vermont Writing Collaborative, 2008).

Sentences

CHAPTER 2
Sentences
Learning the Fundamentals

When I was teaching third grade, I would routinely assign paragraphs and essays. Students would write at length, but they almost always included phrases that they clearly thought were sentences and in fact were not. They seemed to believe phrases qualified as complete sentences if they put a capital at the beginning and a period at the end.

I was surprised that students had made it to third grade without having grasped the concept of a complete sentence—and I wasn't sure how to get the concept across in a way that translated into their writing. I didn't realize that my attempts at writing instruction were like trying to build a house starting with the roof.

Little did I know then that it's not just third graders who often haven't yet learned how to distinguish between a complete, coherent sentence and a group of words that doesn't express a complete thought—or, at the other extreme, a group of words that goes on beyond the boundaries of what a sentence should be. Many high school students also haven't acquired that knowledge, through no fault of their own.

If you want your students to write good paragraphs and compositions, you need to start building a solid foundation first—just the way you would start building a house. In writing, that foundation consists of sentences.

The importance of spending plenty of instructional time working with sentences can't be stressed enough. Students need to move from writing the way they speak to using the structures of written language. At one high-poverty high school, students' writing quality improved dramatically after just four months of instruction in TWR sentence strategies.[1]

Once students begin to construct more sophisticated sentences, they'll enhance not only their writing skills but also their reading comprehension.[2] In addition, sentence-level work will lay the groundwork for your students' ability to revise and edit when they tackle longer forms of writing.

To understand the value of sentence-level work, it helps to think about the concept of working memory—the aspect of our consciousness that takes in and tries to make sense of new information. As we've mentioned, the capacity of working memory is extremely limited, and writing imposes a heavy burden on it. Scientists refer to that kind of burden as **cognitive load**. If students are trying to juggle too many new things in working memory at the same time, the resulting cognitive load can prevent them from learning to write well and from understanding, analyzing, and retaining the content they're writing about. The most effective way to modulate that cognitive load is to begin writing instruction at the sentence level—and to provide built-in guardrails that help focus students' attention on what we want them to absorb.

If students are unfamiliar with the topic they're trying to write about, that adds to cognitive load. That's why it's important to introduce new writing strategies, including sentence-level ones, in the context of familiar material, freeing up cognitive capacity for understanding and retaining the strategies.

It's also important to bear in mind that different aspects of literacy impose different levels of cognitive load. Listening and speaking—which are components of literacy—don't in themselves impose any cognitive load because humans have evolved to do those things naturally. Reading and—especially—writing, on the other hand, can impose heavy cognitive loads. That's why it's important to model new strategies and have students practice them initially as a whole class, with the teacher's guidance.

At the same time, the concept of cognitive load helps explain how sentence-level work lays the crucial foundation for writing at length. As we mentioned, if you have knowledge of the topic you're writing about, that will lessen your cognitive load. But it's also important to have knowledge of how to do things like vary your sentence structure or use certain words to connect your thoughts. When students acquire that kind of knowledge through repeated practice with sentence-level activities, they have more cognitive capacity available for the many other aspects of writing that come into play when they're writing at length.

Another benefit of sentence-level instruction is that it can familiarize students with the complex syntax of written language. Reading complex text aloud to students and ensuring they're hearing the sentences can help—but it's even more powerful to teach students how to use those structures in their own writing.

Almost all the sentence-level strategies described in this book build and deepen knowledge. In fact, they do that even more effectively than lengthier writing assignments for inexperienced or struggling writers, who may be so overwhelmed by the mechanical demands of writing that they lack the capacity to focus on the meaning of what they're trying to write about.

Sentence-level work can also enable students to construct sentences that are informative, complex, and interesting. Many students, when asked to compose a sentence, may write something like this:

He led the Salt March.

The goal of TWR sentence-level strategies and the activities that support them is to enable students to write something more like this:

In 1930, Gandhi, a political and spiritual leader, led the Salt March to protest Great Britain's tax policies.

The second sentence has an **appositive** and is expanded to answer the questions *who*, *when*, and *why*. If you teach all these elements explicitly through TWR sentence-level strategies, your students will be able to construct far more sophisticated and informative responses. The second sentence also demonstrates far more content knowledge than the first one.

In this chapter, we'll describe activities that help students understand some basic sentence-level concepts. In later chapters, we'll cover activities that help students learn to craft more complex sentences.

What Makes a Sentence a Sentence? Correcting Fragments, Scrambled Sentences, and Run-Ons

WHY PRACTICE SENTENCE-DEFINING AND WORD-ORDERING?

- Helps students understand the concept of a complete sentence and discern sentence boundaries
- Helps students understand correct word order
- Provides practice with capitalization, punctuation, and using new spelling and vocabulary words
- Can serve as a comprehension check
- Helps more proficient students understand the meanings of subjects, predicates, and prepositional phrases
- Encourages careful reading and proofreading

A sentence consists of a group of words that includes a **subject** and a **predicate** and expresses a complete thought. Younger students and those who haven't yet developed good writing skills often struggle with the concept of a complete sentence. Everyone uses sentence fragments or incomplete sentences in spoken language, and students may continue to use them as they learn to write.

A **fragment** is a group of words that is not a grammatically complete sentence. Usually a fragment lacks a subject, verb, or both (e.g., "went shopping" or "to the store"), or it is a dependent clause that is not connected to an independent clause (e.g., "After I do my homework").

As we mentioned earlier, simply giving students these definitions isn't likely to help them write complete sentences. For many students, definitions are too abstract. They need to spend time hearing and reading complete sentences alongside sentence fragments and distinguishing between the two. Teachers also need to ask their students questions about fragments that will guide them to turn the fragments into complete sentences.

When you introduce your students to the concept of a complete sentence as opposed to a fragment, explain that while fragments may be fine in conversation, writing requires more precision. Help students understand that need for precision by giving them examples of sentence fragments and asking them what element is missing. Your students may need a lot of practice working with examples you provide before they can recognize fragments in their own writing.

Laying the Groundwork: Fixing Fragments Orally

Initially, when you give examples of fragments, it's best to present them orally rather than in writing. For example, you might say to the class:

ran to the park

With Level 1 students, avoid using technical grammatical terms such as *subject* and *predicate*, which may just confuse them. To guide them to supply a subject, you could ask, "Does that tell us *who* ran to the park? We need to know how to make these words into a complete sentence."

If you're teaching Level 2 students, you might say, "The subject (or predicate) is missing in this fragment. Can you make it into a complete sentence?"

Another example could be:

Sam and Dan

You might say, "We need to know *what they did.* Let's make this fragment into a complete sentence." Students would then supply a verb (such as *ran*) and perhaps a predicate (*ran to the park*) to create a sentence.

If you give your students examples of fragments orally that are related to the content they're studying, it will have the added advantage of deepening their knowledge of the content. These examples can be more or less challenging, depending on the complexity of the content and the knowledge demands of the fragment you choose to give them.

When you make up fragments, it's important to *anticipate the correct responses* and be sure that your students have the knowledge they need to repair them. When they retrieve that knowledge, they'll be further reinforcing it in long-term memory.

Level 1 Example

If you've been teaching your students about the civil rights movement, and you're not sure of their grasp of the material, you might give them this fragment:

> *helped organize freedom summer*

Your students could then draw on the content they've learned to turn the fragment into a sentence, such as the following:

> *Fannie Lou Hamer helped organize Freedom Summer.*

Level 2 Example

If you're teaching a class on World War I and you want to assess what your students learned about the long-term impact of the Treaty of Versailles, you might give them this fragment:

> *contributed to the rise of fascist regimes*

Your students may respond with the following:

> *The harsh terms of the Treaty of Versailles contributed to the rise of fascist regimes.*

Writing Activities with Fragments

Once your students know how to distinguish fragments from sentences through oral practice, have them practice with written examples.

Fragments or Sentences?

Begin by giving your students a list that includes fragments and complete sentences, and tell them to mark the sentences with an *S* and the fragments with an *F*. Have them add correct capitalization and punctuation to the sentences. They should then convert the fragments into complete sentences with appropriate capitalization and punctuation. **When creating the list, be careful not to capitalize or punctuate either the fragments or the sentences.**

If you've been teaching your students about Greek mythology, you could give them a list such as the following. After marking these examples *F* or *S*, students should convert the fragments into sentences and add the correct punctuation and capitalization to the sentences.

DIRECTIONS: Write *S* if the words form a complete sentence. Capitalize and punctuate the sentences. Write *F* if the words are a sentence fragment. Change the fragments into sentences with correct capitalization and punctuation.

1. __*F*__ built a labyrinth for king minos

   Daedalus built a labyrinth for King Minos.

2. __*F*__ daedalus and his son

   Daedalus and his son were imprisoned by King Minos of Crete.

3. __*S*__ icarus was excited to be free

   Icarus was excited to be free.

4. __*F*__ destroyed icarus's wings

   The heat of the sun destroyed Icarus's wings.

Changing Fragments to Sentences

A science teacher might want to review the periodic table and also help students reinforce their understanding of sentences. She might give them the following two fragments and ask them to change them into sentences with proper punctuation and capitalization:

DIRECTIONS: Change the fragments to complete sentences, adding correct capitalization and punctuation.

1. the periodic table

   The periodic table is an organized array of elements.

2. has atomic number 56

   Barium has atomic number 56.

⚠ BE CAREFUL

Keep the following points in mind when you're creating sentence fragment activities for your students:

- Don't capitalize or punctuate either the fragments or the sentences. For example, give students the fragment "beyond the forest" rather than "Beyond the forest." Give them the sentence "beyond the forest there was a clearing" rather than "Beyond the forest, there was a clearing." Capitalizing and punctuating only the sentences would give away which examples are which!

- Be careful not to use commands (e.g., "run quickly") when you're giving students examples of fragments. Commands can be complete sentences. If you're not sure whether an example could be a command, try doing the "please" test: if you can put "please" in front of it and have it make sense, it's a command.

- Avoid using kernel sentences (e.g., "they argued") as examples of fragments because they are complete sentences.

- If you give students a fragment that you intend to be a subject, don't include a verb (e.g., "Nelson Mandela was").

- If you give students a fragment that you intend to be a predicate, include the verb (e.g., "was the mythological founder of Rome").

- Start with fragments that just have subjects or predicates; hold off on using prepositional phrases ("on the ship") or dependent clauses ("after the study was published").

- Make sure your students already have been exposed to the information they will need to complete sentence fragments.

- Don't just lift a fragment directly from a sentence in a text students have read. That would turn the activity into a fill-in-the-blank exercise rather than one that requires them to retrieve information and put it in their own words.

- Before creating a fragment, first create the anticipated response you would like students to develop from the fragment.

Differentiating Fragment Activities

If some of your students need extra support:

- Capitalize the proper nouns.
- Use only subjects and predicates as fragments initially.

Solve the Puzzle: Unscrambling Scrambled Sentences

Rearranging jumbled groups of words into coherent sentences helps students grasp several fundamental concepts: the nature of a complete sentence, the order in which words should be sequenced, and the rules of punctuation and capitalization. When the activity is embedded in curriculum content, students also will be deepening their understanding of that content and of new vocabulary words they've learned.

Scrambled sentences can include statements, questions, and exclamations, but should *avoid commands*. With commands—such as "Get the book"—the subject (*you*) is implied rather than stated explicitly, and that can be confusing.

Use between four and six words per sentence for Level 1 students and between seven and ten words for Level 2 students. As with fragment activities, you should generally not include any capitalization or punctuation in your scrambled groups of words.

Here are some examples of scrambled sentences with anticipated student responses. In the Level 1 examples, we've put the first word in bold as an example of how you can help students who need more support.

Level 1 Example

DIRECTIONS: Rearrange the words into sentences. Add the correct capitalization and punctuation.

1. salt contain water **oceans**

   Oceans contain salt water.

2. are continents **there** seven

   There are seven continents.

Level 2 Example

DIRECTIONS: Rearrange the words into sentences. Add the correct capitalization and punctuation.

1. river land around belonged the mississippi to france

   Land around the Mississippi River belonged to France.

2. louisiana cost the dollars purchase million fifteen

   The Louisiana Purchase cost fifteen million dollars.

⚠ BE CAREFUL

Keep the following points in mind when you're creating scrambled sentence activities for your students:

- Avoid too many function words (*the*, *an*, and so on) when creating scrambled sentences.

- Make sure that the number of words in student-facing material is equal to the number of words in the anticipated response.

- There should be only one correct way to arrange the scrambled words.

Differentiating Scrambled Sentence Activities

For Level 1 students who need additional support:

- Capitalize proper nouns.
- Write the first word in bold letters.

Put the Brakes On: Correcting Run-On Sentences

Run-on sentences are seen frequently in student writing. There's no quick solution, but there are a few effective ways to help students become aware of run-ons and learn how to correct them.

Try putting a run-on sentence on the board daily, preferably embedded in content or relating to a subject students have already learned about. First, ask a student to read the sentence aloud, without pausing, and then ask the class what's wrong with it. After doing this a few times, you can just put run-ons on the board and have students correct them without hearing them read aloud. Continue to do this as a daily warm-up activity until students start correcting them in their writing.

For example, if you are reading *Bridge to Terabithia*[3], you could give students the following run-on sentence to correct:

> *Leslie showed Jess the kingdom of Terabithia, it was a magical place in the woods where they could be themselves, they were king and queen of this land, it was their escape from the real world.*

If the word *and* is the biggest culprit in the run-ons your students write, tell them to go back and look at every *and* they've put into a sentence. Then have them ask themselves whether they're joining two ideas that should be in separate sentences.

Another technique that could help is to give students a list of sentences, some of which are run-ons. Have them identify the run-ons and divide them into sentences.

To Sum Up

- Embed sentence activities in the content you're teaching as much as possible to check students' comprehension and deepen their understanding.

- Use sentence activities to teach grammar and conventions.

- When introducing a new activity, begin by modeling it and having students practice it orally.

- Have students practice activities with sentence fragments, scrambled sentences, and run-on sentences to help them grasp the concept of a complete sentence.

- When assigning sentence fragments, be sure that students have the information they need to turn the fragments into complete sentences.

1. What are important things to remember when creating sentence fragment activities?

2. What are important things to remember when creating scrambled sentences activities?

3. How can correcting run-on sentences be addressed?

4. What are some ways fragment and scrambled sentences activities could be differentiated?

5. Create fragment and scrambled sentence activities based on content you will be teaching.

Notes

1. T.A.M. Vroom, *Adolescent Writing Instruction: A Return to the Sentence* (New York: St. John's University, 2021).

2. S. Graham and M.A. Hebert, *Writing to Read: Evidence for How Writing Can Improve Reading* (A Carnegie Corporation Time to Act Report) (Washington, DC: Alliance for Excellent Education, 2010).

D.D. Neville and E.F. Searls, "A Meta-Analytic Review of the Effect of Sentence-Combining on Reading Comprehension," *Reading Research and Instruction* (1991), 31(1): 63–76.

F. O'Hare, *Sentence Combining: Improving Student Writing Without Formal Grammar Instruction* (NCTE Committee on Research Report Series, No. 15) (Urbana, IL: NCTE, 1973).

P.A. Wilkinson and D. Patty, "The Effects of Sentence Combining on the Reading Comprehension of Fourth-Grade Students," *Research in the Teaching of English* (1993), 27(1): 104–125.

R.P. Zipoli, "Unraveling Difficult Sentences: Strategies to Support Reading Comprehension," *Intervention in School and Clinic* (2017), 52(4): 218–227.

3. K. Paterson, *Bridge to Terabithia* (New York: HarperCollins, 2008).

CHAPTER 3

Sentence Expansion and Note-Taking

Elaborating on Information

As part of a tenth-grade science unit on climate change, Mr. Yates had assigned his class an article about using biofuels instead of fossil fuels. He had found the article on a website that offered science texts at a high school level, and, after reading it himself, he thought his students would find it engaging.

The article explained that biofuels, which are made from plants, are thought to be more climate-friendly than fossil fuels. But, in fact, as the article detailed, many biofuels end up being just as bad for the climate, if not worse, because a lot of fossil fuel is required to produce them.

The next day, Mr. Yates gave his students a do-now question at the beginning of class to assess their understanding of the article: "Why are the most commonly used biofuels not climate-friendly?"

The answers were disappointing. "They make the earth warmer," a student named Michelle wrote, with no further explanation. A few students wrote responses that were impressively complete, but Mr. Yates noted they were all strikingly similar. He then realized why: students had simply copied their sentences from the article.

How can a teacher like Mr. Yates help his students truly understand what they read—and demonstrate their understanding in writing? It's often not enough to merely ask them a question about a text they've read. They may need to be taught how to engage in activities that require them to think analytically about the content of the text and enable them to craft responses that reflect their thinking. Two such strategies are sentence expansion and note-taking, both of which we'll describe in this chapter.

Expanding Students' Knowledge and Responses

WHY PRACTICE SENTENCE EXPANSION ACTIVITIES?

- Enables students to anticipate what a reader needs to know and then to provide that information
- Checks comprehension
- Teaches note-taking strategies (key words and phrases, abbreviations, and symbols)
- Develops the ability to summarize
- Reinforces academic knowledge

Sentence expansion is one of the best techniques available to help students process new information in a manageable way, enabling them both to understand it and to transfer it to long-term memory. It can also help them gauge what information they need to include to make their writing intelligible to a reader who lacks extensive prior knowledge of the subject.

HERE'S HOW SENTENCE EXPANSION WORKS:

1. Give your students a brief—but complete—sentence called a kernel sentence. At the same time, select appropriate question words for them to respond to from this list: *who, what, when, where, why,* and *how.*

2. Then have your students provide answers to those question words in the form of notes. (In the second part of this chapter, we'll cover how to help students acquire the skill of note-taking.)

3. Finally, have students convert those notes into a complete sentence.

Level 1 Example

DIRECTIONS: Expand the sentence.

It sprouts.

What? *seed*

When? *after it gets water + sunlight*

Where? *soil*

EXPANDED SENTENCE: *After it gets water and sunlight, a seed sprouts in the soil.*

Level 2 Example

DIRECTIONS: Expand the sentence.

Mesopotamians built ziggurats.

When? *ancient times*

Where? *center of city-states*

Why? *provide earthly homes for gods & goddesses*

EXPANDED SENTENCE: *In ancient times, Mesopotamians built ziggurats at the center of city-states to provide earthly homes for gods and goddesses.*

Creating a Kernel Sentence

To familiarize your students with the concept of sentence expansion, use a simple, declarative sentence as your example of a kernel sentence. It should have only one verb and no modifiers. You might use something like "Jane ran." or "The candidates will debate." As with the other strategies, when you introduce it, it's not necessary to embed the example in the content you're teaching. It is important, though, to use a kernel that's grounded in a topic your students have knowledge about.

When creating kernel sentences, make sure that you're not using a sentence fragment or omitting an object. To get the most out of this exercise—especially later when you embed it in content—**the kernel must be a complete sentence**. "She enjoys," for example, is not a sentence and can't be used as a kernel—it doesn't express a complete thought. **Avoid using commands**, such as "Run fast," because students may have trouble determining who or what the subject is.

Choosing Question Words

It's helpful to post a chart of the question words at eye level in your classroom. The questions words should be listed in the order shown in Exhibit 3.1:

Who?

What?

When?

Where?

Why?

How?

Exhibit 3.1

Sentence expansion may seem simple, but it requires writers to put themselves in the place of the reader and figure out what the reader needs to know.

KEEP IN MIND THE FOLLOWING TIPS WHEN DEVELOPING SENTENCE EXPANSION ACTIVITIES:

- **You don't need to use all the question words with each kernel.** When introducing the sentence expansion strategy, it's a good idea to present just one, two, or three.

- **The question words *when, where,* and *why* are the best to use when introducing kernel sentences to Level 1 students.**

- **The teacher should ALWAYS be the one to supply the question words—not the students.** However, when writing independently, students should be able to expand sentences by selecting the question words they believe will give the reader the most relevant information.

- **The question words you choose will depend on the kernel you're using and the information you want your students to add.** For example, if you use the kernel "Jim ran," you won't use the question word *who*, because the reader already knows the answer. However, if the kernel is "He ran," it would make sense to use the question word *who*.

- **The question words *who* and *what* will always correspond to a pronoun in the kernel.** If you write the kernel, "It sank," the response to the question word *what* would be, "the *Titanic*." Try to use only one pronoun in a kernel.

- **Students need to have enough information about the topic to expand the sentence.** If they don't know anything about the *Titanic*, for example, they won't know what "It" refers to in the kernel "It sank." They will also need the information required to answer the question words.

- **When expanding a sentence, students should begin it with the response to *when*.** This gives them practice with a construction that is common in writing but not in speech.

- **When expanding sentences, students should not add information beyond what is included in the kernel or in their responses to question words. They should also not delete information from the kernel.**

- **The question word *how* can indicate a response that is an adverb:**

  Ailish walked into the house *slowly*.

  Or it can describe how something is done (by):

  Sarah figured out the answer *by* using her calculator.

TECHNICAL TIP

Formatting counts! When your students provide written answers to the question words you give them, they will be writing in note form rather than complete sentences. That means you'll need to provide them with worksheets that have *dotted* lines after the question words.

In TWR, dotted lines are *always* used for notes (key words and phrases, abbreviations, and symbols), and solid lines are *always* used for complete sentences. Make sure your students understand the difference between what is expected on the dotted lines and the solid ones. We describe how to provide instruction in writing notes in the following section.

Students' expanded sentences need to be grammatically correct, with appropriate capitalization and punctuation.

Examples of Sentence Expansion in Content

Once your students have the idea of sentence expansion, it's time to give them a sentence expansion activity that's embedded in content you're currently teaching. You have to decide what you want your students to learn from the activity, anticipate their responses, and assess whether they have enough knowledge to produce the responses you're looking for.

Always remind your students that they should begin to expand with *when* if it is one of the question words.

English

If you're reading *Animal Farm*[1] by George Orwell, you might consider the following activity:

DIRECTIONS: Expand the sentence.

He called a meeting.

Who?   _Old Major_ ....

When?   _3 days b/4 he died_ ....

Where?   _Manor Farm_ ....

Why?   _encourage animals to revolt_ ....

EXPANDED SENTENCE: _Three days before he died, Old Major called a meeting at Manor Farm to encourage the animals to revolt._

Math

If you're teaching math and covering the distributive property, you might give your students the following problem:

$2(x + 6) = 14$

Then you could give students a hypothetical student's answer along with the kernel:

She made a mistake.

Students would then have to answer the question words *who*, *when*, and *why*. The resulting expanded sentence might look like what is shown here:

	Jasmine's Work
Problem	$2(x + 6) = 14$
Step 1	$2x + 6 = 14$
Step 2	$2x + 6 = 14$ $- 6 = - 6$ $2x = 8$
Answer	$\dfrac{2x}{2} = \dfrac{8}{2}$ $x = 4$

DIRECTIONS: Expand the sentence.

She made a mistake.

Who?   *Jasmine*

When?   *Step 1*

Why?   *didn't distribute 2 to both terms inside ()*

EXPANDED SENTENCE: *In step 1, Jasmine made a mistake because she didn't distribute the 2 to both of the terms inside the parentheses.*

History

DIRECTIONS: Expand the sentence.

She became pharaoh.

Who? _Hatshepsut_

When? _after husband died_

Why? _b/c stepson too young to rule Egypt_

EXPANDED SENTENCE: _After her husband died, Hatshepsut became pharaoh because her stepson was too young to rule Egypt._

Science

DIRECTIONS: Expand the sentence.

They make good barriers.

What? _lipids_

Where? _around cells_

Why? _non-polar_

EXPANDED SENTENCE: _Lipids make good barriers around cells because they are non-polar._

The following supporting activities can help deepen student understanding of why, when, and how to use this strategy.

Level 1 Sentence Expansion Scaffolds

If you're reading *Charlotte's Web*[2] by E.B. White, you might consider the following activity:

DIRECTIONS: Which word tells *who, what, when, where,* or *how?*

farms	_where_	quickly	_how_
rabbits	_what_	yesterday	_when_
carefully	_how_	inside	_where_
the fair	_where_	Charlotte	_who_
Mr. Arable	_who_	newspaper	_what_

DIRECTIONS: Identify what the underlined words tell: *who, what, when, where, why,* or *how?*

Leonardo da Vinci was born in <u>Italy.</u>	_where_
<u>At the age of 14</u>, da Vinci became an artist's apprentice.	_when_
<u>The Medici family</u> employed da Vinci for years.	_who_
<u>Between 1503 and 1519</u>, da Vinci painted the *Mona Lisa.*	_when_
Da Vinci moved to France <u>because he was invited by King Francis I.</u>	_why_

DIRECTIONS: Identify the question word(s)—*who, what, when, where, why,* and/or *how*—that were used to expand each kernel sentence.

KERNEL: They tag butterflies.

EXPANDED SENTENCE: Scientists tag butterflies because they want to track their travel routes.

QUESTION WORDS: *who, why*

KERNEL: Monarch butterflies migrate.

EXPANDED SENTENCE: At the end of October, monarch butterflies migrate to Southern California and Mexico.

QUESTION WORDS: *when, where*

Level 2 Sentence Expansion Scaffolds

If your class is reading *Frankenstein*[3] by Mary Shelley, you might consider the following activity:

DIRECTIONS: Underline and then identify the question word(s)—*who, what, when, where, why,* and/or *how*—that were used to expand each kernel sentence.

KERNEL: She published *Frankenstein*.

EXPANDED SENTENCE: In 1818, Mary Shelley published *Frankenstein*.

QUESTION WORDS: *when, who*

KERNEL: He is feverish.

EXPANDED SENTENCE: Every night, Dr. Frankenstein is feverish because he is obsessed with finding the secret of life.

QUESTION WORDS: *when, who, why*

Differentiating Sentence Expansion Activities

If your students need additional support:

- Put a star next to the word *when* on the worksheet to remind students to start their expanded sentences with their answer to that word.

DIRECTIONS: Expand the kernel sentence.

She won the Nobel Peace Prize.

Who? *Malala*

★ When? *2014*

Why? *because she fought for girls' education*

EXPANDED SENTENCE: *In 2014, Malala won the Nobel Peace Prize because she fought for girls' education.*

- Number the question words in the order you want students to use the answers in their expanded sentences.

DIRECTIONS: Expand the kernel sentence.

She won the Nobel Peace Prize.

(2) Who? *Malala*

(1) When? *2014*

(3) Why? *because she fought for girls' education*

EXPANDED SENTENCE: *In 2014, Malala won the Nobel Peace Prize because she fought for girls' education.*

⚠ BE CAREFUL

It's important to be especially careful when giving students sentence expansion activities—there are many ways to create unintended confusion. Remember these guidelines:

- **Tell your students not to expand the kernel** by adding information that is not in their responses to the question words, or by substituting other words for those that are in the kernel (unless it's a pronoun) or deleting information from it.

- **The question word *when* should refer only to a specific time or time period, not in the sense of *whenever*** (e.g., "When I eat too much, my stomach hurts.").

- **If you will be using *who* or *what* as question words, include a corresponding pronoun in the kernel.** If one of the question words is *who*, and the answer is "Lincoln," the kernel should read, "He issued an order." If one of the question words is *what*, and the answer is "the book," the kernel should read, "It was stolen."

- **Commands should not be used as kernels.** "Ride cars" or "Go fast" can be confusing because the subject is implied. If you ask *who*, it's not clear what response you're expecting.

- **Fragments can't be kernels!** "In the school yard" and "Irrigation of deserts" are not kernels.

- **Keep kernels brief (three or four words).**

- Even though you want students to begin their response with *when*—if that's one of your question words—**always list the question words on the worksheet in the same order as they appear on the wall chart: *who, what, when, where, why,* and *how.*** This sequence of the terms is commonly used, and it's helpful for students to get used to it.

- **Remember that you, NOT the students, choose the question words**. If students choose their own question words, they may leave out important information. Once they become more experienced writers, they can come up with question words to expand sentences when they're revising their own writing.

The Power of Note-Taking: Key Words and Phrases, Abbreviations, and Symbols

We often assume that students will just figure out how to take notes efficiently, but that's not always the case. Considering how frequently we're required to take notes throughout our lives, we believe that giving students a solid foundation in note-taking will benefit them in multiple ways. That foundation should include teaching students how to identify important words and phrases and how to use symbols and abbreviations. Many students need explicit instruction in how to distill information into note form, using abbreviations and symbols.

WHY PRACTICE NOTE-TAKING?

- Helps students distinguish essential from nonessential material
- Boosts comprehension
- Enables the absorption and retention of information
- Promotes analytical thinking
- Enables students to outline paragraphs and compositions before drafting them

Converting text or speech to notes is one of the most valuable skills you can teach your students. It's far more than just a quick way to get information down on paper—although it does serve that purpose. It's a way of enabling students to process and understand what they've read, heard, and learned.

Changing sentences to notes requires students to extract the most important words and phrases and render them in a different mode of expression. That exercise prevents rote copying, ensures comprehension, and promotes absorption and retention of information. For more information on these benefits of note-taking, see the Ask the Experts section.

Learning to identify key words and phrases in a text and reduce them to notes is also a crucial step in the Hochman Method. Your students will need to know how to use key words and phrases to respond to the question words you provide for sentence expansion activities. They'll use the same technique to produce outlines for paragraphs and compositions—and to take notes on their reading or what they're learning in class.

As students gain more experience, they will create their own unique note-taking style. However, initially it's crucial to introduce them to specific techniques and give them plenty of practice with them.

Note-taking is not only a valuable skill; it's also a powerful way to boost comprehension and reinforce knowledge.

Introducing Students to Note-Taking

As with all TWR activities, when you're introducing students to note-taking, model the activity first. Although it's not essential to embed the sentences in the content of the curriculum at this point, it will provide an opportunity to boost students' learning when you do—assuming it's content that has already been covered.

The following sequence for modeling note-taking activities can be done with the whole class. Each step can be followed by independent practice. (The example below would be appropriate for students in fourth grade and up. For grades 1–3, only key words and phrases should be used for notes—not symbols and abbreviations.)

1. **Underline key words and phrases in a sentence.** (Be sure the sentence has several substantive words and phrases.)

   The <u>magma chamber</u> is a <u>zone</u> of <u>molten rock</u>.

2. **Convert a sentence into notes.**

   The magma chamber is a zone of molten rock.

   magma chamber = zone/molten rock ....

3. **Convert given notes into a sentence.**

   ↑ gases → magma blasting through Earth's surface ....

   The increase of gases leads to magma blasting through Earth's surface.

Introduce your students to common abbreviations such as *b/c* for *because*, *w/* for *with*, and *w/o* for *without*. Remind them that when they're writing notes, they should omit words such as *the*, *and*, and *a*.

The following chart lists some of the most frequently used symbols. Note that the = sign can also be used to indicate an appositive.

Symbols

+ OR **&**	**and**
=	**means that, equals, same as**
→	**leads to, results in, cause-effect**
↑	**increase, growth, rise**
↓	**decrease, decline**
/	**new idea**
>	**more than**
<	**less than**
☆	**important**

Consider posting this chart where students can refer to it. See Appendix B for a more extensive chart of common abbreviations and symbols.

RESOURCE

Abbreviations and Symbols
Appendix B

⚠ BE CAREFUL

- Don't try to teach students to underline and take notes from texts with simple, unelaborated sentences. In these materials, often many of the words and sentences are equally meaningful, making the task of identifying the most important ideas or words impossible. This is especially true of material that has been adapted for younger or struggling readers.

- When using abbreviations and symbols, make sure you don't use slashes to break up a thought cluster. For example, you would not want students to write notes on the Continental Congress like this:

❌ INCORRECT NOTE-TAKING:

Continental Congress = meeting/of/states

We're not providing Level 1 examples of note-taking activities because Level 1 students should mainly use key words and phrases under a teacher's guidance, when engaging in sentence expansion activities and creating Single-Paragraph Outlines. The latter are described in detail in Chapter 6.

Level 2 Examples

DIRECTIONS: Change the sentences into notes (key words, phrases, abbreviations, and symbols).

1. The assassination of Franz Ferdinand, the archduke of Austria, led to World War I.

   assassination of Franz Ferdinand = archduke of Austria → WWI

2. At the beginning of World War I, the Allies were France, the United Kingdom, and Russia, while the Central Powers were Germany and Austria-Hungary.

   beg. of WWI/Allies = France, UK, + Russia/Central Powers = Germany + Austria-Hungary

DIRECTIONS: Change the notes into sentences.

1. Neolithic Rev. = 1st Agricultural Rev. → civilization

   The Neolithic Revolution, the first Agricultural Revolution, led to civilization.

2. invention of new tools → easier farming + ↑ food supply

   The invention of new tools led to easier farming and an increased food supply.

ASK THE EXPERTS

Research has shown that note-taking generally improves learning, for two reasons.

- Note-taking produces more engagement with content, leading to better retention and comprehension.

- There's a second boost when (or if) students review their notes to study the material.

Teaching students how to use key words, phrases, abbreviations, and symbols helps by making it easier for students to distill and write down information.

It's easier for students to take notes when reading or when listening to a recorded lecture. They can pause to think and write down information rather than having to do that while trying to keep up with what the teacher is saying. In fact, one way teachers can make note-taking during class easier is to pause, giving students time to take notes. They might also have students use a break to look over and revise their notes, perhaps with a partner or in a small group. Studies have shown that when students revise their notes, they retain more information—especially if that happens *during* a class rather than after it's over, or during a pause in reading.[4]

Another way to make note-taking easier is to alert students to how many points you'll be making or to simply say something like, "This is an important point—be sure to add it to your notes."[5] Research has found that providing students with complete, well-written notes *after* they've taken their own notes can significantly boost their learning.[6]

Teachers can also provide "guided notes," such as an outline that includes some information but leaves space for students to fill in notes on key points. That approach can substantially increase student achievement across all grade levels, including for students with disabilities.[7] Simply giving students complete, prewritten notes, however, is unlikely to work well.

There's also been research on the relative advantages of taking notes by hand rather than on a laptop or other digital device. Students can take notes faster on a laptop, which enables them to pay more attention to what the teacher is saying. However, taking notes on a computer can result in a transcript of what is being said rather than a summary of important points. Taking notes by hand may lead to deeper processing of the material, since students need to analyze the information and extract what is most important.[8]

Whether using a laptop or taking notes by hand is better may depend on the student and the material. If the material is complex and hard to follow, it might make more sense for students to type their notes, giving them more time and cognitive capacity to attend to what the teacher is saying.[9] They can then go over their notes and, if necessary, revise later.

Bear in mind that note-taking can impose a heavy burden on **working memory**, especially if a student is trying to take notes during a live lecture. That's because the student has to understand what the teacher is saying, figure out the key points, possibly connect them to points that have already been made, summarize or paraphrase the information—and then write it down while the teacher is moving on to the next point. All of that can impose a significant cognitive load, possibly *diminishing* understanding and retention.[10]

In the months that followed Mr. Yates's disappointing experiences with the articles on biofuels, he guided his students through sentence expansion activities and taught them the skills of note-taking: how to identify the key words in a sentence, how to use arrows to indicate cause and effect, and how to abbreviate common words like *because*. He had posted a chart of symbols and abbreviations on the classroom wall, and students had become accustomed to using them.

The class had moved on from climate change to animal behavior. One day, Mr. Yates assigned an article about why sharks sleep and told students to take notes on it during and after reading, using the skills they'd learned. He also gave them a kernel sentence to expand, with question words: "They sleep."

The next day in class, he gave them a do-now question: "What can data on shark sleep tell us about the function of sleep in animals generally?"

Michelle—who had given a minimal answer to the question on biofuels months before—wrote this: "Scientists did an experiment showing that sharks use less energy when they sleep, which means they have a lower metabolic rate. The scientists say that supports their hypothesis that sleep helps animals, including humans, conserve energy."

As Mr. Yates read through Michelle's response and others, he found himself smiling. The students hadn't just parroted the article, and their answers showed they had truly understood its content. He felt he had helped set them up for success in eleventh grade—and beyond.

To Sum Up

- List question words on a wall chart in this order: *who, what, when, where, why,* and *how.*

- Provide kernel sentences that express complete thoughts but are **not** commands, questions, or fragments.

- Level 1 students should start expanding sentences using the question words *when, where,* and *why.*

- There should be only one pronoun in a kernel.

- Students should write answers to question words in note form on dotted lines and write their expanded sentences on solid lines.

- Students should begin their expanded sentences with *when* if it is one of the question words.

- Students' expanded sentences should not add, delete, or substitute information (unless it's replacing a pronoun).

- Use sentence expansion activities to help students anticipate what the reader needs to know.

- Use sentence expansion activities to check students' comprehension of content.

- Note-taking is a powerful strategy for gaining and retaining knowledge.

- Below mid–third grade, note-taking should be limited to key words and phrases. After that point, begin to add symbols and abbreviations at your discretion.

BOOK DISCUSSION QUESTIONS

1. Why should students practice expanding sentences?

2. What are important things to remember when creating sentence expansion activities?

3. What are ways sentence expansion activities can be scaffolded and differentiated for students?

4. Create a sentence expansion activity based on content you will be teaching.

5. Why should students learn how to take notes?

6. What are the steps to introducing students to note-taking?

7. What can you do to ensure students become effective note-takers?

Notes

1. G. Orwell, *Animal Farm* (Glasgow: William Collins, 2021).

2. E.B. White, *Charlotte's Web.* 1st ed. (New York: Harper & Brothers, 1952).

3. M. Shelley, *Frankenstein* (New York: Penguin Classics, 2012).

5. J. Gonzalez, "Note-Taking: A Research Roundup," *Cult of Pedagogy Blog* (9 September 2018), https://www.cultofpedagogy.com/note-taking/.

5. Gonzalez, "Note-Taking."

6. Gonzalez, "Note-Taking."

7. Gonzalez, "Note-Taking."

8. C. Kuepper-Tetzel, "Factors of Effective Note-Taking: Application of Cognitive Load Theory," *The Learning Scientists Blog* (13 September 2018), https://www.learningscientists.org/blog/2018/9/13-1.

9. Association for Psychological Science, "Take Notes by Hand for Better Long-Term Comprehension" (14 April 2014), www.psychologicalscience.org/news/releases/take-notes-by-hand-for-better-long-term-comprehension.html.

   P.A. Mueller and D.M. Oppenheimer, "The Pen Is Mightier than the Keyboard: Advantages of Longhand over Laptop Note Taking," *Psychological Science* (2014), 25(6): 1159–1168, http://pss.sagepub.com/content/25/6/1159.

10. A. Piolat, T. Olive, and R. Kellogg, "Cognitive Effort during Note Taking," *Applied Cognitive Psychology* (2005), 19: 291–312, 10.1002/acp.1086.

CHAPTER 4

Sentences

Introducing Variety and Complexity

At the beginning of the school year, Mr. White gave his third graders a prompt to get a sense of their writing ability: "Please write a paragraph about the best part of your summer."

The response from Lola in Exhibit 4.1 was pretty typical.

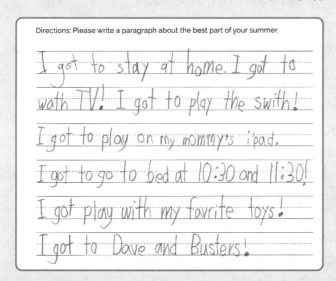

Directions: Please write a paragraph about the best part of your summer.

I got to stay at home. I got to wath TV! I got to play the swith! I got to play on my mommy's i'pad. I got to go to bed at 10:30 and 11:30! I got play with my favrite toys! I got to Dave and Busters!

Exhibit 4.1

Mr. White tried to focus on the positive. Lola had written complete sentences, and she'd spelled most of the words correctly. Her capitalization and punctuation were also exemplary, and she had even used an apostrophe. In addition, the entire paragraph was focused on the topic of the prompt.

On the other hand, the sentences in Lola's paragraph all had the same simple structure. One ended in an exclamation point instead of a period, but that was about it for variety. Basically, her paragraph was just a list.

In previous years, Mr. White had tried to help his students create more complex sentences, but his suggestions—for example, not to end almost every sentence with an exclamation point—hadn't had much effect.

He had also tried encouraging students to create sentences that were more like those in the children's literature they read, but they didn't seem to know how to do that. In fact, it wasn't always clear they understood those complex sentences.

The fact is, some students may not know how to vary their sentence structure unless they've been explicitly introduced to different types of sentences and how to use them. Once they're aware of the possibilities, they're in a much better position to create engaging prose that incorporates a range of structures, including complex sentences with multiple clauses.

And, as we've mentioned, teaching students how to construct complex sentences can also boost their reading comprehension.[1] Because the syntax, or sentence structure, of written language is more complex than that of spoken language, it's often unfamiliar and confusing for students. Written sentences may have multiple clauses, and the subject and verb may be separated by a lot of other information. That can lead students to assume, for example, that the word closest to the verb is the subject of the sentence even when it's not.

Even children's books often use more complex syntax than adult conversation.[2] As the grade levels go up and students are expected to read texts with increasingly complex syntax—including original historical documents—lack of familiarity with complex syntax can pose a serious barrier to comprehension.

The following excerpts from children's literature, a classic work of fiction, and a historical document illustrate the complexity and length of sentences that students may encounter and find difficult to understand.

Next morning when the first light came into the sky and the sparrows stirred in the trees, when the cows rattled their chains and then roosters crowed and the automobiles went whispering along the road, Wilbur awoke and looked for Charlotte.[3]

Charlotte's Web by E.B. White

In consideration of the day and hour of my birth, it was declared by the nurse, and by some sage women in the neighborhood who had taken a lively interest in me several months before there was any possibility of our becoming personally acquainted, first that I was destined to be unlucky in life; and secondly, that I was privileged to see ghosts and spirits; both these gifts inevitably attaching, as they believed, to all unlucky infants of either gender, born toward the small hours on a Friday night.[4]

David Copperfield by Charles Dickens

When in the course of human events, it becomes necessary for one people to dissolve the political bonds which have connected them with another, and to assume among the powers of the earth, the separate and equal station to which the Laws of Nature and of Nature's God entitle them, a decent respect to the opinions of mankind requires that they should declare the causes which impel them to the separation.[5]

The United States Declaration of Independence

Lack of familiarity with complex syntax is a widespread problem. According to one study of around 25,000 American students, only 10 percent of eighth graders are able to "evaluate complex syntax."[6] It's also a problem that isn't limited to historically disadvantaged groups or struggling readers. One Harvard English professor found that when she taught *The Scarlet Letter*, her students "were really struggling to understand the sentences as sentences—specifically, they were having trouble identifying the subject and the verb."[7]

Students need to learn to walk before they can run, though. Before moving on to concepts like **subordinating conjunctions**, **transitions**, and **appositives**, let's start with the fundamentals.

The Four Basic Sentence Types

All sentences, no matter how complex, can be boiled down to these four types:

Declarative sentence (statement)
Sets forth an idea or argument; the most common type of sentence.
Example: Theodore Roosevelt created five national parks.

Imperative sentence (command)
Gives advice or instructions or expresses a request or an order.
Example: Visit a national park.

Interrogative sentence (question)
Makes an inquiry and always ends with a question mark.
Example: How can the national parks be protected?

Exclamatory sentence (exclamation)
Expresses force or a strong emotion and ends with an exclamation point.
Example: National parks must be protected!

WHY PRACTICE SENTENCE-TYPE ACTIVITIES?

- Enables students to vary sentence structure
- Provides one of the three strategies for creating topic and concluding sentences
- Introduces students to developing questions
- Helps students learn correct punctuation
- Reinforces spelling, vocabulary, and academic knowledge

Introducing students to the four sentence types will pay off when it comes time for them to write paragraphs and essays and you ask them to vary their sentence structure.

Distinguishing between the Sentence Types

After explaining the four different sentence types, have your Level 1 students practice distinguishing between them. Explain that *S* stands for *statement*; *Q*, for *question*; *E*, for *exclamation*; and *C*, for *command*. You might give them the following activity:

DIRECTIONS: Identify the sentence type (S, Q, E, C).

___S___ Tony doesn't want to go.

___Q___ Does Tony want to go?

___E___ Don't go, Tony!

___C___ Go now.

You can use sentence-type activities to teach punctuation. For example, you can give students different types of unpunctuated sentences and ask them to add the appropriate punctuation. Tell them that commands can end with a period or an exclamation point.

DIRECTIONS: Add the correct punctuation to each sentence:

Anna doesn't want to go ___.___

Does Anna want to go ___?___

Don't go, Anna ___!___

Using Sentence-Type Activities to Assess and Reinforce Knowledge and Vocabulary

If you are teaching the word *fluctuate*, you can ask students to write each sentence type using the word in any of its forms. They might give the following answers:

DIRECTIONS: Write a sentence of each type using the word *fluctuate* in any form.

Statement: *Climate change is causing extreme fluctuations in the weather.*

Question: *What causes body temperature to fluctuate?*

Exclamation: *Fluctuating weather patterns can be dangerous!*

Command: *Prepare for extreme fluctuations in weather.*

Not all topics lend themselves to all four sentence types. To determine which sentence types are appropriate for a particular activity, remember to always anticipate student responses.

In a math class, students could write the following sentences with the word *diagram*.

DIRECTIONS: Write a sentence of each type using the word *diagram*.

Statement: *The diagram represents 1/2.*

Question: *Is a diagram a visual representation?*

Command: *Draw a diagram that has four sides and measures 360 degrees.*

As an alternative to putting one word into the four sentence types, consider using several words that are relevant to what your students are studying.

Level 1 Example

> **DIRECTIONS:** Write each sentence type using the following words.
>
> register (command)
> _Register to vote._
>
> elections (statement)
> _There are national, state, and local elections._
>
> vote (exclamation)
> _Every vote counts!_
>
> democracy (question)
> _How are citizens represented in a democracy?_

Level 2 Example

> **DIRECTIONS:** Write two statements and two questions using the following words.
>
> prophase (statement)
> _Prophase is one of the phases of mitosis._
>
> eukaryotic cells (statement)
> _Mitosis can only occur in eukaryotic cells._
>
> mitosis (question)
> _What are the five phases of mitosis?_
>
> chromosome (question)
> _How many chromosomes does each cell produced by mitosis have?_

Differentiating Sentence-Type Activities

If some of your students need extra support or an additional challenge, here is a possible modification:

- Ask more advanced students to create all four sentence types, while asking others to create only statements and questions.

How to Develop Knowledge and Skills? A Good Question

RESOURCE

Expository
Writing Terms
Appendix A

It's as important for students to learn how to generate questions as it is for them to learn how to answer them. When students formulate questions, they're developing higher-level cognitive functions while at the same time focusing on the main idea of the content that provides the basis of their question.

For example, imagine that you needed to formulate a question about the paragraph you just read. You might need to read it several times, asking yourself what it's really all about. Perhaps you'd come up with the following:

Why is it important for students to learn how to generate questions?

or:

What skills or abilities do students develop when they formulate questions?

If you embed question activities in the content your students are learning, you'll encourage them to retrieve information from long-term memory, read and reread text closely to ensure their recollection is correct, and think deeply about what they're learning.

Developing Questions about Images

An excellent way of introducing your students to the skill of developing questions is to show them a picture and ask them to come up with two or three questions based on what they see. If the picture is related to the content of the curriculum—for example, a political cartoon or a depiction of a historical event in a history class—and you ask students to write both questions and responses, you'll also be able to check your students' understanding of the material.

Level 1 Example

You could give your Level 1 students the following picture to practice developing questions when they are being introduced to the book *Ox-Cart Man*.[8]

DIRECTIONS: Write three questions about the picture.

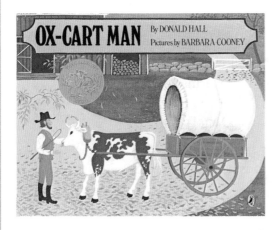

1. <u>When does this story take place?</u>

2. <u>Why is there a cow pulling the cart instead of a horse?</u>

3. <u>What's going to go in the cart?</u>

Level 2 Example

You could give Level 2 math students the following activity:

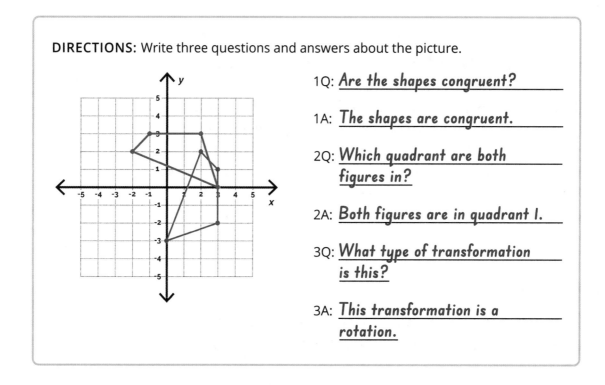

DIRECTIONS: Write three questions and answers about the picture.

1Q: *Are the shapes congruent?*

1A: *The shapes are congruent.*

2Q: *Which quadrant are both figures in?*

2A: *Both figures are in quadrant I.*

3Q: *What type of transformation is this?*

3A: *This transformation is a rotation.*

Using Expository Terms

Appendix A ("Expository Writing Terms") lists terms that call for a specific type of response—for example, *analyze* or *compare*. The following activity will help students understand the different meanings of these terms when they encounter them on tests or in text. If they've used the terms *enumerate* and *summarize* in formulating their own prompts, they're less likely to become confused when they see directions using those terms. You can ask your students to formulate test or assignment instructions using the expository terms and then respond to them.

RESOURCE

Expository
Writing Terms
Appendix A

Depending on grade level and the content the class is studying, students might come up with the following. Asking students to provide the answers is optional.

Level 1 Example

DIRECTIONS: Write three directions using the words *compare*, *summarize*, and *describe* about *frogs* and *toads*.

1: <u>Compare frogs and toads.</u>

2: <u>Summarize the differences between frogs and toads.</u>

3: <u>Describe the appearances of frogs and toads.</u>

Level 2 Example

DIRECTIONS: Write three directions and answers about *absolute rulers* using the words *describe*, *enumerate*, and *explain*.

1: <u>Describe the role of absolute rulers in medieval Europe.</u>

1A: <u>Absolute rulers had total control over their countries.</u>

2: <u>Enumerate possible reasons for opposition to absolute rulers.</u>

2A: <u>First, people had no political power. Second, the rulers controlled the practice of religion. Lastly, they had total control over the economy.</u>

3: <u>Explain why absolute rulers believed they were entitled to their power.</u>

3A: <u>Absolute rulers believed that they had a divine right to rule.</u>

Conjunctions, Complexity, and Clauses

Conjunctions include words such as *because* and *but*. Using conjunctions to connect words, phrases, and clauses provides more information for the reader and helps make writing clear and linguistically rich.

A **clause** is a group of words in a sentence that contains a subject and a verb. There are two types of clauses:

- An **independent (main) clause** represents a complete thought and can stand alone as a sentence. For example, in the sentence *The teacher was happy because I did my homework*, *The teacher was happy* is an independent clause.

- A **dependent (subordinate) clause** does not express a complete thought and could not stand alone as a complete sentence. In the previous example, *because I did my homework* is a dependent clause.

Conjunction activities enable students to craft more complex sentences. As students do so, they also develop the ability to understand such sentences when they encounter them in their reading.

Simple but Powerful: *because, but, so*

A powerful TWR sentence activity is known as *because-but-so*. It's a great illustration of how an exercise that seems simple can actually require students to think analytically.

WHY PRACTICE BASIC CONJUNCTIONS?

- Develops the ability to write extended and elaborated responses
- Checks student comprehension
- Develops analytical thinking
- Fosters close reading
- Provides practice in using new vocabulary words correctly
- Reinforces academic knowledge and vocabulary

This is how you should proceed: give students **sentence stems**—the beginning of a sentence—and have the students turn them into three separate sentences, using each conjunction. This approach requires them to engage in far more specific and focused thinking than just asking them to respond to an open-ended question. Think about the difference between asking students, "Why do seeds need light to grow?" and framing the assignment as follows:

Seeds need light to grow because _____

Seeds need light to grow, but _____

Seeds need light to grow, so _____

Make sure your students understand the meanings of each conjunction. You could explain it to them this way:

- *because* explains why something is true, why something happened, or why a certain condition exists

- *but* indicates a change of direction

- *so* tells us what happens as a result of something else—in other words, a cause and its effect

As with other TWR activities, the content of *because-but-so* drives its rigor. When you adapt the activity to the content you're teaching, be sure to anticipate student responses and ensure that your students have enough content knowledge to complete the activity successfully.

In addition to guiding your students to create compound and complex sentences, this activity will prod them to think critically and deeply about the content they're studying and encourage them to refer back to the text. It will also provide you with a precise check of your students' comprehension.

DIRECTIONS: Complete the following sentence stems.

The Nile was beneficial to ancient Egyptians because *it provided fertile soil for farming.*

The Nile was beneficial to ancient Egyptians, but *annual floodwaters caused destruction.*

The Nile was beneficial to ancient Egyptians, so *the river was worshiped as a god.*

You can also use this activity to give students practice with new vocabulary or spelling words. Embed those words in the stems you create. For example, if your students have just learned the word *mediocre*, you can give them the following sentence stems:

DIRECTIONS: Complete the following sentence stems.

The critic thought the restaurant was mediocre because *the menu was limited.*

The critic thought the restaurant was mediocre, but *others believed it was excellent.*

The critic thought the restaurant was mediocre, so *he rated it 3 stars instead of 5 in his review.*

Depending on the content you're teaching and the ability of your students, you could also give students different stems about the same topic to complete rather than the same one with all three conjunctions.

DIRECTIONS: Complete the following sentence stems.

Diversity in a gene pool is better for survival because *more favorable phenotypes are more likely to survive and produce offspring.*

Evolution occurs slowly over long periods of time, but *that is not the case with bacteria resistant to antibiotics.*

Populations tend to grow and exceed their limited resources, so *competition results in differential survival.*

With Level 1 students, practice this activity orally before having students try it in writing. To introduce the idea, start with a simple stem embedded in familiar content or common knowledge—for example, "The teacher was happy _____." Students might respond orally with answers such as these:

The teacher was happy because _we raised our hands._

The teacher was happy, but _she still gave us homework._

The teacher was happy, so _she gave us a longer recess._

Once your students grasp the concept, embed the activity in content you're currently covering. If your class is studying Abraham Lincoln, you could give students the stem, "Abraham Lincoln was a great president because _____." The activity would look like this:

DIRECTIONS: Complete the following sentence stems.

Abraham Lincoln was a great president because _he kept the country united._

Abraham Lincoln was a great president, but _critics have called him a dictator because of his broad use of emergency powers._

Abraham Lincoln was a great president, so _more books have been written about him than any other American president._

You might just focus on one conjunction at a time with Level 1 students by giving students two or three different stems to complete with *because*. If students have been reading *Malala's Magic Pencil*,[9] you might give them the following activity:

DIRECTIONS: Complete the following sentence stems.

Malala wished for a magic pencil because _she wanted to use it to bring peace to the world._

Dangerous men tried to silence Malala because _her voice became so powerful._

Malala wrote about her life because _she wanted more people to know what was happening to girls in her city._

Differentiating Basic Conjunction Activities

You can easily modify the *because-but-so* activity to accommodate students at different ability levels. Give all students the same stem, but ask more proficient students to provide complete sentences for all three conjunctions while asking others to write a sentence for only one or two.

⚠ BE CAREFUL

Keep the following points in mind when creating and assigning *because-but-so* activities:

- **Formatting matters!** The underlined blank space for completing the stem should appear on the same line as the conjunction itself, **not** on a separate line below it. Otherwise, students may capitalize the word after the conjunction and write another sentence instead of a clause.

  INCORRECT FORMATTING:

  The war was won because

   The colonists were determined to protect their country.

  INCORRECT FORMATTING:

The conjunctions should **not** be given as a list without repeating the stem:

 The war was won because

        but

        so

Students may try to put all three conjunctions in one sentence:

 The war was won because the colonists were determined to protect their country but there were many casualties so the United States was able to gain its independence.

It's important to follow the correct format for *because-but-so* activities as shown in the examples—supplying the stem for each sentence and following each conjunction with a solid blank line that students should use to complete the sentence.

✓ The war was won because *the colonists were determined to protect their country.*

✓ The war was won, but *there were many casualties.*

✓ The war was won, so *the United States was able to gain its independence.*

- Anticipate your students' responses when developing activities with these conjunctions. Always complete the stems yourself before asking your students to do so.

- Students should not create stems because they may omit information that is important to include.

- Be sure students know the word *so* isn't being used in the sense of "I admire Nelson Mandela *so much*." Instead, it introduces a phrase that tells us what happened as a result of something else.

- Be mindful of the difference between *so* (shows cause and effect) and *so that* (often gives a reason instead of a result). For example:

  ▶ Hammurabi created a written code of laws **so that** he could establish justice in Babylon.

  ▶ Hammurabi created a written code of laws, **so** Babylon experienced a period of stability.

- Not every text will lend itself to activities using all three conjunctions. For example, if a text provides only positive information about Abraham Lincoln's presidency, students will have difficulty completing the *but* sentence shown in the example. In that case, you should only give students the conjunctions *because* and *so.*

- If students use *because*, *but*, and *so* to begin sentences, they're likely to write a fragment rather than a complete sentence. As they become more competent writers, they can begin to use these conjunctions to start sentences.

- Make sure students follow *but* with contrasting information on the same topic rather than providing information on a different topic.

- Tell students they need to place a comma before *but* when it connects two independent clauses. A comma is not needed before *but* when it connects an independent clause and a fragment (dependent clause).

- As always, make sure that students have had the opportunity to acquire the information they will need to complete the activity.

Adding Complexity: Subordinating Conjunctions

WHY PRACTICE SUBORDINATING CONJUNCTIONS?

- Promotes the use of complex sentences
- Improves reading comprehension by familiarizing students with syntax they'll encounter in their reading
- Enables students to vary sentence structure
- Reinforces academic knowledge and vocabulary
- Encourages close reading and references to text
- Checks student comprehension
- Enables students to extend their responses
- Provides a strategy for creating topic and concluding sentences

A subordinating conjunction is a word like *before* or *unless* that introduces a dependent (subordinate) clause and signals the relationship between that clause and the main idea. For example, in the sentence *Although I drank a glass of water, I was still thirsty*, the subordinating conjunction *although* introduces a clause relating to *I was still thirsty*. Subordinating conjunctions are often used in written language but not as frequently in spoken language. In conversation, we would be more likely to say *I drank a glass of water, but I was still thirsty.*

The following subordinating conjunctions are used frequently to begin sentences in writing. They are listed in Exhibit 4.2 in the order in which they are taught to Level 1 students (they can be taught to Level 2 students in any order):

1. After	6. Although
2. Before	7. Whenever
3. If	8. Since
4. When	9. While
5. Even though	10. Unless

Exhibit 4.2

Subordinating conjunctions can occur at the beginning, middle, or end of a sentence. However, it's best to begin instruction using them at the beginning of a sentence, which is why they're capitalized in the preceding chart. Once your students learn to use subordinating conjunctions, they'll be able to place them elsewhere. They'll also be able to write extended responses that are rich in complexity and content.

When students begin writing paragraphs and essays, they can use subordinating conjunctions to create topic or concluding sentences that are interesting and informative.

Introducing Students to Subordinating Conjunctions

To develop your students' skill in using subordinating conjunctions, give them introductory dependent clauses that you've created and ask them to complete the sentences. As with sentence stems using *because-but-so,* this approach demands more analytical thinking and precision than merely asking open-ended questions.

For example, there is a significant difference between asking a student "Why was the Industrial Revolution important?" and asking them to complete the following stems:

Although the Industrial Revolution brought many benefits, _____

Before England embarked on the Industrial Revolution, _____

When a stem begins with *although,* students need to find contrasting or contradictory information. If they use *before,* they need to demonstrate their understanding of the chronology of events.

Level 1 Examples

Students in primary grades can practice completing stems, either orally or in writing, based on books you've introduced in read-alouds. With Level 1 students, it's best to start with conjunctions that depend on chronology (*before*, *after*) or the conjunction *if*.

If you've been reading them the book *Chicks and Salsa*,[10] for example, you could give them the following stems, and students might provide these answers:

DIRECTIONS: Complete each sentence stem.

Before the chickens made salsa, *they crept into the garden to get tomatoes and onions.*

After the ducks were inspired by the chickens, *they took cilantro from the garden to make guacamole.*

If you've read your students the book *From Seed to Plant*,[11] the stems and answers might look like these:

DIRECTIONS: Complete each sentence stem.

Before a flower can make seeds, *it has to be pollinated.*

If a seed isn't on or in soil, *it will not sprout.*

After a seed germinates, *the root grows down into the soil.*

Level 2 Examples

If you're teaching English and your students have been reading *Metamorphosis*,[12] you might give them the following stems to complete, and they might provide the answers shown:

> **DIRECTIONS:** Complete each sentence.
>
> Although Grete is benevolent toward Gregor, *she is repulsed by him.*
>
> Since she wants Gregor to eat, *Grete begins a monotonous feeding routine.*
>
> If Grete had not shown compassion toward Gregor, *he probably would have died sooner.*

When students are learning about *buoyancy* in a science class, the stems and answers might look as follows:

> **DIRECTIONS:** Complete each sentence stem.
>
> If an object has a higher average density than a liquid, *the object is not buoyant enough to float.*
>
> When an object has a larger surface area touching a liquid, *the liquid exerts more upward force on the object.*

Connecting Ideas: Transitions

WHY PRACTICE TRANSITION ACTIVITIES?

- Helps students identify and show the relationship between ideas
- Provides logical connections between sentences, paragraphs, and sections within compositions
- Enables students to signal how a reader should react to or process the information presented
- Makes writing more readable and engaging
- Reinforces academic knowledge and vocabulary

Transitions are often called *signal words* because they signal, or indicate, a relationship between ideas. They can make text smoother and help minimize the confusion that brief or unelaborated statements can cause.

Explain to students that, as a general rule, when transitions appear at the beginning of a sentence, they are followed by a comma. The term *transition* can refer to words that appear in the middle of a sentence, but we'll be using the term to refer to words at the beginning of a sentence. (See Exhibit 4.3.)

RESOURCE

Transition Words and Phrases
Appendix C

Types of Transitions

Time and sequence—provide sequence of events, steps in a process

Conclusion—express a summary, cause-and-effect relationship, point of view, solution

Illustration—give examples, provide details, explain or elaborate on a statement

Change of direction—signal contrasting thoughts

Emphasis—prove a point or statement; reaffirm something previously stated

Exhibit 4.3   Transition Words and Phrases

TECHNICAL TIP

It's a good idea to display the following posters of frequently used transitions as easy references and reminders for students to use them. These posters list the transition words and phrases that students are most likely to encounter in texts and literature. A more extensive table of transition words and phrases can be found in Appendix C.

Time & Sequence 1

first	also
second	in addition
last	before
next	later
finally	after

Time & Sequence 2

initially	currently
previously	earlier
soon	meanwhile
later on	during
at last	simultaneously
additionally	furthermore

Conclusion

in conclusion	consequently
to conclude	finally
in closing	therefore
in summary	thus
clearly	in the end
as a result	ultimately

Illustration

for example	as an illustration
for instance	to illustrate
such as	particularly
specifically	in particular

Change of Direction

however	but
even though	yet
in contrast	instead
on the other hand	on the contrary
although	

Emphasis

in particular	primarily
certainly	particularly
obviously	moreover
most important	notably
in addition	keep in mind

Introducing Transitions

The best way to introduce students to transitions is through the sentence-level activities we describe in this chapter. Students will eventually use transitions to connect sentences and paragraphs.

When introducing students to transitions, begin with time-and-sequence, conclusion, and illustration transitions.

Time-and-Sequence Transitions

These are transition words and phrases such as *first*, *second*, and *finally*. Students will find them helpful when writing narratives that relate a chronological series of events or steps in a process. They are especially helpful when explaining a solution to a math problem, describing a process in science, writing a summary of a plot, or tracing the timeline of an event.

You may want Level 1 students to stay with simple time-and-sequence transitions such as *first*, *second*, and *finally*, along with *then* and *next* (category 1A in Appendix C). More advanced students can use words such as *initially* and *previously* (category 1B in Appendix C).

One way to have students practice using transitions is to give them a sentence followed by a transition word or phrase that introduces the next sentence. Students can complete the second sentence in a way that fits the transition word you've provided. Alternatively, you can provide the second sentence but leave a blank space for them to supply an appropriate transition.

Level 1 Example

The class trip to the Museum of Natural History was interesting. First, **we visited the insect exhibit.**

or

The class trip to the Museum of Natural History was interesting. **First,** we visited the insect exhibit.

Level 2 Example

There are a number of factors to consider when choosing sunglasses. Initially, *you need to be careful that the lenses absorb 99–100% of UVA and UVB rays.*

or

There are a number of factors to consider when choosing sunglasses. *Initially,* you need to be careful that the lenses absorb 99–100% of UVA and UVB rays.

Conclusion Transitions

Students should use conclusion transitions to introduce the last sentence in a paragraph or the first sentence of the concluding paragraph in a composition.

Conclusions can simply summarize the ideas in a piece of writing, in which case a transition like *in summary* would be appropriate. Other conclusions focus on a solution or the author's point of view. More advanced students can practice deciding when it would be better to conclude with a summation or a statement that goes beyond that.

Some conclusion transitions, like *as a result* and *therefore*, should be used to introduce the endings of cause-and-effect paragraphs and compositions. These cause-and-effect transitions are marked in Appendix C with an asterisk.

Level 1 Example

Often plastic waste is not recycled and ends up in the ocean. As a result, *many sea animals may become extinct.*

or

Often plastic waste is not recycled and ends up in the ocean. *As a result,* many sea animals may become extinct.

Level 2 Example

This example assumes students have read *Hatchet*.[13]

The smoke from the fire keeps the mosquitoes and birds away from Brian's shelter. Therefore, *he is able to maintain his food supply.*

or

The smoke from the fire keeps the mosquitoes and birds away from Brian's shelter. *Therefore,* he is able to maintain his food supply.

Illustration Transitions

Illustration transitions are used to give examples, to support a detail, or to explain or elaborate on a statement with evidence. For example, one illustration transition is—in fact—*for example*. Illustration transitions can be introduced to students who are at the higher end of Level 1. Younger students can be introduced to the phrase *for example* if it's done orally as a whole-class activity, under a teacher's guidance.

Level 1 Example

Each of the gods had his or her area of responsibility. For example, *Apollo was the god of music and the sun.*

or

Each of the gods had his or her area of responsibility. *For example,* Apollo was the god of music and the sun.

Level 2 Example

The Agricultural Revolution changed people's lives. Specifically, *humans began to farm and plant on their own fields.*

or

The Agricultural Revolution changed people's lives. *Specifically,* humans began to farm and plant on their own fields.

If you're teaching Level 2 students who have no trouble using the three categories of transitions just described, introduce them to two other kinds of transitions: change of direction and emphasis.

Change-of-Direction Transitions

Change-of-direction transitions introduce contrasting thoughts. They are important signals to use in compare-and-contrast as well as in argumentative writing.

Remind students that some change-of-direction transitions, such as *although* and *even though*, need to be used as subordinating conjunctions that introduce a dependent clause, not a sentence. For example, "Although zoos are popular attractions, critics believe they are cruel to the animals."

Level 1 Example

The zebra is related to a horse. However, *they are not the same species.*

or

The zebra is related to a horse. *However,* they are not the same species.

Level 2 Example

Red blood cells carry nutrients throughout the body. In contrast, *white blood cells fight infection.*

or

Red blood cells carry nutrients throughout the body. *In contrast,* white blood cells fight infection.

Emphasis Transitions

Emphasis transitions can be introduced at the same time as change-of-direction transitions. They prove a point or statement or reaffirm something the writer has already stated. They are often used in argumentative and opinion writing, letters of complaint, and formal requests. These transitions can also be used as conclusion transitions.

Consider giving Level 1 students only the following transitions: *in addition, most importantly, in particular.*

Level 1 Example

Helen liked to read in Braille. In particular, <u>*she loved the book*</u> *Little Women*.

or

Helen liked to read in Braille. <u>*In particular,*</u> she loved the book *Little Women*.

Level 2 Example

This example assumes students have read *The Crucible*.[14]

Dozens of people in Salem are accused of witchcraft. Notably, <u>*Rebecca Nurse and John Proctor, highly respected members of the community, are accused.*</u>

or

Dozens of people in Salem are accused of witchcraft. <u>*Notably,*</u> Rebecca Nurse and John Proctor, highly respected members of the community, are accused.

Mix It Up: Using Transitions from Different Categories

After students have become familiar with different categories of transitions, you can have them choose from among several types. The following examples show transitions from the time-and-sequence, illustration, and conclusion categories.

DIRECTIONS: Connect the following sentences using the given transition words.

In addition   For example

Specifically   As a result

1. Augustus Caesar introduced many economic reforms. **_In addition,_** he focused attention on political and social issues.

2. The rule of Augustus improved the status of women. **_Specifically,_** women had rights and could own property.

3. Roman engineers made major changes within the Roman Empire. **_For example,_** the engineers paved streets and designed sewage systems.

4. Augustus Caesar's reforms were a great success. **_As a result,_** Rome experienced over 200 years of peace and prosperity.

If students have been reading *Jumanji*,[15] you might give them the following activity.

DIRECTIONS: Complete the second sentence following the transition word.

1. Many scary things happened while Judy and Peter played *Jumanji*. Specifically, *a lion tried to attack Peter.*

2. *Jumanji* came with specific instructions. For example, *the first player to reach the end must yell "Jumanji" to win and end the game.*

3. Monkeys tore apart the kitchen. Then, *a monsoon came.*

4. A rhinoceros stampede came through the living room. Also, *a python wrapped itself around the fireplace.*

Differentiating Transition Activities

If some of your students need more support than others in using transitions, you can give them a word bank of possible transitions—or tell them what category of transition they need to supply and have them consult Appendix C, "Transition Words and Phrases."

RESOURCE

Transition Words and Phrases
Appendix C

⚠ **BE CAREFUL**

You may find that your students fill in the blank after a transition word with a fragment rather than a complete sentence. If that happens, tell them to cover up the transition word and make sure that the rest of the sentence can stand alone.

Appositives:
Another Name for a Noun

An **appositive** is a second noun, or a phrase or clause equivalent to a noun, that is placed beside another noun to explain it more fully. For example:

✓ One World Trade Center, the tallest building in New York City, is also known as the Freedom Tower.

In this example, "the tallest building in New York City" is the appositive.

An appositive usually follows the noun it describes, as in the previous example, but it can also precede it:

✓ The tallest building in New York City, One World Trade Center, is also known as the Freedom Tower.

Students may have trouble grasping the concept of appositives. They may confuse them with **relative clauses**, which begin with *who, that, which, where,* or *when,* and include a verb—a construction more likely to be found in spoken language. For example:

✗ One World Trade Center, which is the tallest building in New York City, is also known as the Freedom Tower.

It may be helpful for your students to know that most appositives begin with *a*, *an*, or *the*.

To help students identify the appositive in a sentence, tell them that it's a phrase that can be removed or covered up without making the entire sentence incomplete. If we omitted the phrase "the tallest building in New York City" in the first example about the World Trade Center, we would still have a complete sentence:

> One World Trade Center is also known as the Freedom Tower.

Use your judgment about whether your students are ready to learn about appositives. In our experience, they should not be introduced before the middle of third grade or beginning of fourth grade.

Before teaching your students appositive activities, be sure to give them an explanation of the purpose appositives serve. For example, you could say that appositives:

- always follow or come before a noun and help to describe it further;
- further define or describe a person, place, or thing;
- are set off by commas if they appear in the middle of a sentence; and
- can help them create more effective topic and concluding sentences because they give the reader more information.

Adding an appositive is the third strategy for creating topic and concluding sentences (see Exhibit 4.4).

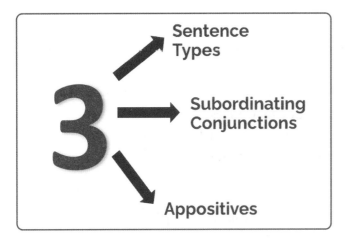

Exhibit 4.4 Three strategies for creating topic and concluding sentences

The most effective way to introduce students to appositives is the following sequence:

1. Identify appositives.
2. Match appositives.
3. Fill in appositives.
4. Brainstorm appositives.
5. Given an appositive, write a sentence.
6. Given a topic, write a sentence with an appositive.

1. Identify Appositives

Give students examples of sentences containing appositives and have them underline them. Remember that for these activities, an appositive should not include a verb.

DIRECTIONS: Underline the appositive in the sentence.

Louis XIV, *an absolute monarch of France*, built the Palace of Versailles as a symbol of royal power.

---

2. Match Appositives

You can create a matching activity based on a text your class has been studying. For example, if your class has been reading *Flowers for Algernon*,[16] you could list the major characters on the left side of the sheet and a noun phrase that describes each of them on the other—not in the same order, of course.

DIRECTIONS: Match each noun with the appositive that best describes it.

1. *b* Alice Kinnian
2. *e* Dr. Strauss
3. *d* Burt Seldon
4. *a* Algernon
5. *c* Dr. Nemur

a. a white mouse
b. Charlie's teacher
c. a professor of psychology
d. a graduate student
e. a neurosurgeon

---

3. Fill In Appositives

Next, you can have your students fill in blanks with appositives in sentences that you create. For students who may not be able to insert an appositive independently, a word bank will help them choose the appropriate one.

The following example assumes students have read *A Raisin in the Sun*.[17]

DIRECTIONS: Use an appositive to complete each sentence.

1. Beneatha thinks George Murchison, **_a wealthy classmate_**, is not marriage material.

2. Ruth, **_Travis's mother_**, wants her son to be independent and responsible.

3. Beneatha met Asagai, **_a student from Nigeria_**, on her college campus.

4. Asagai brings Beneatha a gift, **_robes from Nigeria_**.

---

4. Brainstorm Appositives

Have students suggest appositives for a particular topic.

DIRECTIONS: Brainstorm appositives for the given topic.

TOPIC: Marie Curie

a famous physicist

winner of the Nobel Prize

a renowned chemist

a Polish scientist

an inventor

the scientist who discovered radium

---

5. Given an Appositive, Write a Sentence

Given an appositive for a topic your class has been studying, have students write a sentence incorporating that appositive.

> **DIRECTIONS:** Write a sentence using the given appositive.
>
> a Greek city-state
> _Athens, a Greek city-state, valued education and democracy._
>
> a great philosopher
> _Socrates, a Greek philosopher, created a method of questioning._
>
> a series of contests
> _The Olympics, a series of contests, were held in honor of the Greek gods._

6. Given a Topic, Write a Sentence with an Appositive

> **DIRECTIONS:** For each topic, write a sentence using an appositive.
>
> natural selection
> _Natural selection, a process of evolution, results in species with favorable traits._
>
> artificial selection
> _Artificial selection, a process carried out by humans, is used to replicate favorable traits._

Out of Many, One: Sentence-Combining

Sentence-combining involves giving students a series of short declarative sentences and having them find various ways of combining those sentences into one longer, compound or complex sentence. Extensive research has found it to be a highly effective way of teaching grammar. It also gives students greater control over **syntax**, which is the way words are put together and ordered in sentences.[18]

If you've taught your students how to use conjunctions, appositives, and subordinating conjunctions, they'll be able to draw on those techniques in finding ways to combine sentences. They'll also be able to practice using pronouns.

To introduce students to sentence-combining, give them a series of short, declarative sentences that can be combined into one longer, complex sentence. Begin with just two or three sentences, adding more as students' skills develop.

For example, you could give your students the following short sentences:

> Tania took the subway every day.
>
> Tania did not like the subway.
>
> Tania needed to get to work.

There are a variety of ways these sentences could be combined into one longer sentence. You could, for example, put the second sentence first and introduce it with a subordinating conjunction.

> Although Tania did not like the subway, she took it every day because she needed to get to work.

You could also begin with the second sentence and use basic conjunctions to connect it to the other two.

> Tania didn't like the subway, but she took it every day because she needed to get to work.

Once students feel comfortable with the concept of sentence-combining, it's time to start embedding the activity in the content you're teaching.

Level 1 Example

This example assumes students have read *Fourth Grade Rats.*[19]

DIRECTIONS: Combine the given sentences in one sentence.

Joey stopped wearing tattoos.

Joey stopped acting like a rat.

Joey stopped wearing tattoos and acting like a rat.

Level 2 Example

If you've been teaching your students about two of the ancient civilizations of India, you could give them the following sentences to combine:

DIRECTIONS: Combine the given sentences in one sentence.

Mohenjo-Daro and Harappa were twin cities.

Mohenjo-Daro and Harappa used urban planning.

The cities had a system of plumbing.

Mohenjo-Daro and Harappa were twin cities that used urban planning and had a system of plumbing.

Students may not need knowledge of the content to engage in sentence-combining activities. In the preceding example, even if you've never heard of Mohenjo-Daro and Harappa, you can create a complex sentence because you've been given all the information you need in the simple sentences.

Since it doesn't necessarily require students to retrieve information from long-term memory, sentence-combining may not be as powerful in reinforcing and deepening knowledge as some other TWR activities.

However, sentence-combining activities are still a good use of students' time. In some cases, they will need to draw on their knowledge of the topic to combine the simple sentences effectively, and they will always be reinforcing their knowledge of grammar and syntax.

Using Sentence Activities to Teach Grammar and Conventions

As TWR's Principle 5 states, grammar is best taught in the context of student writing. In fact, for many students, that's probably the *only* way they'll learn to use the grammar and conventions of written English. And sentence activities are the most effective vehicle for teaching those skills. If you wait until students are writing paragraphs and compositions, the number of mechanical errors can be overwhelming for you and for your students.

Naturally, we don't expect students to master all the conventions of written English at once, but there's no reason to hold off on gradually introducing the fundamentals.

If you're working with Level 1 students, you may need to start by teaching them to begin each sentence with a capital letter and end it with a period. As your students progress, you can introduce the use of question marks and exclamation points. Once they have a grasp of those conventions, you can begin to focus on the capitalization of proper nouns.

When introducing students to the first subordinating conjunctions they'll encounter—*before, after, if,* and *when*—show them that the comma should go after the dependent clause. For example:

After it stops raining, I'm going to take a walk.

In addition to giving students examples of sentences like these, you'll also need to ensure that they're placing commas correctly in their own writing.

⚠ BE CAREFUL

Be careful not to overload Level 1 students with grammatical terms. It can become confusing and overwhelming to try to learn these terms while they are also thinking about spelling, sentence structure, and word choice. They can practice applying correct grammar and conventions without necessarily learning their labels.

TWR's method does teach certain grammatical terms, such as *appositive*, that are useful as a kind of shorthand for concepts that are key parts of the method. If you want to suggest a specific way of varying sentence structure, it's easier to say "Try adding an appositive" than "Try adding a phrase describing the noun."

But TWR doesn't teach grammatical terms just for the sake of teaching them. For example, the method doesn't require teaching the concept of a prepositional phrase, which is a construction students are likely to be using naturally.

Weave It In: Integrating Sentence Activities into Daily Instruction

Given that the ability to craft a good sentence is the necessary foundation for all good writing, it's important to offer as many opportunities as possible for students to practice writing sentences, even after they have progressed to writing paragraphs and compositions. In addition, **sentence activities can be powerful boosts to students' understanding and retention of content.** If students have already learned how to use appositives, for example, constructing them in the context of new material will both provide a review of the grammatical concept and help students understand and remember the new material.

Once you and your students have become acquainted with various TWR sentence activities, you'll find there are many ways to use them in your classroom—no matter the grade level or the subject you're teaching. A few possibilities are outlined here.

At the beginning of class, you can give students a do-now to review material you've taught previously.

Although Egyptians built the pyramids, _____

Mid-lesson, you may want to pause and have students do a **stop-and-jot** by asking them to develop a question about what they've learned so far.

You could also have students **turn-and-talk** to complete a *because-but-so* activity.

Egyptians built pyramids because _____

Egyptians built pyramids, but_____

Egyptians built pyramids, so_____

At the end of class, consider having students fill in an exit slip responding to highlights in the lesson.

Egyptians built pyramids. As a result, _____

As a quiz, you can ask students to complete the following activities:

Write a sentence using this appositive: *huge monuments in the Egyptian desert.*

or

Write a sentence with an appositive about the topic of *Egyptian pyramids.*

If you weave these kinds of sentence-level activities into your instruction on a daily basis, you'll be giving your students the tools they need to create effective paragraphs and compositions, while at the same time boosting their understanding of the content you're teaching.

To Sum Up

- Familiarize students with the four sentence types—statement, command, question, and exclamation—to equip them to vary their sentence structure and provide the first strategy for creating effective topic and concluding sentences.

- Have students develop questions about texts or pictures to spur them to read closely and deepen their content knowledge.

- Give students sentence-stem activities with *because, but*, and *so* to enable them to think critically and to use and understand more complex sentences in their writing and reading.

- Have students practice beginning sentences with subordinating conjunctions (*although, since*, etc.) to familiarize them with the syntax used in written language, help them extend their responses, and give them a second strategy for constructing topic and concluding sentences.

- Have students practice using the various types of transition words to signal the connections between their ideas and create smoothly flowing prose.

- Introduce students to appositives to help them give a reader more information and provide a third strategy for creating effective topic and concluding sentences.

- Have students practice sentence-combining to teach grammar and conventions and to help them create compound and complex sentences using varied structures.

- Embed sentence activities in the content you're teaching as much as possible to check students' comprehension and deepen their understanding.

1. Explain the benefits of teaching students each of the following strategies:

   ▶ sentence types
   ▶ developing questions
   ▶ because-but-so
   ▶ subordinating conjunctions
   ▶ transitions
   ▶ appositives
   ▶ sentence-combining

2. What are ways some of the strategies in this chapter can be differentiated?

3. How can grammar be addressed with these strategies?

4. Create topic and concluding sentences with the three sentence strategies: sentence types, subordinating conjunctions, and appositives. Try using topics from your curriculum.

5. Create an activity for each of the sentence strategies presented in this chapter based on the content you teach.

Notes

1. C.M. Scott, "A Case for the Sentence in Reading Comprehension," *Language Speech and Hearing Services in Schools* (2009), 40: 184–191.

   C.M. Scott and C. Balthazar, "The Role of Complex Sentence Knowledge in Children with Reading and Writing Difficulties," *Perspect Lang Lit.* (2013, Summer), 39(3): 18–30, PMID. 25821532; PMCID: PMC4373700.

2. J.L. Montag and M.C. MacDonald, "Text Exposure Predicts Spoken Production of Complex Sentences in 8- and 12-Year-Old Children and Adults," *Journal of Experimental Psychology: General* (2015, April), 144(2): 447–468, doi: 10.1037/xge0000054. PMID: 25844625; PMCID: PMC4388064.

3. E.B. White, *Charlotte's Web*, 1st ed. (New York: Harper & Brothers, 1952).

4. C. Dickens, *David Copperfield* (New York: Modern Library, 2000).

5. U.S. National Archives and Records Administration, "Declaration of Independence: A Transcription."

6. S.F. Reardon, R.A. Valentino, and K.A. Shores, "Patterns of Literacy among U.S. Students," *Future of Children* (2012, Fall), 22(2), https://files.eric.ed.gov/fulltext/EJ996185.pdf.

7. N. Heller, "The End of the English Major," *The New Yorker* (2023, February 27), https://www.newyorker.com/magazine/2023/03/06/the-end-of-the-english-major.

8. D. Hall, *Ox-Cart Man*, 1st ed. (New York: Viking Press, 1979).

9. M. Yousafzai, *Malala's Magic Pencil* (New York: Little, Brown and Company, 2017).

10. A. Reynolds, *Chicks and Salsa,* 1st U.S. ed. (New York: Bloomsbury Children's Books, 2005).

11. G. Gibbons, *From Seed to Plant* (New York: Holiday House, 1991).

12. F. Kafka, *Metamorphosis* (London: Penguin Classics, 2016).

13. G. Paulsen, *Hatchet* (New York: Simon & Schuster, 2008).

14. A. Miller, *The Crucible: A Play in Four Acts* (New York: Penguin Books, 2015).

15. C. Van Allsburg, *Jumanji* (Boston: Houghton Mifflin, 1981).

16. D. Keyes, *Flowers for Algernon* (New York: HarperCollins, 2007).

17. L. Hansberry, *A Raisin in the Sun* (New York: Random House, 1997).

18. S. Graham and D. Perin, *Writing Next: Effective Strategies to Improve Writing of Adolescents in Middle and High Schools. A Report to Carnegie Corporation of New York* (Washington, DC: Alliance for Excellent Education, 2007).

   B. Saddler, *Teacher's Guide to Effective Sentence Writing* (New York: The Guilford Press, 2012).

19. J. Spinelli, *Fourth Grade Rats* (New York: Scholastic, 1991).

Writing at Length

CHAPTER 5

Planning before Writing

Determining the Shape of What's to Come

Ms. Allen, a seventh-grade ELA teacher, noticed that whenever she asked her students to produce a written response to a prompt, certain things were bound to happen.

Some students just put their heads down on their desks, seeming to give up before they had even started.

Others would start scribbling industriously, raising Ms. Allen's hopes. But when she collected their papers, she was usually disappointed to find pages of disorganized thoughts, often barely understandable.

And then there was Tyler. Normally good-humored and likable, Tyler seemed to undergo a personality transformation when he was asked to write. He would leave his seat and start poking other students, disrupting the entire class and ignoring Ms. Allen's requests that he sit down. At times, he would simply take an extended bathroom break, returning only after the time allotted for the writing assignment was over.

Eventually, Ms. Allen realized that Tyler wasn't just misbehaving. He was desperate to avoid revealing his inability to write. The students who put their heads down on their desks were less disruptive, but they felt the same way. And the others who produced pages of unintelligible prose? They didn't even realize they weren't able to write coherently.

Ms. Allen wondered how students could get to seventh grade without knowing how to write a paragraph, let alone an essay. Everyone expected them to have already acquired those skills. If they hadn't, they felt they were failures—and for some kids, like Tyler, that painful feeling led them to act out.

Students like those in Ms. Allen's classroom *can* learn to write effective paragraphs and essays if they're taught how to plan carefully first.

If you're about to embark on a road trip, try a new recipe, develop a football play—or engage in just about any complex, multi-step task—you need to have a plan. Without one, it is far more likely that your efforts will be disappointing at best and end in failure at worst. Yet, when we teach our students to write in lengthier forms such as paragraphs and compositions, we don't often help them come up with the kind of plan they need to produce an effective piece of writing.

Some people say that planning will constrain students' creativity. To the contrary, we've found that teaching students to plan can actually *enhance* their creativity. If students are working from a plan, they're liberated from the need to figure out the overall structure of what they're writing as they go along. As a result, they have the mental space they need to conjure up vivid imagery or relevant details.

True, some authors prefer to simply free-write as a first step in their writing process, allowing their thoughts to take them where they will. But that approach doesn't work for most students, for at least two reasons. First, most students are not experienced writers. They may still be struggling with figuring out everything from punctuation or word choice to larger questions such as the overall organization of their thoughts. If they're asked to plunge into a longer piece of writing with no outline to follow, they'll need to juggle all these tasks at once. As we explained in Chapter 1, they're likely to be overwhelmed.

Second, the free-writing approach to drafting is best suited to relatively free-form genres such as memoirs, poems, plays, short stories, or (perhaps) novels. That's not the kind of writing most of us are expected to produce in college or the workplace. What we are asked to do, in countless situations, is to explain, inform, justify, enumerate, summarize, and describe. (A comprehensive list of these expository writing terms can be found in Appendix A.)

RESOURCE

Expository Writing Terms
Appendix A

Even many experienced writers find planning to be essential if they're going to communicate effectively. As compared to more creative forms of writing, explanatory, argumentative, and analytical pieces demand that authors figure out in advance where they're going to end up and chart a clear and logical course that will lead a reader there.

As a classic writing handbook points out, "planning must be a deliberate prelude to writing. The first principle of composition, therefore, is to foresee or determine the shape of what is to come and pursue that shape."[1]

In short, if you want your students to be able to move from writing effective sentences to writing coherent paragraphs—and, ultimately, compositions—you'll need to teach them how to plan before they write, using the linear outlines that we present in Chapters 6 and 9. As with revising—which we'll turn to in Chapter 7—planning/outlining is a stage of writing that rarely receives enough instructional time and attention.

Offloading the Cognitive Burden: Why Planning Is Crucial

Why is it so important for students to plan before they write? Largely because of the demands that writing places on **executive functions,** which are cognitive processes that enable us to plan, monitor, and successfully achieve our goals. They are housed primarily in the prefrontal cortex of the brain and enable us to perform a series of actions that are essential to good writing. The abilities associated with executive functions begin to develop in early childhood, but they don't reach their peak until we are in our mid-20s. That means that virtually all students in kindergarten through twelfth grade are working with executive function abilities that are still a work in progress.

When assigning writing tasks, teachers need to be keenly aware of the demands they place on a student's executive functions, including working memory. These functions enable a writer to do the following tasks:

- **Strategize.** For beginning or less experienced writers, the teacher, not the student, selects the topic. Selecting a topic demands the ability to foresee consequences. A topic shouldn't be so narrow that there is too little material to write about. If the topic is too broad, a great deal of skill is needed to sort essential from non-essential information.

- **Initiate a series of actions.** After a topic is selected, students need to find textual evidence to support a topic sentence or thesis statement.

- **Outline.** Students must be able to develop an outline that provides a road map for presenting a body of information, an explanation, or an argument. When students plan by creating an outline, they will have more cognitive resources to devote to tasks like self-monitoring and instituting needed changes.

- **Organize.** Students need to sequence information in the outline in the order that suits a particular piece of writing, whether it's a narrative, an argument, or a comparison of two or more different things.

- **Resist distractions.** The typical classroom and home are full of potential distractions, and the modern era—with its screens and ubiquitous internet connections—seems to have made students' attention spans shorter than ever.

- **Sustain effort.** Students must maintain the stamina necessary to focus on the writing task at hand.

- **Self-monitor.** When working on a draft, students need to continually assess it to ensure they're not going off track. They must be able to identify non-essential, less essential, and essential information.

- **Institute needed changes.** Although students can make changes while creating an outline, most often they will do so while writing or revising a draft. Changes can range from reorganizing an entire sequence of ideas to executing smaller modifications such as choosing more accurate words, varying sentence structure, and inserting transitions.

A key component of executive functioning is working memory, the aspect of our consciousness where we try to make sense of new information. As we discussed in Chapter 2, writing places a heavy burden on working memory—a burden that scientists call cognitive load. Depending on the topic, even constructing sentences can impose a heavy cognitive load on inexperienced writers. Writing at length only increases that load, and it can impose a significant burden even if students have good sentence-level skills. Yet students who are still struggling with the basics of writing, at all grade levels, are frequently asked to compose not only paragraphs but entire essays.

Teachers need to be aware that executive functions are compromised by attention deficit disorders and stress. Stress can be caused by many factors, and nearly all students experience it to some extent. Those who are most likely to experience the levels of stress that interfere with executive functions include students who have language and learning disabilities, those who are still learning English, and those who live in chronically stressful conditions, such as those associated with poverty. Students who are under a great deal of pressure to succeed or who have suffered loss also can experience significant stress.

However, writing—and especially composing lengthy writing assignments—is such a complex activity that virtually *all* students will experience some level of stress while engaging in it. That's why it's particularly important for them to have a clear, written plan before they begin writing at length. Such a plan enables writers to "offload" some of the burden that writing at length imposes on working memory.[2]

> **TEACHER TIP**
>
> Students can and should learn to plan and outline paragraphs as a whole class even while they're becoming familiar with the various sentence-level skills described in this book. Inexperienced writers can learn a lot from outlining, both about the topic at hand and about how to organize ideas logically when they are guided to do so. However, students shouldn't be expected to outline, draft, and revise longer writing independently until they've acquired the sentence-level skills they need to do so.

Identifying Topic, Audience, and Purpose

To plan a paragraph or a composition, your students need to understand three things: the topic they're writing about, the readers they're trying to communicate with, and the reason they're writing. Initially, you'll need to lead them in class discussions since most students will find it difficult to identify these elements on their own.

Choosing a Topic

It's best to choose a topic that is part of the core curriculum and that students have already learned something about.

Sometimes students are expected to follow a separate writing curriculum that provides little information about the topics they're supposed to write about. However, it's virtually impossible to write about a topic you know little or nothing about.

Students are also often asked to write about their personal experiences or opinions—for example, an essay on whether the cafeteria should serve chocolate milk. While students may have the knowledge to engage in that kind of writing, they miss out on the opportunity to use writing to build and deepen their knowledge.

Even when choosing topics from the core curriculum, it's crucial to determine if students have enough background knowledge about the topic before they begin the planning process. If students need more information, class discussions should help them acquire it or help them identify the best sources to provide it. Students need *some* knowledge to begin planning a piece of writing, but in the process, they may identify gaps in their knowledge and they may take the opportunity to fill those gaps.

Determining the Audience

One of the more challenging aspects of writing for many students is to imagine themselves in the mind of an intended reader. They may struggle to anticipate what that reader would need or want to know and modify their writing accordingly. For example, a paragraph describing Washington, DC, that's directed at an audience of first-time tourists will be very different from one aimed at people who already live or work there.

Of course, in the context of the classroom, the audience is primarily you, the teacher—and ideally, you'll know at least as much about the topic as your students. But students need to be reminded that in some situations they'll need to tailor the structure, facts, word choice, and arguments in their writing to the kinds of readers they're planning to reach. Even though their teacher may know a lot about the topic, it's important for students to learn how to write for other audiences who don't.

For example, older students can imagine they're writing about a topic relating to climate change for an audience of third graders. Then have them imagine writing about the same topic for an audience of climate-change skeptics. Would they choose different language? Would they need to explain more information for one group as opposed to another? Would they make different points?

The intended audience will also determine the tone a writer adopts. Your tone is likely to be different if you're addressing someone you know well as opposed to someone else. On the left in Exhibit 5.1 is an example of a note that I wrote to my husband while dashing out the door, and the example on the right is a note that I wrote to a friend who was staying with us.

— NOTEPAD —	— NOTEPAD —
GET MILK	Hi Christine, I had to rush out to a meeting. If you don't mind, would you please pick up some bread for us? I'll be back soon. Thank you! xo Judy

Exhibit 5.1

In most cases, students should adopt a fairly formal tone in their writing assignments since that's the tone they'll usually be expected to take in college and in the workplace.

Writing prompts and test questions may not specify the audience students should have in mind. In that case, students should generally assume that the reader is someone without a great deal of specific information about the topic.

Sometimes the prompts themselves will define how much information students need to provide. If a prompt reads "*Summarize* the plot of *Animal Farm*," students will need to relate the key points of the entire plot as if the audience knows nothing about it. If, on the other hand, a prompt reads "*Analyze* Squealer's role on the farm," students should focus only on that aspect of the novel.

Understanding the Purpose

Are students trying to persuade the reader to adopt a certain position, or are they simply narrating a series of events? The purpose of a piece of writing influences many of the choices students will make in planning it. A paragraph that is intended to persuade a reader usually has a different kind of topic sentence than one that is describing a situation, place, or person. Similarly, the concluding sentence of a persuasive piece of writing might be a call to action rather than a summary of what's been said.

Writers will also organize details differently depending on their purpose. If they're writing about a series of events or a process, it will make sense to narrate them in chronological order. But if they're trying to persuade a reader to adopt a particular point of view, they will probably want to begin with their "soft" arguments and end with their strongest.

The language you use when creating a writing prompt or posing a question for students can signal the particular purpose of the writing you're looking for, so acquaint your students with the various expository terms and their meanings (see Appendix A). For example, if you ask them to *justify* something, this means the purpose of their writing is argumentative. If you're teaching Level 2 students, you might use some of the following expository terms to help students identify the purpose of a writing assignment:

RESOURCE

Expository
Writing Terms
Appendix A

> **Contrast** the candidate's positions with those of his opponent.
>
> **Summarize** the plot of *The Scarlet Letter*.
>
> **Discuss** the symbolism in the setting of *Lord of the Flies*.
>
> **Analyze** the relationship between Finny and Gene in *A Separate Peace*.

Even younger Level 1 students can practice responding to some of the expository terms. For example:

Explain why Mr. Falker was a good teacher.

Discuss why the disappearance of sea ice is affecting penguins.

Describe the garden where Mary meets Ben.

Summarize Chapter 2.

A Guide to Purpose: Three Types of Writing

Identifying the purpose of a piece of writing determines much of the tone and organization of the paragraph or composition.

To help students identify purpose in writing, TWR emphasizes three types of paragraphs and compositions: **expository**, **narrative**, and **opinion** or **argumentative**. In the real world, of course, a single piece of writing often contains more than one of these types at a time. But when students are first learning to write at length, they need practice with one type of writing at a time. Later, when they've become comfortable with the demands of each type, they can begin to blend them in the way experienced writers often do.

Expository Writing

Classes in English, social studies, and science tend to generate assignments that require expository writing. Therefore, most of the time spent on writing instruction should be devoted to teaching students how to do it well.

Expository writing may explore:

- presenting a problem and a solution
- analyzing a cause-and-effect relationship
- providing a description or giving directions
- comparing and contrasting two concepts, events, or individuals and drawing a conclusion based on the facts presented

When introducing compare-and-contrast assignments, be aware that organizing those kinds of essays can challenge the skills of many writers. It can be even more difficult to write a single paragraph interweaving two points of view.

Narrative Writing

Narrative writing relates a process, a biography, or event in chronological or sequential order, and is usually organized with transition words that signal time or sequence, such as *first, next, then, later,* and *finally* (see Appendix C, "Transition Words and Phrases"). In general, narratives are written in either the first person (as a participant) or third person (as an observer).

RESOURCE

Transition Words
and Phrases
Appendix C

Narrative writing involving fictional stories or personal experience is not the focus of the Hochman Method. Rather, the kind of narratives we cover might include summarizing a plot in English class, explaining the steps for solving a problem in math, tracing a process in science, enumerating the important milestones in a biography, or identifying what led up to a historic event in social studies.

Opinion Writing and Argumentative Writing

We discuss opinion writing and argumentative writing in detail in Chapter 10, but we'll provide a brief overview of these types of writing here. Opinion writing, usually assigned to elementary students, seeks to change how the reader thinks or feels without providing evidence or opposing views. By contrast, argumentative writing presents both sides of an issue, appeals to logic, and gathers evidence and reasons for supporting one side or the other. The conclusion usually proposes the action or point of view that the writer would like the reader to take.

Education experts consider argumentative writing the most complex and cognitively demanding form of composition.[3] As they become more experienced writers, students may be required to support their claims with evidence and weigh the pros and cons of each side. Perhaps most challenging, they must be able to accurately represent a position with which they may not agree, then take an opposing position and justify it to the reader.

Most argumentative assignments are given in middle and high schools. Students might be asked to criticize an author's technique or to evaluate the importance of a historical event. But most state writing standards call for students to begin writing "opinion pieces" in the early elementary grades, so it's a good idea to begin instruction in this kind of writing earlier than middle school.

However, it may be more difficult to find opinion and argumentative assignments for young children that are embedded in the content of the curriculum. If necessary, you might have to assign opinion pieces on non-curricular topics such as "Homework on Weekends." But if a school is using an elementary curriculum that is rich in content—and especially, in historical topics—it may well be possible to have students engage in curriculum-based opinion writing.

Before your students begin to write an outline for an opinion or argumentative paragraph or composition, have them engage in class discussions about their topic. That kind of dialogue or debate can help them determine and refine their own opinions and formulate arguments that their intended audience would find persuasive.

To Sum Up

- Writing at length places heavy demands on the aspects of cognition known as executive functions and working memory.

- Before students can plan a piece of writing, they need to identify the topic, the audience, and the purpose.

- Encourage students to write for different audiences, possibly requiring them to alter their topic, their tone, and their word choice.

- As students acquire sentence-level skills, they can begin learning to outline, draft, and revise, BUT only as a whole-class activity.

- Introduce students to the meaning of expository terms such as *enumerate* and *justify* to help them understand the purpose of an assignment or a prompt.

- Provide assignments in the three types of writing: expository, narrative, and opinion or argumentative.

BOOK DISCUSSION QUESTIONS

1. How have you encouraged or taught students to plan before they write?

2. Why should students create outlines before they write a draft?

3. How do the executive functions impact writing?

4. Describe three things students should think about before writing.

5. Describe the three types of writing.

Notes

1. W. Strunk and E.B. White, *The Elements of Style* (New York: Longman, 1999), p. 15.

2. O. Chen, F. Paas, and J. Sweller, "A Cognitive Load Theory Approach to Defining and Measuring Task Complexity through Element Interactivity," *Educational Psychology Review* (2023), 35: 63.

3. R.P. Ferretti and W.E. Lewis, "Best Practices in Teaching Argumentative Writing," *Best Practices in Writing Instruction*, 2nd ed. (New York: The Guilford Press, 2013), pp. 113–140.

CHAPTER 6

A Simple, Linear Guide

Introducing the Single-Paragraph Outline

It was more than halfway through the school year, and Ms. Chen was getting anxious. Her tenth graders were still struggling to produce even brief coherent written responses to the prompts she gave them. That was especially true if she asked them to incorporate evidence from the text or analysis into their answers.

She felt like she'd tried everything. She'd broken the writing process into different components, having them take notes on their reading and use sticky notes or index cards to record the evidence they planned to use. She'd had them create concept maps to help them organize their thoughts. It looked like they had some great ideas.

But when she got their finished products, she was dismayed to see that students usually provided undigested chunks of information without much in the way of analysis. And it was rare to see a paragraph that had a clear topic sentence—or even anything that actually resembled a paragraph. Sentences followed one another in no particular order, and students often wandered away from their topic. She'd tried other kinds of graphic organizers—Venn diagrams and webs—but nothing seemed to work.

Ms. Chen sometimes wondered if her efforts to scaffold the writing process had only made things worse. It seemed that many students found the multiple sticky notes and the bubbles in their concept maps more overwhelming than helpful. She had run out of ideas for ways to help them express themselves in a clear, coherent paragraph. How could she send them off to eleventh grade without that essential skill?

Graphic organizers such as thought webs, Venn diagrams, and bubble maps may be helpful for brainstorming, vocabulary instruction, or helping students grasp certain concepts. However, they don't provide an effective template for transferring those ideas into a coherent piece of writing. A crucial step is missing: taking the material in the bubbles, webs, or boxes and figuring out what is most important, what is least important or irrelevant, and how to put the ideas and points in a logical order.

Some teachers may have tried the Harvard Outline, with its main ideas, sub-ideas, sub-sub-ideas, Roman numerals, and capital and lowercase letters. Although it has the advantage of a linear structure, and it can serve as a great study guide, we've found that the Harvard Outline doesn't translate well into paragraphs or essays. It goes to the other extreme from the free-form bubble map, requiring such high-level categorization and classification skills that students can get bogged down and confused in the planning process. Even if they do manage to complete such a detailed outline, they may find it difficult to convert the complex structure to written text.

What Ms. Chen didn't realize was that before asking her students to write, she needed to help them through the process of constructing a simple outline. If she had, she might have found that her students' paragraphs were far clearer and more coherent.

Teachers may feel pressure to have students write multiple-paragraph compositions, especially at higher grade levels. But teaching students to outline and write a single coherent paragraph first is a crucial investment of time and energy. In one study done with seventh and eighth graders, students who used TWR's Single-Paragraph Outline achieved better results than those who used a concept map or no planning tool at all—and the students who got the highest writing scores not only used the outline but also had been explicitly taught how to use it. Students also preferred the outline. Of those who used it, 85 percent said it made writing a paragraph easier.[1]

Learning to use certain text structures in the context of a single paragraph—such as problem/solution or cause/effect—will help equip students to plan and write essays using those structures later on. And once students are familiar with TWR outlines, they can easily replicate them on scratch paper when asked to provide written responses on tests, or when planning essays and compositions independently.

Remember that students should continue to practice sentence-level strategies while learning to outline and draft paragraphs. You also don't have to wait for students to "master" sentence-level strategies before introducing them to the Single-Paragraph Outline. These activities can and should be done in tandem.

Defining Terms

A **paragraph** is a group of sentences that includes details supporting a specific point. A well-written paragraph will display the following characteristics:[2]

- **Structure.** The sentences in the paragraph are sequenced in a way that ensures clarity for the reader.

- **Coherence.** The sentences are logically connected with transition words that signal that connection, including indications of a change of direction or emphasis.

- **Unity.** Every sentence supports the main idea of the paragraph.

- **Well-constructed sentences.** The sentences are grammatically correct and clear, and their types and structures vary (some simple, others compound or complex).

Guiding Students to Create Effective Outlines

WHY PRACTICE DEVELOPING THE SINGLE PARAGRAPH OUTLINE (SPO)?

- Provides structure (beginning, middle, and end)
- Eliminates repetition
- Improves ability to stick to the topic
- Enables students to distinguish essential from nonessential material
- Provides a guide for placing ideas in logical order
- Promotes analytical thinking
- Provides a template that students can easily duplicate on their own
- Enables students to revise more easily than if they start with a draft
- Modulates the cognitive load imposed by writing at length
- Reinforces content knowledge

RESOURCE

Single-Paragraph Outline
Appendix G

Exhibit 6.1 shows a blank SPO (this template is also available full-size in Appendix G):

T.S. _____

_____

1. ....

2. ....

3. ....

4. ....

C.S. _____

_____

Exhibit 6.1   Blank Single-Paragraph Outline

The simple linear format of the SPO benefits all students.

Solid lines tell students to write complete sentences for the **topic sentence (T.S.)** and the **concluding sentence (C.S.)**. Dotted lines tell students to write notes for supporting details.

Exhibit 6.2 is an example of an SPO a student has completed—and after that, the paragraph the student might write based on it.

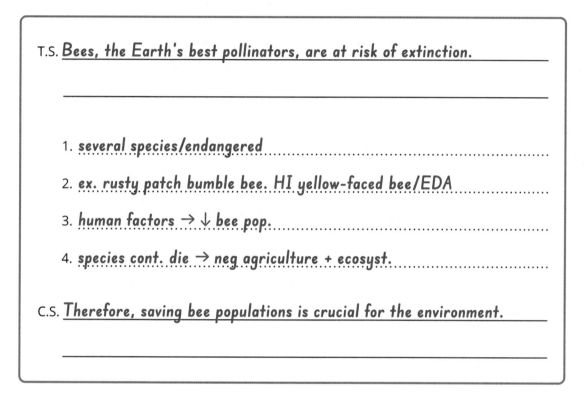

T.S. *Bees, the Earth's best pollinators, are at risk of extinction.*

_____

1. *several species/endangered*
2. *ex. rusty patch bumble bee. HI yellow-faced bee/EDA*
3. *human factors → ↓ bee pop.*
4. *species cont. die → neg agriculture + ecosyst.*

C.S. *Therefore, saving bee populations is crucial for the environment.*

_____

Bees, the Earth's best pollinators, are at risk of extinction. Several species are listed as endangered. For example, the rusty-patched bumble bee and seven varieties of the Hawaiian yellow-faced bee have been classified as endangered under the Endangered Species Act. Human factors like pesticides and habitat loss are causing a major decline in bee populations. If bee species continue to die, there will be negative effects on our agriculture and ecosystems. Therefore, saving bee populations is crucial for sustaining the environment.

Exhibit 6.2   Example SPO

This chapter provides you with strategies and activities to use when guiding your students to eventually create outlines and paragraphs on their own.

SPO Scaffolding Activities

The ultimate objective is to enable students to produce an outline independently. However, handing them a blank SPO without first teaching them the necessary underlying skills won't produce that outcome.

Before students can construct an SPO on their own, they will need to learn the steps leading up to that task: creating a topic sentence, including and sequencing relevant details, and crafting a concluding sentence.

A topic sentence expresses a paragraph's main idea. Make sure students understand that the sentences in the body of a paragraph should provide details that relate to the general idea contained in the topic sentence.

When you're modeling using notes for detail sentences, remember not to write full sentences on the dotted lines. Usually, when Level 1 students are ready to create SPOs independently, they should also use only key words and phrases for notes, but more experienced writers can add symbols and abbreviations (see Appendix B).

RESOURCE

Symbols and Abbreviations
Appendix B

When writing in note form on the detail lines, tell students that the notes don't necessarily indicate just one sentence. Specifically, an example or a quotation included on the same dotted line could be written as more than one sentence in the paragraph.

A concluding sentence may restate the main idea of the paragraph, although it shouldn't just be a repetition of the topic sentence. Alternatively, depending on the type of paragraph, a concluding sentence might express a point of view or a call to action.

> **WHY PRACTICE DEVELOPING TOPIC AND CONCLUDING SENTENCES?**
> - Enables students to make generalizations
> - Promotes analytical thinking
> - Enables students to identify key information or concepts
> - Reinforces academic knowledge and vocabulary

Developing topic and concluding sentences requires students to consider a collection of facts and information and decide what characteristics unite them—in other words, to develop the ability to make generalizations. Many of the activities that follow will help students in identifying and creating both topic and concluding sentences. Once students have created an effective topic sentence, constructing the concluding sentence is often an easier job.

Sequence of SPO Scaffolding Activites:

1. Create an SPO with the whole class.
2. Distinguish a T.S. from details.
3. Identify T.S. and sequence details.
4. Given T.S., select relevant details from a list.
5. Eliminate irrelevant detail(s) from a list or SPO.
6. Given T.S., generate details.
7. Practice the three strategies for writing a T.S. and C.S.
8. Given topic/prompt, generate T.S.
9. Given details, generate T.S.
10. Given T.S. and details, generate C.S.
11. Given topic/prompt, construct SPO independently.

1. Create an SPO with the Whole Class

You should have your students practice the steps involved in creating an SPO before asking them to develop one themselves, but it's helpful to demonstrate the entire process first so they know where they're headed. When modeling the SPO for Level 1 students, consider selecting topics that are not complicated or don't require searching for new information.

Level 2 students can begin learning how to construct SPOs based on a current curriculum topic if most students in the class have already acquired enough information about it to help generate topic and concluding sentences and details.

There are two ways to develop an SPO with the whole class. One, as shown in the following example, is to have students come up with a topic sentence and then narrate a series of details related to it, perhaps in chronological order.

Level 1 Narrative Example

T.S. _Try growing bean plants at home._

first   1. _holes in bottom of container_

next   2. _put soil in and dig holes_

then   3. _put seeds in and cover_

finally   4. _water every day_

C.S. _It is exciting to watch seeds grow into plants!_

Try growing bean plants at home. First, you should put holes in the bottom of a container. Next, put soil in it and dig holes. Then, you put seeds in the holes and cover them with soil. Finally, be sure to water your plants every day. It is exciting to watch your seeds grow into plants!

Level 2 Narrative Example

T.S. *It is easy to find the pH balance of a liquid.*
_____

first   1. *clean container* ....

next   2. *fill w/ few in. of liquid* ....

then   3. *dip test strip/few sec.* ....

finally   4. *compare color/litmus scale* ....

C.S. *If you follow these simple steps, you can determine if a liquid is*

acidic, neutral, or alkaline.
_____

It is easy to find the pH balance of a liquid. First, thoroughly clean the container you are using. Next, fill the container with a few inches of the liquid you are testing. Then, dip the test strip in the liquid for a few seconds. Finally, compare the color you see to the litmus scale. If you follow these simple steps, you can determine if a liquid is acidic, neutral, or alkaline.

The second way to develop an SPO involves brainstorming. The steps that you would take are:

1. Identify a topic, audience, and purpose.

2. Help students brainstorm 10–15 details about a topic and organize them into categories.

3. Generate a topic sentence on the solid line on the top of the outline using one of the three TWR strategies (sentence types, subordinating conjunctions, appositives).* **This can be done before the brainstorming if preferred.**

4. Select, categorize, and sequence details and write them in note form on the dotted lines. (See Chapter 3 for a discussion of TWR note-taking techniques.) *Note that every brainstormed item does not have to be included on the SPO.*

5. Generate a concluding sentence using one of the three TWR strategies (sentence types, subordinating conjunctions, appositives) on the solid line at the bottom of the outline.**

*Level 2 students can use all three: sentence types, subordinating conjunctions, and appositives. Level 1 students should begin with sentence types and then three of the subordinating conjunctions: *before, after, if.*

**A concluding transition may be appropriate to use at the beginning of the concluding sentence.

Level 1 Brainstorming Example

TOPIC: Winter

soup	cold + icy	sweaters
New Year's Eve	coats and scarves	ice-skate, ski, sled
hot chocolate	holiday foods	lip balm
cozy blankets	boots	make a snowman
hats + gloves	cloudy	snowy

T.S. _Winter is a unique time of year._

1. cold, snowy, cloudy days
2. coats, sweaters, hats, gloves
3. hot chocolate, soup, holiday foods
4. skiing, sledding, making a snowman

C.S. _Clearly, winter is an exciting season!_

Level 2 Brainstorming Example

TOPIC: Achievements of Aztecs

herbal treatments → cure diseases

Ist. civ/dev edu syst → all children attended

adv. calendar → improved farming

adv. math syst → used area for construction

built pyramids/temples for ceremonies

built chinampas = floating gardens → crops ↑

T.S. <u>The Aztecs, a Mesoamerican civilization, had many outstanding</u>

<u>achievements.</u>

1. <u>adv. math system → used area for construction</u>
2. <u>Ist civ./dev edu system → all children attended</u>
3. <u>built pyramids/temples for ceremonies</u>
4. <u>built chinampas = floating gardens → crops ↑</u>

C.S. <u>The contributions of the Aztecs had a great impact on subsequent</u>

<u>civilizations.</u>

Now that students have an idea of what the end product looks like, it's time to introduce them to the steps involved in creating an SPO. Each step has value in itself and will help students think more analytically, find important points more efficiently, and take notes more effectively. In addition, each step requires modeling by the teacher, as well as oral and collaborative practice, before students can engage in it independently.

Once students have learned these steps, they not only will be ready to construct an SPO independently but also will have most of the skills they'll need when they move on to planning compositions.

2. Distinguish a T.S. from Details

To help students understand the concept of a topic sentence, present them with three or more sentences and ask them to identify the topic sentence and the sentence or sentences that provide supporting details. You could start with three sentences and ask students to mark one with *T.S.* for *topic sentence* and the other two with *D* for *detail.*

This example assumes that the students have read *Miss Nelson Is Missing!*[3]

Level 1 Example

DIRECTIONS: Identify the topic sentence using *T.S.* and the supporting details using *D.*

__D__ Students had to do lots of homework.

__T.S.__ Ms. Swamp was a very strict teacher.

__D__ She cancelled story hour.

The next example is embedded in content relating to medieval Europe.

Level 2 Example

DIRECTIONS: Identify the topic sentence using *T.S.* and the supporting details using *D.*

__D__ Art and literature began to reflect the times by including themes of death.

__D__ Many landowners were ruined financially due to a lack of laborers to cultivate the land.

__T.S.__ The Bubonic Plague, a dreadful disease, had a significant impact in Europe.

__D__ One third of Europe's population, 25 million people, died.

__D__ Since many laborers died, many families lost their means of survival.

3. Identify T.S. and Sequence Details

You can increase the level of difficulty by giving students groups of three to five sentences and asking them to first identify the topic sentence and then put the remaining sentences in a logical sequence. This activity will help them understand how to sequence ideas or events within a paragraph.

In this activity, the transition words signal the sequence of the detail sentences.

Level 1 Example

> **DIRECTIONS:** Identify the topic sentence using *T.S.* and number the supporting details in the correct order.
>
> __2__   Then, the seed sprouts a plant with flowers.
>
> __T.S.__   The growth of a pumpkin is interesting.
>
> __3__   Finally, the flowers disappear, and the pumpkin grows!
>
> __1__   First, a seed is planted in the ground.

Students who have been studying the Mughal Empire might complete the following activity.

Level 2 Example

> **DIRECTIONS:** Identify the topic sentence using *T.S.* and number the supporting details in the correct order.
>
> __1__   Babur started the empire and removed the Delhi Sultanate.
>
> __3__   Jahangir continued the policy of tolerance toward Hindus along with most of Akbar's policies.
>
> __2__   After Babur, Akbar, the greatest Mughal Emperor, laid the foundation for many future leaders.
>
> __T.S.__   There were many rulers of the Mughal Empire.
>
> __4__   Shah Jahan also continued Akbar's policies and built the Taj Mahal.

4. Given T.S., Select Relevant Details from a List

Provide students with two different topic sentences and a list of details. Have students write each detail under the topic sentence it belongs with.

Level 1 Example

> **DIRECTIONS:** Write each detail under the appropriate topic sentence.
>
> | | | |
> |---|---|---|
> | long lines | play games | buy souvenirs |
> | lots of walking | overcrowded | water rides |
>
> T.S. Amusement parks are exciting.
>
> 1. *play games* ....
>
> 2. *buy souvenirs* ....
>
> 3. *water rides* ....
>
> T.S. Amusement parks are exhausting.
>
> 1. *long lines* ....
>
> 2. *lots of walking* ....
>
> 3. *overcrowded* ....

Level 2 Example

DIRECTIONS: Write each detail under the appropriate topic sentence.

occurs in 4 steps

1 diploid cell → 4 haploid cells

used to reprod. somatic cells

daughter cells clone = gen. identical

males make 4 sperm/females only 1 egg

crossing over during proph. 1 → genetically unique cells

seq. of 2 divisions

1 diploid cell → 2 diploid cells

T.S. Mitosis, a step in the cell cycle, results in the division of the nucleus.

1. *occurs in 4 steps* ....

2. *daughter cells clone = gen. identical* ....

3. *1 diploid cell → 2 diploid cells* ....

4. *used to reprod. somatic cells* ....

T.S. Meiosis, a type of cell reproduction, is the process organisms use to make gametes, sperm, and eggs.

1. *crossing over during proph. 1 → genetically unique cells* ....

2. *seq. of 2 divisions* ....

3. *1 diploid cell → 4 haploid cells* ....

4. *males make 4 sperm/females only 1 egg* ....

5. Eliminate Irrelevant Detail(s) from a List or SPO

Some students have difficulty distinguishing relevant from irrelevant details or go off topic when they write. If some of your students fall into that category, have them underline or put *T.S.* next to the topic sentence in a list and then cross out the detail that has the least connection to the topic sentence.

This example assumes that the students have read *The Snowy Day*.[4]

Level 1 Example

> **DIRECTIONS:** Identify the topic sentence (T.S.) and cross out the irrelevant detail.
>
> _____   He made a snowman.
>
> *T.S.*   Peter had a wonderful time on a snowy day.
>
> _____   ~~Peter had a dream that the snow melted.~~
>
> _____   He made snow angels.

Level 2 Example

> **DIRECTIONS:** Identify the topic sentence (T.S.) and cross out the irrelevant detail.
>
> _____   Then, subtract 15 from both sides of the equation.
>
> _____   ~~There is only one variable in the equation.~~
>
> _____   Divide both sides by 3 to solve for x.
>
> *T.S.*   Follow 3 steps to solve $3(x+5) = 45$.
>
> _____   Distribute the 3 inside the parentheses to get $3x + 15 = 45$.

6. Given T.S., Generate Details

In this activity, you provide students with a topic sentence that you've created on a blank SPO template and have them generate three or four details to go with it.

For a Level 1 group, you might start with the following sentence.

Level 1 Example

DIRECTIONS: Using key words and phrases, write details for the given topic sentence.

T.S. Dogs are popular pets.

1. protective
2. loyal
3. playful

If you've been teaching Level 2 students about the Incan Empire, you could give them the following sentence.

Level 2 Example

DIRECTIONS: Using key words and phrases, write details for the given topic sentence.

T.S. Although the Incan Empire was in power for less than one hundred years, parts of its culture lives on today.

1. Quechuan language
2. celebrate winter solstice
3. textile making
4. irrigation + architecture

7. Practice the Three Strategies for Writing a T.S. and C.S.

When students were doing sentence-level work, they learned strategies to help them create topic sentences. When first explaining how to use these strategies for topic sentences, you should provide the topic and make sure it's one that students are familiar with.

If you are guiding Level 2 students through the formulation of topic sentences, tell them about all three strategies (see Exhibit 6.3). If you're teaching Level 1 students, just discuss the first two—sentence types and subordinating conjunctions—and limit the latter to the conjunctions *before*, *after*, and *if*.

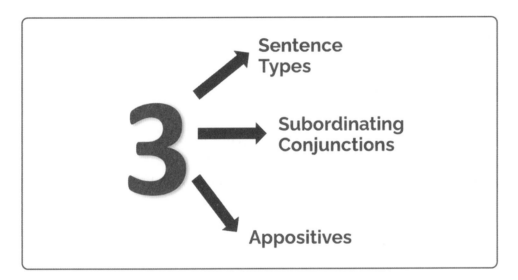

Exhibit 6.3   Three strategies for creating topic and concluding sentences

- **Use a sentence type.**
  Students may use a statement, a question, an exclamation, or (possibly) a command. For example, the topic sentence for a paragraph about Washington, DC might be, *Have you ever been to Washington, DC?* Note that while exclamations and commands can be helpful for younger students who are learning to write paragraphs, middle and high school students should generally not use them for topic sentences.

- **Begin with a subordinating conjunction.**
  A Level 1 student might use a subordinating conjunction such as *before* to form a topic sentence. For example: *Before you get a dog, you need to make preparations.* A Level 2 student might use a more

sophisticated conjunction such as *although*—as in *Although the New Deal did not solve all of the nation's problems, it saved the United States from economic collapse.*

- **Include an appositive.**
  A paragraph about New York City could start with *New York, the nation's largest city, is visited by many tourists.* A paragraph about Genghis Khan might begin *Genghis Khan, a powerful Mongol leader, created a large empire.*

Have your students practice using these strategies to transform boring topic sentences into engaging, informative ones.

These three strategies are also useful in formulating concluding sentences—which we'll address further on in this chapter.

8. Given a Topic/Prompt, Generate T.S.

After students have had practice writing topic sentences using the three strategies, give them a topic and ask them to create two or three topic sentences for it. Level 1 students are expected to write topic sentences using only sentence types and the subordinating conjunctions *before*, *after*, and *if*.

If students have been studying endangered species, you might give them the following activity.

Level 1 Example

> **DIRECTIONS:** Write two topic sentences about the topic: one using a sentence type and one starting with a subordinating conjunction.
>
> **TOPIC:** Endangered sea turtles
>
> Sentence Type
> <u>Why are sea turtles endangered?</u>
>
> Subordinating Conjunction
> <u>Since sea turtles are endangered, steps must be taken to protect them.</u>

Level 2 Example

If your Level 2 students have been studying the environment, you might give them the topic *climate change* and ask them to write three topic sentences using each of the three strategies: sentence types, subordinating conjunctions, and appositives. They might come up with the following sentences.

DIRECTIONS: Write three topic sentences about the topic: one using a sentence type, one starting with a subordinating conjunction, and one including an appositive.

TOPIC: Climate change

Sentence Type
What is the leading cause of climate change?

Subordinating Conjunction
Since climate change has rapidly worsened weather extremes, steps must be taken to reverse it.

Appositive
Climate change, a deviation from usual weather or temperature, has become an urgent problem.

---

9. Given Details, Generate T.S.

Provide students with an SPO without topic sentence. The details should be presented in note form. Notes for Level 2 students should include key words and phrases, abbreviations, and symbols, while notes for Level 1 students should use just key words and phrases. This activity will require students to synthesize a number of details to come up with a topic sentence that brings them all together.

Level 1 Example

If Level 1 students have been learning about the life cycle of a butterfly, you could give them an SPO such as the following one and have them provide a topic sentence.

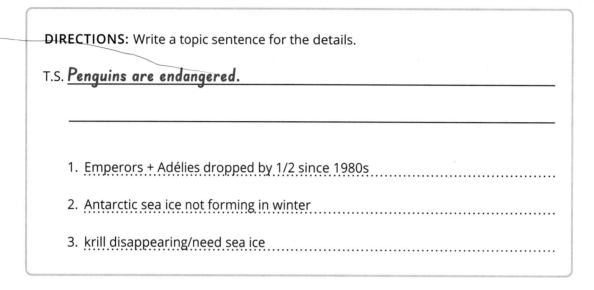

DIRECTIONS: Write a topic sentence for the details.

T.S. *Penguins are endangered.*

    1. Emperors + Adélies dropped by 1/2 since 1980s

    2. Antarctic sea ice not forming in winter

    3. krill disappearing/need sea ice

Students might use the details shown in the following example—and the knowledge that enables them to identify the era being discussed—to generate a topic sentence.

Level 2 Example

DIRECTIONS: Write a topic sentence for the details.

T.S. *The Mayans were a complex Mesoamerican civilization.*

    1. present-day Mexico/Yucatan Peninsula

    2. polytheistic/sun + moon + rain gods

    3. accurate calendar + math + pyramids

    4. possible drought + famine/disease

10. Given T.S. and Details, Generate C.S.

The same basic techniques that have enabled students to craft effective topic sentences will work for concluding sentences—with one twist. A concluding sentence should echo the idea of the topic sentence but not repeat it verbatim.

In some types of writing, the concluding sentence should introduce something new—perhaps a call to action or a personal opinion. However, in many cases, a paraphrase or summary of the topic sentence can serve as the concluding one. Consider the following examples.

Level 1 Example

> **DIRECTIONS:** Write a concluding sentence for the following topic sentence and details.
>
> T.S. <u>What makes summer a special season?</u>
>
> _____
>
> 1. warm weather
> 2. shorts and T-shirts
> 3. watermelon and ice cream cones
> 4. baseball, fishing, swimming
>
> C.S. <u>*In conclusion, summer is an enjoyable time of year!*</u>
>
> _____

Level 2 Example

DIRECTIONS: Write a concluding sentence for the following topic sentence and details.

T.S. <u>The Renaissance was a time of tremendous advancements in many areas.</u>

_____

art   1. <u>Michaelangelo/DaVinci</u> ....

education   2. <u>Gutenberg/printing press</u> ....

inventions   3. <u>watches/microscope</u> ....

science   4. <u>Copernicus/Galileo → astronomy</u> ....

C.S. *The 14th–17th centuries marked a time of major cultural change in Europe.*

As we discussed in Chapter 4, one way to make a sentence sound more like a concluding one is to introduce it with an appropriate transition, such as *finally* or *in conclusion.*

It's best if the topic and concluding sentences don't repeat the same structure. For example, if the topic sentence includes an appositive, then encourage students to use a different structure for the concluding sentence—perhaps a subordinating conjunction or an exclamation.

11. Given Topic/Prompt, Construct SPO Independently

If students have been reading *Mae Among the Stars,*[5] you might give them the following activity.

Level 1 Example

DIRECTIONS: Complete an SPO for the topic.

TOPIC: Mae Jemison

T.S. _Mae Jemison dreamed of going to space._

1. _read books about space_
2. _teacher suggested being nurse_
3. _followed dream_
4. _became astronaut_

C.S. _Mae Jemison made her dream come true!_

Level 2 Example

DIRECTIONS: Complete an SPO for the topic.

TOPIC: Spanish-American War

T.S. _The Spanish-American War of 1898 marked a turning point in both American and Spanish history._

1. _Cuba wanted independence from Spain/US support_
2. _sinking USS Maine/Havana Harbor → tensions ↑_
3. _Apr 1898 US declared war on Spain_
4. _US victory/Dec 1898 Treaty of Paris → ended war_

C.S. _The Spanish-American War led to the end of Spanish colonial rule and signaled the emergence of the United States as a global power._

SPO: Text Structures

An SPO enables students to use almost any text structure, including the following standard ones:

- Narrative
- Descriptive
- Problem/solution
- Cause/effect
- Pro/con
- Compare-and-contrast
- Opinion/persuasive

You can choose one of the following outlines for a whole-class introduction to adapting the SPO for different text structures, using the sequence of steps described in the preceding sections. If your students have sufficient knowledge about something they've already studied or are studying, you can embed the activity in that content.

Narrative

T.S. _In 1912, the sinking of the Titanic, a luxury ship, was a disaster._

1. _built for safety/"unsinkable"_
2. _speed/ignored signals → hit iceberg_
3. _only 20 lifeboats/confusion_
4. _1500 died/most 1st & 2nd class survived_

C.S. _Many lessons were learned from this catastrophe._

Descriptive

T.S. <u>Sailing first class on the Titanic was an incredible experience for</u>

<u>its millionaire passengers.</u>

1. <u>cabins = 5 rooms</u>
2. <u>several restaurants + lounges</u>
3. <u>high speed telegraphs/elevator</u>
4. <u>gym, pool, Turkish baths</u>

C.S. <u>The Titanic was the most luxurious passenger ship of its time.</u>

Problem/Solution

T.S. <u>Even though Galileo invented the telescope, Newton and Herschel</u>

<u>implemented many modifications that make it what it is today.</u>

Problem	1. <u>shape of lens/blurry images</u>
Solution	2. <u>made longer → increased magnification 50-100x</u>
Problem	3. <u>fuzzy images + rainbow colors</u>
Solution	4. <u>used mirrors to prevent rainbow colors</u>

C.S. <u>The telescope, an optical instrument designed to make distant objects</u>

<u>appear nearer, continues to help us study the sky today.</u>

Cause/Effect

T.S. <u>As a result of France's purchase of Louisiana, major changes</u>

<u>took place.</u>

Cause   1. 1800/Napoleon = leader France/Spain returns to LA

Effect   2. US alarmed/feared allies w/ Britain

Cause   3. France @ war w/ GB/Nap needed $ → sold LA to US

Effect   4. Westward Expans./US doubled in size

C.S. <u>The Louisiana Purchase, a critical event in U.S. history, strengthened</u>

<u>and expanded the nation.</u>

Pro/Con

T.S. <u>Although he was difficult to work with, Isaac Newton made important</u>

<u>contributions to science.</u>

−   1. accusations of plagiarism

−   2. paranoid about sharing work/sabotaged others

+   3. 1687/published "Math Principles" → redemption

+   4. achievements = gravity + calculus

C.S. <u>In summary, despite his flaws, Newton is remembered as a scientific</u>

<u>genius.</u>

Compare and Contrast

T.S. _Frogs and toads, while similar in many ways, also exhibit distinct differences._

Similar	1.	amphibians/live near water
Similar	2.	lay eggs/undergo metamorphosis
Different	3.	frogs = smooth + moist skin/prefer wetter environments
Different	4.	toads = rough + dry skin/can tolerate drier habitats

C.S. _Although they have similarities as amphibians, frogs and toads differ in their physical appearance and habitats._

Opinion/Persuasive

T.S. _Since the penny is no longer a useful denomination, it is time to get rid of it._

1. centuries of inflation → value of penny ↓
2. costs > penny to mint
3. penny = nuisance → slows down lines
4. nickel = lowest denomination → easier transactions

C.S. _Write to your congressional representative to get the penny retired!_

Turning an Outline into a Draft

After your students have put together a coherent SPO, they are ready to convert the outline into a draft. They'll need to expand their notes on the dotted lines into complete sentences and add those sentences to the topic and concluding sentences they've already written.

When students convert their SPOs into a draft, the resulting paragraph will be logically organized, on topic, and non-repetitive. At the same time, though, it may not be engaging to a reader. To make their writing flow, students will need to apply the revision techniques that we'll introduce in the next chapter. Those techniques will draw on skills they've acquired through sentence-level activities.

Bear in mind that leading your students through the process of developing an SPO and later having them complete one independently is a valuable exercise in itself, regardless of whether it results in a written paragraph. Creating an outline deepens and cements students' knowledge of the content it relates to and develops their ability to make generalizations and put information into a logical sequence. **Be sure to give your students plenty of opportunities to develop outlines without turning them into drafts and final copies.**

Differentiating SPO Activities

- For students who need more support in completing an SPO, you can provide the topic or the concluding sentences—or both—and have them write in notes for the details. Students who need less support can come up with their topic and concluding sentences independently.

- Have some students use only key words and phrases for their notes on the dotted lines, while having others use abbreviations and symbols as well.

- If some students need more help coming up with details, you could provide them with cues in the margin while letting others come up with detail categories on their own.

To Sum Up

- The SPO is linear and simple, enabling students to order details that support the main idea and eliminate irrelevant information.

- Model the process of creating an entire SPO as a whole-class activity for both Levels 1 and 2 before introducing activities that focus on the SPO scaffolds.

- To help students understand the concept of a topic sentence and learn to organize and sequence details, use the SPO scaffolding activities.

- Build on students' knowledge of sentences to introduce the strategies for constructing topic and concluding sentences: sentence types, subordinating conjunctions, and (for Level 2 students) appositives.

- Guide students through the process of creating non-repetitive concluding sentences.

- As with sentence activities, it's important to keep circling back to the SPO scaffold activities to reinforce the skills used to develop SPOs and to serve as comprehension checks.

1. Why is the linear structure of the Single Paragraph Outline (SPO) the best plan for students?

2. Explain why it's important to write supporting details as notes on an outline instead of complete sentences.

3. What important skills will students develop as they practice creating topic and concluding sentences?

4. What techniques can help students avoid repeating their topic sentence verbatim when writing their paragraph's concluding sentence?

5. What benefits will students get from creating an outline, even if they don't turn it into a draft or a final copy?

6. What are some ways to differentiate an SPO activity for students who need more practice completing an outline?

7. How do outlines promote analytic thinking?

8. Try creating an SPO based on content you have taught.

Notes

1. D. Zoleo, "Examining the Use of Linear Outlines to Support Student Writing," *Theses and Dissertations* (2021): 214.

2. J. Langan, *English Skills, Instructor's Edition,* 6th ed. (Boston: McGraw-Hill, 1997).

3. H. Allard, *Miss Nelson Is Missing* (New York: Houghton Mifflin Co., 1977).

4. E.J. Keats, *The Snowy Day* (London: Puffin Books, 1976).

5. R. Ahmed, *Mae among the Stars* (New York: HarperCollins, 2018).

CHAPTER 7

Revision

Putting It All Together

Over the course of the school year, Mr. Chambers's fifth-grade students had acquired an impressive array of sentence-level skills. They'd learned how to use basic and subordinating conjunctions and transition words, and they'd practiced adding appositives and using question words to expand kernel sentences. Mr. Chambers had also led them through the process of constructing a Single-Paragraph Outline (SPO), and they seemed to have grasped it.

At the end of a unit on insects, Mr. Chambers asked his students to write a paragraph on the life cycle of the butterfly. He was looking forward to seeing how they would apply the strategies they'd learned to their independent writing.

But when he started reading through what his students had produced, his heart sank. The paragraph written by a student named Mara was typical:

The life cycle of a butterfly has four stages. The first one is the egg stage. The second one is the larva stage. The third one is the pupa stage. The last one is the adult stage. The life cycle of the butterfly is very interesting.

The essential information was there—barely. Mara had also written complete sentences, stayed on topic, and created topic and concluding sentences. But the paragraph was wooden and boring.

Mr. Chambers was sure Mara knew how to construct more complex, varied, and informative sentences as well as how to use transitions to make her writing flow. She and her classmates had done a good job with all of those strategies when given sentence-level activities to work on, or when Mr. Chambers made specific suggestions to, for example, add an appositive to a sentence. But it seemed that, for some reason, they weren't able to apply those strategies to their own writing independently.

What could he do, Mr. Chambers wondered, to enable them to internalize these strategies and become better independent writers? After all, he wasn't always going to be there to suggest that they add an appositive or use a subordinating conjunction.

It's crucial to teach students specific writing strategies and then have them use activities you've modeled and created to practice those strategies. It's also crucial to give them targeted feedback on their writing. But that kind of practice and feedback is often not enough to enable them to produce fluent, graceful writing on their own. Of course, they need to learn how to edit their writing. But first, and more important, students need to learn how to revise it.

WHY PRACTICE REVISION ACTIVITIES?

- Leads to smoothly flowing, logically connected prose in paragraphs and compositions
- Provides a way of incorporating substantive changes into a piece of writing
- Enables students to use skills gained from sentence activities and outlining when writing at length

Students may find revision challenging unless it's presented as a step-by-step process. Providing them with an array of activities—which we'll demonstrate in the following sections—will help.

Revising versus Editing: An Important Distinction

Many people see the concepts of revising and editing as one and the same since both processes are necessary to improve a piece of writing. For experienced writers, revising and editing may overlap, but when working with your students you should teach the two processes separately. Understanding the distinction between the two is a crucial first step in helping your students transform a boring and disjointed piece of writing into one that engages the reader and flows smoothly.

Revising: Improving the Substance

Revising means clarifying or altering the content or structure of a draft. At its core, revising requires writers to put themselves in the shoes of a reader, anticipating what information that reader will need or want to know and determining how to communicate it as effectively as possible.

Revising is what all good writers do, sometimes repeatedly, to make their writing clear, accurate, and fluid. It can be as simple as substituting a powerful adjective for one that falls flat or as complex as reorganizing the sequence of ideas in an essay to make an argument stronger. For beginning writers, it often involves turning simple rudimentary sentences into rich, complex ones or elaborating on vague ideas with details and examples. For many writers, it may mean eliminating unnecessary verbiage or streamlining convoluted sentence structure.

To revise, students will build on the planning they engaged in when creating their SPOs. They will also draw on the skills they learned when practicing the sentence-level activities, including harnessing the power of transitions to make their writing flow.

Editing: Polishing the Prose

Editing, although important, is often a less complex process. It involves identifying and then correcting errors in grammar, punctuation, capitalization, syntax, and spelling.

Most teachers focus on editing, probably because they are more comfortable with the mechanics and rules of writing. Similarly, if you ask students to improve on a piece of writing, they're likely to make mechanical changes because, when they know the rules, it's easier; adding a comma or capitalizing a proper noun isn't nearly as complex as imagining what a reader needs to know or reorganizing the content of their writing. But it's revising that deserves the lion's share of instructional time and students' mental effort. To the extent that students do revise, they rarely engage in it with the specificity it requires.

Experienced writers usually revise and edit simultaneously. However, it's best if students focus on revising *before* they edit. Only after students grow familiar with the process of revising should they be expected to edit, proofread, and otherwise refine their work. Revising may change the wording and structure of a piece of writing, so there's no point in fine-tuning words and passages that may disappear in the next draft. Editing an assignment before it has been revised is like icing a cake before it's fully baked.

However, that doesn't mean that you should wait until students have reached the editing stage to start correcting their mechanical errors. Even if your objective is to help your students revise their work, you can still point out spelling and punctuation errors without shaping an entire lesson around them. At the end of this chapter, we'll go into further detail on how and when editing should be done.

Revision Activities

The following activities support students' ability to revise their work.

Enriching Simple Sentences through Sentence Expansion

When your students convert the notes on their outlines into sentences on their drafts, they may produce only brief, simple statements, as Mara did, especially if they're beginning writers. Although short declarative sentences can provide emphasis and make facts clear, a steady succession of them makes for wooden prose.

How can you guide students to expand these sentences into ones that are longer and richer?

Remind them that when they've engaged in sentence expansion exercises, they've used question words such as *who, what, when, where, why,* and *how* to transform kernels into complex, information-packed sentences (see Chapter 3). Now they can use the same kinds of questions to expand the brief sentences in their drafts in order to provide more information to the reader—and, if they need some help, you can provide the appropriate question words as prompts.

For example, let's say one of your students starts to use their outline to draft a paragraph about the book *Frindle*[1] by Andrew Clements. They might produce this simple sentence:

> Nick Allen called a pen a "frindle."

At that point, you can ask: "Do you remember *why* he called it a 'frindle'?"

The student might respond: "Because he wanted to perform a language experiment and annoy his language arts teacher."

"Great!" you can say. "How about expanding the sentence to include that information?"

That prompt enables the student to turn their simple sentence into this:

> Nick Allen called a pen a "frindle" because he wanted to perform a language experiment and annoy his language arts teacher.

Introducing Sentence Variety

Another way your students can liven up a boring draft is to vary their sentences in length and type. Remind students of the four different sentence types they can use (statement, question, exclamation, and command) and the possibility of beginning a sentence with a subordinating conjunction (see Chapter 4).

Perhaps, for example, one of your students writes a sentence about colonial America that's followed by another sentence or two using a similar structure:

> Colonists needed a way to travel and to water their crops. They settled near rivers.

You might say, "How about combining those two sentences? And how about beginning with a subordinating conjunction?" The student might then write the following:

> Since the colonists needed a way to travel and a way to water their crops, they settled near rivers.

If you've been regularly assigning your students activities that give them practice with the various sentence-level strategies—embedded in the content they're studying—these techniques will be fresh in their minds.

Revisiting Topic and Concluding Sentences

If your students have completed an SPO, they've already engaged in the process of creating interesting and informative topic and concluding sentences and writing them on an outline. As we detailed in Chapter 6, there are three basic strategies for creating a topic sentence:

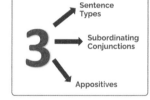

- Choose one of the sentence types.
- Begin the sentence with a subordinating conjunction.
- Add an appositive.

You may consider activities in which you would ask students to improve a boring topic sentence as shown in the examples below.

Level 1 Example

> **DIRECTIONS:** Improve the following topic sentence using the three strategies: a sentence type, a subordinating conjunction, and an appositive.
>
> **In this paragraph, I am going to tell you all about summer.**
>
> 1. *Enjoy summer!*
>
> 2. *Although summer is a fantastic season, heat waves can be dangerous.*
>
> 3. *Summer, a fantastic season, is popular with students because there is no school.*

Level 2 Example

DIRECTIONS: Improve the following topic sentence using the three strategies: a sentence type, a subordinating conjunction, and an appositive.

This paragraph is going to be about Genghis Khan.

1. Genghis Khan was one of the most powerful leaders in history.

2. Although there have been many memorable leaders, Genghis Khan was one of the most powerful.

3. Genghis Khan, a powerful Mongol leader, created a large empire.

Choosing Vivid, Varied, and Precise Words

One way of enlivening a sentence is to use strong and varied nouns and verbs, as well as modifiers and descriptive phrases. At first, you may need to show Level 1 students where to place adjectives and descriptive phrases in sentences, but eventually students will be able to find the correct placement on their own.

If students favor overused, easy-to-spell adjectives such as *fun*, *nice*, or *good*, encourage them to find descriptive words that are more specific. You can brainstorm with students, provide them with a list of suggested alternative words, or explain how to use a thesaurus. Instead of *fun*, for example, a student might substitute *exciting* or *sensational*. Instead of *good*, you might suggest *enjoyable* or *fantastic*. It's often a pleasant surprise to see the better choices students make when they brainstorm for more precise and varied alternatives.

If students have been reading *Because of Winn-Dixie*,[2] you might give them the following activity:

Level 1 Example

DIRECTIONS: Brainstorm a list of adjectives for the bolded word below.

Opal is a **nice** girl.

friendly   respectful

generous   compassionate

helpful   kind

Level 2 Example

DIRECTIONS: Brainstorm a list of more precise words or phrases for each of the following bolded words or phrases.

1. **A long time ago**, people fought for freedom.

   During the Revolutionary War   In the late 18th century

   From 1775 to 1783   During the colonial period

   After the Boston Tea Party   During the American War of Independence

2. A long time ago, **people** fought for freedom.

   the Continental Army   colonists

   the New England colonies   revolutionaries

   the Sons of Liberty   Americans

Two of the basic conjunctions, *but* and *so*, lead to more sophisticated words that students should be encouraged to use in their independent work. Remember that students should use the more sophisticated words in Exhibit 7.1 at the beginning of their sentences rather than in the middle.

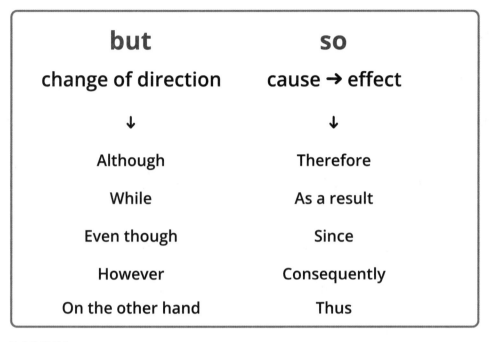

but	so
change of direction	cause → effect
↓	↓
Although	Therefore
While	As a result
Even though	Since
However	Consequently
On the other hand	Thus

Exhibit 7.1

Using Transitions to Create Flow

Your students should be familiar with the transition words and phrases we discussed in Chapter 4. If you guide them to insert appropriate transition words and phrases during the revision process, their writing will become significantly more fluid and coherent. To demonstrate how powerful these brief insertions can be, show your students examples in literature or expository writing and have them identify where transitions are used.

A transition may begin a sentence, creating a link between that sentence and the one that has preceded it, or link thoughts within a sentence. Transitions can also underscore a theme or idea that knits the paragraph's various sentences together.

If your students have trouble deciding what kind of transition to use when revising, you can suggest a specific category from Appendix C for them to look at. With enough practice, they'll be able to find the right kind of transition independently.

RESOURCE

Transition Words
and Phrases
Appendix C

Transitions—when used correctly—are vital to the creation of coherent paragraphs and compositions. As a reminder, the basic types of transitions and their functions are shown in Exhibit 7.2.

Types of Transitions

Time and sequence—provide sequence of events, steps in a process

Conclusion—express a summary, cause-and-effect relationship, point of view, solution

Illustration—give examples, provide details, explain or elaborate on a statement

Change of direction—signal contrasting thoughts

Emphasis—prove a point or statement; reaffirm something previously stated

Exhibit 7.2   Transition Words and Phrases

TECHNICAL TIP

The table of transitions in Appendix C describes the functions of the five types of transitions. It is not an exhaustive list, but the words and phrases we've focused on are the ones students are most likely to encounter in texts and literature. Consider giving students a copy of Appendix C to refer to when they are revising.

Introducing the Unelaborated Paragraph

We often notice that students can apply TWR techniques when a teacher provides them with structure, but then have difficulty when writing independently. This issue usually emerges when students revise their drafts. A student might, for example, improve a sentence by adding an appositive when you specifically suggest that strategy, but he won't come up with the idea on his own.

An effective way to solve this problem and see improvement in students' independent writing is by using the **unelaborated paragraph**. Students may be reluctant to change their own writing after they've already invested some effort in getting it down on paper. They may be far more likely to practice revision strategies on a piece of writing composed by someone else.

WHY PRACTICE REVISING UNELABORATED PARAGRAPHS?

- Helps students learn to use TWR strategies with careful scaffolding and then apply them to their own writing independently
- Enables them to practice revision techniques on text for which they don't feel a sense of ownership
- Deepens their understanding of content
- Reinforces academic knowledge and vocabulary

The idea is to give students a bare-bones paragraph consisting of four to six simple sentences and then guide them through the process of improving it.

Unelaborated paragraphs should have no errors in spelling, capitalization, punctuation, or grammar so that students can focus on revision, not editing.

To enrich and expand the sentences and make the paragraph flow, students will be drawing on the sentence-level strategies they've learned, including their knowledge of transitions, and getting practice in using varied vocabulary. Your directions to students for revising the paragraph should draw only on skills that you have explicitly taught them.

As with all TWR activities, introduce the unelaborated paragraph as a whole-class activity, under your guidance. Ideally, it should be embedded in content students have studied. If that's not possible, choose a subject students know well. If they don't have a command of the subject, students won't be able to provide the details they'll need to improve and expand the paragraph.

Here is a Level 1 example of what it might look like as students revise an unelaborated paragraph.

Level 1 Example

Ms. Gold used the following unelaborated paragraph with her Level 1 students about the class's trip to the aquarium:

> The third grade went to the aquarium. We saw lots of fish. We had lunch. The bus ride was fun. It was a very good field trip!

"This is a pretty boring paragraph, isn't it?" Ms. Gold asked after posting the paragraph in her classroom, and the students agreed. "Let's see if we can make it more interesting. *When* did we go to the aquarium?"

"Last week!" the students called out. Ms. Gold added the words *Last week* to the beginning of the first sentence.

"Okay, great!" Ms. Gold said. "But what about this next sentence? *What* could we add to that?"

"We could say, *we saw many different sea creatures,*" a student offered.

"That's a good idea. What about the next sentence? *When* did we eat lunch? *Where* did we eat lunch?"

As she made her way through the paragraph, Ms. Gold continued the process of asking questions and adding students' responses to the board. Other questions she asked included the following:

"Why was the bus ride fun?"

"Can we think of a better word than *good* in the last sentence?"

After this, she gave the students a worksheet that reflected her discussion with the class about how to revise the unelaborated paragraph.

DIRECTIONS: Revise the paragraph using the directions that follow.

The third grade went to the aquarium. We saw lots of fish. We had lunch. The bus ride was fun. It was a very good field trip.

1. Expand T.S. (when?)

2. Sentence 2: Vary vocabulary, be specific (lots, fish)

3. Sentence 3: Expand (when? where?)

4. Sentence 4: Vary vocabulary (fun)

5. Sentence 4: Expand (why?)

6. C.S.: Vary vocabulary (good)

Last week, the third grade went to the aquarium. We saw fantastic sea creatures such as dolphins. Later, we had lunch outside at the picnic tables. The bus ride back to school was great because we had snacks and talked to our friends. It was a wonderful field trip!

More experienced writers will be able to improve unelaborated paragraphs with less scaffolding. But don't stop giving such students unelaborated paragraphs because you think they're too easy! They continue to be an extremely effective activity even for high school students as a check of comprehension and as an opportunity to practice revision.

Level 2 Example

Here is an example of a Level 2 activity. The class was studying the accomplishments of famous women in American history.

DIRECTIONS: Revise the paragraph using the directions that follow.

Eleanor Roosevelt was important. She was married to Franklin Roosevelt. She was the First Lady from 1933 to 1945. She made many contributions. Many people admired her.

1. Improve T.S. and C.S.
2. Expand sentences
3. Use transitions
4. Combine sentences
5. Vary vocabulary
6. Use an appositive
7. Give examples
8. Use a subordinating conjunction

Eleanor Roosevelt, one of the most admired women of the 20th century, was the wife of President Franklin Delano Roosevelt and First Lady from 1933 to 1945. Although she was born into great wealth and privilege, she was extremely aware of the injustices suffered by those less fortunate. She became a passionate advocate for human rights, and is remembered as an author and activist. After FDR's death, President Harry Truman appointed her as a delegate to the United Nations, where she gained worldwide respect and received many honors and awards for her achievements. Truman called Eleanor Roosevelt the "First Lady of the World."

In composing this informative and smoothly flowing paragraph, students are demonstrating their ability to create sophisticated sentences and a sense of organization. At the same time, they are drawing on and deepening their knowledge of the topic.

Differentiating Unelaborated Paragraph Activities

- Provide all students with the same bare-bones paragraph, but give some students fewer instructions for revision. For example, give some students a list of six things to do and limit others to only one or two.
- Make directions explicit as opposed to general. For example:

    Explicit: Use an appositive in the T.S.
    General: Improve T.S.

    Explicit: Add *where* to the fourth sentence.
    General: Expand sentences.

Moving from Unelaborated Paragraphs to Independent Revision

The main goal of giving students unelaborated paragraphs is to enable them to make similar revisions in their own writing without a teacher's prompting.

The following steps will lead students to that goal:

1. Revise an unelaborated paragraph as a class.

2. Give students an unelaborated paragraph with explicit directions and have them work in pairs, small groups, or independently.

3. Have students revise an unelaborated paragraph, without directions, independently, in pairs, or with a small group.

4. Have students revise their own work after getting teacher feedback that reflects the language used in TWR strategies and activities—for example, "add a transition."

5. Have students revise their own work independently, using the techniques they have practiced.

As your students become accustomed to revising their writing, encourage them to revise their drafts more than once. In fact, point out that in most cases, the better the writer, the more times she will rework a draft.

It's important to note that many lessons can end after revisions and edits. A polished final copy of a paragraph or composition is not necessary to achieve the lesson's objectives.

Generally, introductory revision assignments should be kept brief. It's best for Level 1 writers to limit their revisions to one paragraph of five or six sentences. That's also true for more able writers who are still learning how to make substantive revisions. If students write at greater length, they may find it difficult to revise and edit and become discouraged. **Clarity and accuracy, not length, are the goals.**

When students are writing by hand, stress that they should leave room on their papers for revising and editing their drafts by skipping lines. If students are using a computer, they should double or triple space for the same reason. For drafting and revising written work and printing final copies, computers are invaluable—as long as students learn keyboarding skills and become proficient typists. If they have to hunt and peck at a keyboard, students will be distracted during the complex process of composing.

Giving Students Feedback

Feedback on drafts should be tailored to an individual student's level of proficiency. When your students are writing drafts, they may write sentences that need to be expanded. With Level 1 students, your feedback should be explicit. For example, you might insert *when?* or *why?* at specific points in their writing. With Level 2 students, you will be able to just write *expand* on their work. That should encourage them to consult the question word chart you've posted on the wall, which can help them determine which of the question words are relevant to their sentences.

After being taught how to construct sentences, craft SPOs, and use transitions, students should be able to understand the following notes and abbreviations. This kind of feedback is far more helpful than just saying "make it better" or "add more details" and hoping for the best.

BRIEF BUT TARGETED FEEDBACK

<u>when? why?</u> [expand this point]

<u>ext w/ so</u> → [extend with *so*]

<u>ex.</u> [provide an example]

<u>app. in T.S.</u> [use an appositive in topic sentence]

<u>insert transition</u>

<u>sub. conj. in C.S.</u> [begin concluding sentence with a subordinating conjunction]

<u>combine sent. 2 & 3</u>

A teacher might also point out, more generally, places where a student got off track, using words like:

repetitive

irrelevant

Exhibit 7.3 is an example of feedback included directly on the draft.

Exhibit 7.3

Editing: Last but Not Least

Once students have a final draft, it's time to proofread—that is, check for errors in spelling, capitalization, punctuation, and grammar. Many students, especially those at Level 1, will need help spotting those errors and correcting them.

As we discussed in Chapter 1, researchers have unanimously concluded that teaching grammar rules in isolation doesn't work for most students. But that doesn't mean that we shouldn't teach grammar. What *does* work is to teach grammar—along with writing conventions such as spelling and punctuation—in the context of the activities students are assigned or do in class.

In Chapters 2 and 4, we pointed out that it's best, whenever possible, to teach grammar and conventions in the context of sentence-level work, where the number of errors is likely to be more manageable than in lengthier student writing. But even if you've done that, most students will continue to make at least some mechanical errors when they move on to paragraphs and compositions—although perhaps not as many as they would have otherwise. To give your students the skills that will enable them to avoid distracting readers with technical mistakes, continue to identify and correct these errors in your students' drafts.

Saving Time with Proofreading Symbols

RESOURCE

Proofreading Symbols
Appendix D

If you familiarize your students with standard proofreading symbols, such as a caret (∧) to indicate an insertion, you'll be able to use those symbols to give quick and specific feedback on their writing during both the revision and editing stages. (You'll find a list of proofreading symbols in Appendix D.) If you simply circle a grammatical error such as a lack of subject-verb agreement, there's a good chance the student won't understand what the problem is.

Take the time to make sure students know what mistakes they've made and that they know how to correct them. There's no other way to ensure that they'll learn the rules. Using symbols to communicate precisely what the error is will make the revision and editing process much more efficient.

Busy teachers often have difficulty finding the time to provide detailed feedback on students' writing. But if you've laid the groundwork, you can provide shorthand feedback fairly quickly. And students will not only understand your abbreviations but also know how to follow through on the suggestions you've given them.

RESOURCE

Student Revise and Edit Checklist
Appendix E

When students become more adept at revision, you may want to provide them with the "Student Revise and Edit Checklist" in Appendix E, adapting it as necessary to your students' needs and level of ability. Students can then go through the checklist on their own and ensure that their paragraphs and compositions are the best they can be.

To Sum Up

- Revising, or making structural improvements to a draft, should be done before editing, which consists primarily of correcting mechanical errors.

- To help students revise their drafts, remind them to use sentence expansion, sentence types, subordinating conjunctions, appositives, and sentence-combining to vary their sentence structure.

- Encourage students to use vivid and precise words in the revision process.

- Transition words signal the connections between sentences and ideas and create smoothly flowing prose.

- Before students try to revise their own writing, have them practice on unelaborated paragraphs that you provide.

- Use proofreading symbols and abbreviations for TWR strategies so feedback is explicit and brief.

BOOK DISCUSSION QUESTIONS

1. What is the difference between revising and editing? Which should receive the most instructional time? Why?

2. What are the purposes of transition words and phrases in the revision process?

3. Which sentence strategy do you think is referred to most frequently in revision feedback?

4. Explain why unelaborated paragraphs are an effective way to teach revision.

5. Why should unelaborated paragraphs have no spelling, capitalization, or punctuation errors?

6. How can you make your feedback more meaningful for students?

Notes

1. A. Clements, *Frindle* (New York: Aladdin Paperbacks, 1998).

2. K. DiCamillo, *Because of Winn-Dixie* (Cambridge, MA: Candlewick Press, 2000).

CHAPTER 8

Summarizing

Finding the Main Idea of a Text

Ms. Buxbaum's eleventh-grade social studies class had been studying the American Revolution and its aftermath. She'd given her students an article to read on the Constitutional Convention and asked them to summarize it.

Jamal's summary went on for three pages, recounting details such as the names of the first few colonies to select delegates in the early months of 1787, the oppressive heat in Philadelphia that summer, and the introduction and rejection of the New Jersey Plan.

Felicia's summary, on the other hand, was just two simple sentences:

Delegates from the colonies met in Philadelphia. They drafted the Constitution.

Neither of these summaries was exactly what Ms. Buxbaum had in mind. Jamal clearly knew a lot about the Constitutional Convention, but had trouble distinguishing important events from colorful but essentially irrelevant details. And Felicia's summary had left out some crucial information—like when the Constitutional Convention had taken place.

Ms. Buxbaum realized that students like Jamal and Felicia needed more guidance in exactly what a summary should include. But she wasn't sure how to provide it.

Students often have trouble figuring out how much to say and what to focus on when they're asked to summarize. How much is too much? How much is too little? What's important and what's not? Teachers' guides may require students as young as second grade to summarize a chapter or an entire book. Yet even many high school students find it challenging to come up with a good summary, struggling to find the right level of succinctness or detail.

The Power of Writing Summaries

A **summary** is a brief statement that presents the main points of a text, in a concise form, either in writing or orally.

Teachers sometimes underestimate the importance and the challenges of having their students learn to craft effective summaries. Summarizing is so powerful because it requires you to get to the essence of whatever you're trying to summarize. If you transfer a mental or oral summary to written form, it can be especially powerful because you have to think even more intensively about what you want to say. A written summary is also easier to critique and rework. But writing also imposes a greater cognitive load than thinking or speaking, and inexperienced writers can find it challenging to create a written summary without explicit instruction.

Students at any grade or ability level can learn to summarize, although your approach may vary depending on your students' skill level, the complexity and knowledge demands of the text, and other factors. The skills students have acquired through learning to expand a sentence or create a Single-Paragraph Outline (SPO) will give them a valuable boost in writing summaries.

WHY PRACTICE SUMMARIZING?

- Boosts reading comprehension
- Acts as a comprehension check
- Helps generate concise and accurate responses to questions
- Maintains focus on the main idea and most relevant details
- Teaches paraphrasing techniques
- Provides practice synthesizing information
- Enhances the ability to analyze information
- Develops the ability to make generalizations
- Aids in retaining information and vocabulary

Summarizing information is something we all need to do, often many times a day—and not only inside a classroom. Just to name a few examples, summarizing comes into play when we're asked to do any of the following:

- Relate an experience or process
- Describe someone or something
- Sum up a plot
- Give directions
- Present a critical review

The difficulty of summarizing varies with the content, the complexity of the language and syntax, and the depth of knowledge the reader has about the topic. To see what we mean, try summarizing the following paragraph, which appears on the first page of Immanuel Kant's *Critique of Judgement*:[1]

> *We proceed quite correctly if, as usual, we divide Philosophy, as containing the principles of the rational cognition of things by means of concepts (not merely, as logic does, principles of the form of thought in general without distinction of Objects), into theoretical and practical. But then the concepts, which furnish their Object to the principles of this rational cognition, must be specifically distinct; otherwise, they would not justify a division, which always presupposes a contrast between the principles of the rational cognition belonging to the different parts of a science.*

Not so simple, especially if you don't have a graduate-level degree in philosophy!

ASK THE EXPERTS

Reviews of multiple studies have found that summarizing can be a powerful boost to reading comprehension and learning.[2] When students are taught how to create summaries, the research has found that the practice helps them identify the main idea of a text, make generalizations, and retain information.

One review of the research found that the effects were particularly strong in the elementary grades. It also found that writing summaries worked better than simply having students read a text multiple times, read and study it, or receive instruction in reading skills.[3]

Teachers are often told they should have students summarize material, but they're not necessarily told why or how. Now that we've explained why summarizing is important, we'll tell you how to teach this critical skill.

Three Questions to Ask before You Begin

Before you ask your students to start summarizing, there are three questions you'll need to answer first.

- **Do your students have sufficient knowledge of the topic to summarize it?** It's best to embed summarizing activities into the content you're teaching and to ensure that you have spent enough time on that content to enable students to write about it intelligently.

- **What is the purpose of the summary?** Is it a comprehension check you'll collect or a study aid for your students?

- **What is the format?** Will the summary be a single sentence, an outline, or a paragraph?

Two Structures for Summaries

The following two formats, the summary sentence and the SPO, will help your students structure their thoughts about the information they have read, heard, or collected. Which one you use will depend on the text to be summarized, the purpose of the summary, and the ability level of your students. Both formats will require your students to go back into the text, read closely, and find the main idea and most important points.

As always, it's a good idea to complete these activities as a class before asking students to try them on their own.

The Summary Sentence

The first format, the **summary sentence** template, looks a lot like the one your students have used for sentence expansion. The question words are the same, and summarizing draws on many of the same skills as sentence expansion, but there is no kernel sentence provided as a starting point. Instead, students will be summarizing a specific text—a story, a paragraph, a book chapter, or an article.

DIRECTIONS: Complete the summary sentence. It is not necessary to use all the question words. Respond only to the ones that are relevant.

Who/What? *Maya*

(did/will do) What? *built urban centers*

When? *pre-Columbian era*

Where? *throughout their empire*

Why? *N/A*

How? *expertly*

SUMMARY SENTENCE: *During the pre-Columbian era, the Maya expertly built urban centers throughout their empire.*

When you give your students a text to summarize, clarify what you want them to focus on when they create their summaries if the content lends itself to several possibilities. When students are expanding a brief kernel sentence, the focus is clear. But a paragraph, article, or chapter may cover a range of possible subjects. If you want students to focus on one aspect of the text, be sure to make that subject explicit.

For example, let's say you've asked students to summarize an article about tornadoes occurring in a particular state, and you expect them to focus on the damage the tornadoes caused. Some students might choose to focus instead on the timeline of the events or the areas and people that were impacted. Unless you designate the subject, you may not get back the kind of summary you anticipate.

In addition, make sure students know that they won't need to answer all the question words that are listed. When students are still learning to create summary sentences, it's important to guide them through thinking about which question words will be relevant for a specific text and tell them that if a certain word isn't appropriate, they should put "N/A" (not applicable) on the dotted line next to it.

Many newspapers and magazines summarize their articles in a single sentence at the beginning as a way of letting readers know what will follow. Often, book and movie reviews and television shows are summarized in a single sentence. Consider showing your students how frequently this type of brief summary appears.

The end product of the summary sentence activity is an informative, coherent sentence that could often work as the topic sentence of a paragraph. Standing alone, it serves as a way of identifying the main idea of a text.

TEACHER TIPS

- Have students create a summary sentence at the beginning of a class as a do-now activity, based on homework or material that was previously covered.

- Review material that the class has covered. For example, if students have been reading *Macbeth*, try having them summarize one of his soliloquies.

- Students should write their answers to the question words in the form of notes on the dotted lines.

- Begin summary sentences with the answer to the *when* question, if that's appropriate for the text being summarized.

- Single-sentence summaries can be practiced orally, as a whole-class activity, to help students stay concise and on topic.

- Be sure to post the question words prominently.

⚠ BE CAREFUL

Simpler texts, particularly those that have been "modified" or "adapted," are harder to summarize because they include less information and therefore are effectively already summarized. Make sure the text you're giving students to summarize has enough detail and complex language to enable them to distill it.

At the same time, the text shouldn't be so complex that students can't understand it. Text selection can be tricky, so teachers should be the ones to do it rather than the students, at least initially.

Summarizing with the SPO

Students can use the SPO to plan a paragraph that provides a summary. Many of the same skills they learned in connection with the SPO are also involved in developing summaries:

- Distinguishing between essential and nonessential information
- Reducing text to notes or paraphrases
- Organizing the points they want to make
- Synthesizing information and making generalizations
- Rephrasing a topic sentence as a concluding one

When students use the SPO for a summarizing activity, they will be referring to a specific source and mining it for the information they'll need to complete the outline. Students will need to do the following:

- Identify details that support the topic.
- Generate a topic sentence.
- Select and sequence supporting details.
- Write the details as notes on the dotted lines.
- Generate a complete concluding sentence.

When introducing summarizing, a sixth-grade teacher asked his students to read an article about the importance of wearing the right sunglasses.[4] Next, the whole class developed the following SPO. The paragraph following the SPO was written independently.

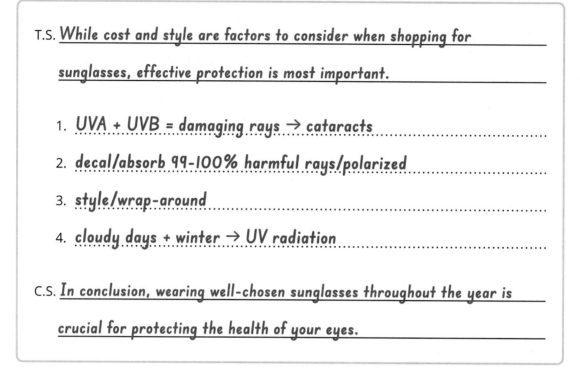

T.S. <u>While cost and style are factors to consider when shopping for</u>

<u>sunglasses, effective protection is most important.</u>

1. UVA + UVB = damaging rays → cataracts

2. decal/absorb 99-100% harmful rays/polarized

3. style/wrap-around

4. cloudy days + winter → UV radiation

C.S. <u>In conclusion, wearing well-chosen sunglasses throughout the year is</u>

<u>crucial for protecting the health of your eyes.</u>

While cost and style are factors to consider when shopping for sunglasses, effective protection is most important. Consumers need to know about the dangers of UVA and UVB rays because they can cause great damage, including cataracts. Look for a decal stating that the glasses are polarized and can absorb 99-100% of harmful rays. Wrap-around styles are best for protecting your eyes on all sides. Many people don't know that UV radiation exists on cloudy days and during the winter. As a result, their eyes can be at risk. To conclude, be diligent when shopping for the safest sunglasses.

To Sum Up

- Summarizing builds on skills students have developed in sentence expansion activities and in creating SPOs.

- Before asking students to summarize, make sure they have sufficient knowledge of the topic to understand the text you're asking them to summarize, and that they can identify the intended purpose and format of the summary.

- Make sure students have had ample practice with sentence expansion before tackling summary sentences, which are significantly more challenging.

- When asking students to complete the templates for the summary sentence, first make sure they understand what to fill in for the "who/what" and "did/will do (what)" lines in order to clearly identify the topic.

- Students who have been introduced to the SPO can use it to summarize specific text.

- Have students practice summarizing both orally and in writing.

BOOK DISCUSSION QUESTIONS

1. How does summarizing enhance comprehension?

2. Describe the three conditions that need to be met before students begin to create a summary.

3. How does the Single-Paragraph Outline (SPO) serve as a guide for writing a summary?

Notes

1. I. Kant, *Kant's Critique of Judgement*, translated with Introduction and Notes by J.H. Bernard, 2nd ed. rev. (London: Macmillan, 1914), http://oll.libertyfund.org/titles/kant-the-critique-of-judgement.

2. National Reading Panel, "Teaching Children to Read: An Evidence-Based Assessment of the Scientific Research Literature on Reading and Its Implications for Reading Instruction," Reports of the Subgroups (2000), https://www.nichd.nih.gov/sites/default/files/publications/pubs/nrp/Documents/report.pdf.

   E.A. Stevens, S. Park, and S. Vaughn, "A Review of Summarizing and Main Idea Interventions for Struggling Readers in Grades 3 through 12: 1978–2016," *Remedial and Special Education* (2018), 40(3), https://doi.org/10.1177/0741932517749940.

3. S. Graham and M. Hebert, *Writing to Read: Evidence for How Writing Can Improve Reading. A Carnegie Corporation Time to Act Report* (Washington, DC: Alliance for Excellent Education, 2010).

4. Ian K. Smith, M.D. "Watching Out for a Shady Deal," *Time* (2 July 2 2001), https://content.time.com/time/subscriber/article/0,33009,1000243,00.html.

CHAPTER 9

Moving On to Compositions

The Transition Outline and the Multiple-Paragraph Outline

As spring rolled around, Ms. Hamilton knew her fifth graders would soon be expected to produce extended written responses to prompts on their end-of-year state reading tests. They would be asked to read a passage on a topic they might or might not be familiar with and to write at length in response to a prompt about that passage.

In an effort to prepare them for the test, Ms. Hamilton had them read an article about the threat of extinction for the honeybee and write about the causes and effects of extinction. The results weren't encouraging.

Ava wrote one long paragraph that basically repeated the same nugget of information—more or less verbatim from the text—over and over. Michael's response included a lot of information about the extinction of dinosaurs but had little to do with honeybees. Brandon related a number of details from the article but listed them in no particular order. And Trina—along with a number of other students—just put her head down on her desk, apparently too overwhelmed by the assignment to even try to come up with a response.

Ms. Hamilton wasn't sure what to do. Was the test expecting too much of fifth graders—or at least of the fifth graders in her classroom? Or was there something missing from her teaching? Whatever the problem, in a few short weeks her kids would be expected to produce extended, coherent written responses to a prompt on a test. And she was pretty sure most weren't going to be able to do it.

If writing is hard, then writing at length only makes it harder. One reason it's important to start writing instruction at the sentence level is that it lessens the heavy load that writing imposes on working memory, freeing up cognitive capacity. But even if students have learned how to construct good sentences, writing at length can still result in an overwhelming cognitive load. Writers may need to juggle many complex items in working memory—for example, keeping track of what they've already said or what they're planning to say next. That's why linear outlines are so important: they can "offload" some of that cognitive burden.

As students reach higher grade levels, they're expected not only to write at length but also to write well about topics beyond their personal experience, which requires them to juggle that content in working memory along with the demands of writing. A heavy emphasis on personal narratives in the elementary grades often leaves students unprepared to meet those kinds of writing expectations in middle and high school.

In response to that problem, many states have adopted standards requiring that students write at length and in a variety of genres beginning in the elementary grades—informational and opinion essays as well as narratives. No longer is it enough for a fourth grader to write a paragraph about his summer vacation or a trip to the zoo. The standards may require him to be able to write, for example, compositions that "introduce a topic or text clearly, state an opinion, and create an organizational structure in which related ideas are grouped to support the writer's purpose."[1]

While it's important to prepare younger students for the writing demands they'll encounter at higher grade levels, the standards tell us only where students need to end up without explaining how to get them there. Writing standards and assignments based on them are rarely grounded in realistic expectations of children's development, nor do they account for the heavy cognitive load that writing imposes on inexperienced writers of any age.

When asked to write at length in an expository mode, students at all grade levels often struggle with sentence structure, organization, clarity, and coherence. Simply handing out longer and more challenging writing assignments doesn't magically give students the skills they need to create well-crafted compositions.

A **composition** (essay) is a series of paragraphs united by a common theme. The characteristics of effective compositions mirror those of effective paragraphs:

- **Structure.** The paragraphs are sequenced in a way that ensures clarity for the reader.

- **Coherence.** The paragraphs are logically connected with appropriate transition words.

- **Unity.** Every paragraph supports the main idea or thesis of the composition.

- **Well-constructed sentences.** The sentences within each paragraph are grammatically correct and clear, and their types and structures should vary (some simple, others compound or complex).

Over the course of many years, my colleagues and I have analyzed countless compositions, research papers, and essays. After looking at both long-term assignments and timed responses to essay questions on tests, we realized that we needed a structured, sequenced method for guiding students to compose longer pieces of writing. A crucial component of that method is to explicitly teach students how to create a linear outline, building on what they've learned about outlining a paragraph.

The Benefits of Outlining

WHY PRACTICE OUTLINING FOR A COMPOSITION?

- Reveals gaps in knowledge or comprehension to both teachers and students
- Develops organizational skills
- Helps in categorizing information
- Provides students with a logical sequence for expository, narrative, and argumentative text structures
- Avoids repetition and irrelevant information
- Promotes well-structured introductions and conclusions
- Develops efficient note-taking skills
- Strengthens the ability to create transitions between ideas and paragraphs
- Reinforces academic knowledge and vocabulary

Creating an outline will help your students cement knowledge they've already acquired and gather new information that builds on it. Once students are familiar with outlines and the associated skills, they'll be able to reproduce outlines on scratch paper during tests and use them to write clearer and more coherent responses.

It's important to remember that, as with the SPO, creating the outline is a powerful activity in itself, regardless of whether a student turns it into a draft or a finished product. And, as always, it's important to continue sentence-level activities while students are learning to create outlines for compositions.

The Transition Outline and Multiple-Paragraph Outline

The Transition Outline (TO), shown in Exhibit 9.1, is designed for students who are ready to write more than one paragraph but not yet ready for the task of writing complete introductions and conclusions.

RESOURCE

Transition Outline (TO), *Appendix L*

A composition based on the TO begins with a single sentence, the **thesis statement**, and ends with a single sentence, the **concluding statement**. Typically, such one-sentence paragraphs are found only in fiction or journalistic writing. Nevertheless, we believe it's important to give students an easier option to introduce and conclude a subject before teaching them how to write more fully developed introductions and conclusions, which we'll describe later in this chapter.

RESOURCE

Multiple-Paragraph Outline (MPO) *Appendix Q*

Some students may be ready to move directly to the more challenging Multiple-Paragraph Outline (MPO), shown in Exhibit 9.2, without first creating TOs.

Transition Outline (TO)

NAME: _____   DATE: _____

TOPIC: _____

THESIS STATEMENT: _____

_____

Main Idea	Details
¶ 1	....
¶ 2	....

CONCLUDING STATEMENT: _____

_____

Exhibit 9.1

Multiple-Paragraph Outline (MPO)

NAME: _____   DATE: _____

TOPIC: _____

THESIS STATEMENT: _____

_____

Main Idea	Details
Introduction ¶ 1	....
¶ 1	....
¶ 3	....
¶ 4	....
Conclusion ¶ 5	....

CONCLUDING STATEMENT: _____

_____

Exhibit 9.2

Students who are familiar with the SPO but not ready for the format of the TO or the MPO can use a Pre-Transition Outline (PTO). The format of the PTO can be found later in this chapter, under "Adapting the TO and MPO: Pre-Transition Outline (PTO)," and in Appendix J.

RESOURCE

Pre-Transition
Outline (PTO)
Appendix J

You will need to use your judgment about what your students are equipped to handle. In classes where there is a significant range of ability, you may decide to provide some students with the TO and others with the MPO, even if all are writing about the same content.

Prepping for the TO and MPO

If you've given your students ample practice creating Single-Paragraph Outlines (SPOs), they will have already acquired some of the prerequisite skills needed for developing a TO on their own. Specifically, they will have learned how to:

- Write supporting details in note form, using key words and phrases, abbreviations, and symbols
- Organize and categorize details

They'll also need to acquire two new skills:

- Generating a thesis statement that summarizes the theme or main idea of an entire essay
- Generating a concluding statement that rephrases the thesis statement

To construct these statements, students will draw on and extend the generalizing abilities they've acquired in summarizing and in composing topic and concluding sentences for the SPO.

Similarly, when it's time to draft and revise a composition using the TO, students who have had experience writing paragraphs will already have acquired some of the skills they need:

- Creating topic sentences
- Using a variety of sentence structures
- Connecting sentences with transition words and phrases

But they will also need to acquire some new skills through repeated practice, including:

- Expanding their use of transition words and phrases to connect paragraphs as well as sentences
- Learning how to smoothly incorporate quotations from text into their writing

Level 2 students who are ready to move on to drafting and revising compositions using the MPO will also need to acquire another, more challenging skill:

- Writing introductory and concluding paragraphs that include not only a thesis statement but also at least two more sentences that provide a larger context for it

When you're introducing students to the TO or the MPO, it's best to base writing assignments on what students have studied previously or are currently learning, as long as they've had time to acquire a good deal of information about the topic. Advanced Level 2 writers can be assigned topics that require research.

We'll begin by explaining how to guide students through the less complex TO process and then discuss how to teach the skills required for the MPO to those Level 2 students who are ready to tackle it. Argumentative compositions, which are particularly challenging, will be discussed in detail in the next chapter.

Introducing Students to the TO

Even after students are comfortable creating an SPO and using it to draft a paragraph, they may still need more support before they're ready for the tasks required to write sophisticated essays. It's not necessary to have them start with three paragraphs and then progress to four or five. The length of a composition should be determined by its topic and content.

Be sure to spend a lot of time developing a TO with the whole class following the sequence illustrated in Exhibit 9.3. As with the SPO, outlines don't necessarily have to be converted into drafts.

Transition Outline (TO)

NAME: _____   DATE: _____

1 TOPIC: _____

2 THESIS STATEMENT: _____

_____

Main Idea	Details
¶ 1 **3**	....**4**....................... ....
¶ 2 **3**	....**4**....................... ....
¶ 3 **3**	....**4**....................... ....

5 CONCLUDING STATEMENT: _____

_____

Exhibit 9.3

THE STEPS FOR DEVELOPING A TO

1. Select a topic and identify the purpose of the composition.

2. Write the thesis statement.

3. Write the main idea of each paragraph as a phrase or category in the Main Idea boxes on the left-hand side of the TO, with the abbreviation T.S. as a reminder to write a topic sentence.

4. Write the details supporting the main idea in the right-hand column for each body paragraph. Use keywords, phrases, abbreviations, and symbols on the dotted lines.

5. Write the concluding statement.

Each step in this sequence is discussed in the following sections.

1. Selecting a Topic and Identifying the Purpose

Students must know a topic well before they'll be able to create a TO about it. Book reports, current events related to scientific or geographic issues, and biographies are all good topics.

The teacher, not the student, should select the topic for the TO, and—at least at first—all students should be writing on the same topic. Students will need practice before they can identify a topic on their own that's appropriate for a composition—one that's neither too narrow nor too broad. The Civil War, for example, is too broad, and a discussion of a specific minor battle might be too narrow. A review of the military career of Ulysses S. Grant or an analysis of the Battle of Gettysburg would work better.

Although students at higher grade levels will be writing about more complex topics, they should not be expected to engage in independent research while learning how to construct a TO. That would impose too great a burden on working memory.

After the topic has been chosen, guide students in identifying the purpose and the type of the composition. Will it be an expository, narrative, descriptive, or opinion essay? More advanced writers can combine these structures, but less experienced writers should stick to a single one. For background on these different types of essays, see the discussion in Chapter 5.

2. Developing a Thesis Statement

A **thesis statement** is **a statement that conveys the main theme of the entire composition**—just as a topic sentence conveys the main idea of a single paragraph. A thesis statement should be written as a complete sentence at the top of the TO. **The thesis statement and concluding statement are the only complete sentences on the TO.**

Constructing a thesis statement requires that students understand the main points they will be making in a composition and the text structure they will adopt. At the same time, they'll need to be able to state their thesis in a single sentence—and one that is not too detailed.

Tyrell wrote a thesis statement that may remind you of sentences composed by your own students:

> *In this essay, I am going to tell you about the many effects of the Civil War.*

Tyrell reveals his topic, but it is not obvious exactly what he is going to tell us.

Students may benefit from a thesis statement that explicitly outlines a **plan of development**. This means that the thesis statement presents the main points of the composition in the order in which they will be addressed in the composition. The plan of development provides a clear road map for the rest of the outline.

With guidance, Tyrell rewrote his statement to include a plan of development:

> *The economic, social, and political effects of the Civil War lasted for generations.*

Exhibit 9.4 is a TO showing Tyrell's thesis statement with a plan of development: *economic, social, political*. Tyrell's thesis statement signals to the reader that the next paragraph of the essay will focus on the economic effects of the Civil War. Then there will be a paragraph on the social effects, and finally a paragraph on the political effects.

Transition Outline (TO)

NAME: _Tyrell_   DATE: _____

TOPIC: _Effects of the Civil War_

THESIS STATEMENT: _The economic, social, and political effects of the_
Civil War lasted for generations.

Main Idea	Details
¶ 1 economic ↓ TS	....
¶ 2 social ↓ TS	....
¶ 3 political ↓ TS	....

CONCLUDING STATEMENT: _____

_____

Exhibit 9.4

When your students are first learning to create thesis statements, tell them they can draw on the three strategies for creating topic sentences that they've already learned:

Statement:
The economic, social, and political effects of the Civil War lasted for generations.

Subordinating conjunction:
Although the Civil War lasted only four years, its impacts on the economic, social, and political structures of the United States were enormous.

Appositive:
The Civil War, a turning point in the country's history, had major economic, social, and political effects.

Students may choose not to include a plan of development, in which case they can experiment with different structures. For example, a thesis statement could simply say:

Theodore Roosevelt's presidency marked the beginning of the United States as a world power.

The essay could then address the specifics—the Panama Canal, the Roosevelt Corollary—contained in that general idea.

You may find it helpful to provide students with examples of different approaches they can use when developing their thesis statements:

A personal judgment:
It is urgent that problems associated with rising sea levels as a result of climate change be addressed worldwide.

Advice or directions:
There are several strategies to combat the effect of rising sea levels.

A statement of consequences (cause and effect):
If climate change is not addressed globally, coastal cities will be in danger.

An interpretation (usually of fiction or poetry):
John Knowles's widely read coming-of-age novel, A Separate Peace, presents themes of friendship, envy, and the effect of social class on relationships.

Compare and contrast:
There are significant differences between the candidates regarding their positions on education.

Even without a plan of development, students will be able to refer back to their thesis statement to stay on track. Every paragraph in the composition should relate to the theme contained in the thesis statement.

3. Developing the Main Idea Boxes

The column on the left side of the TO is headed "Main Idea." The Main Idea boxes are for words or phrases indicating the topic of each paragraph.

Unlike the SPO, the TO does not require students to write out the topic sentences for their paragraphs. However, it can be helpful to have them write the abbreviation T.S. in each Main Idea box to remind them to include topic sentences for each paragraph when they compose their drafts.

Listing the main ideas in the left-hand boxes helps students avoid repetition and ensures that each paragraph relates to the composition's overall theme.

Different types of compositions call for different kinds of main ideas for the body paragraphs, as you can see from the following examples. The order and number of the paragraphs also will depend on the type of assignment.

BIOGRAPHICAL

Thesis statement

- Early life
- Major accomplishment(s)
- Legacy

Concluding statement

BOOK REVIEW

Thesis statement

- Book summary
- Opinion

Concluding statement

CAUSE/EFFECT

Thesis statement

- Causes
- Effects

Concluding statement

PROBLEM/SOLUTION

Thesis statement

- Problem
- Solution

Concluding statement

COMPARE AND CONTRAST

Thesis statement

- Similarities
- Differences

Concluding statement

MAJOR EVENT

Thesis statement

- Background
- Event
- Impact

Concluding statement

4. Developing the Details

The Details boxes are on the right side of the outline. These boxes have dotted lines where students write notes using key words and phrases, abbreviations, and symbols that will form the basis of their body paragraphs. Students should have sufficient background knowledge to provide at least three details for each paragraph.

Make sure students understand that they should write the details for each paragraph in note form rather than in full sentences. Although students need to settle on the order of the paragraphs when creating the TO, the order of the details may not matter at this point. Students can revise their outlines or change the order of the details when it's time to write their drafts.

5. Writing the Concluding Statement

The function of a concluding statement is to restate and reinforce the thesis statement of the composition. A concluding statement usually does one of the following:

- Summarize
- Offer a solution or recommendation
- Pose a question
- Justify a position
- Present a point of view

Here are some examples of possible concluding statements, along with thesis statements for the same essays:

EXAMPLE 1:

Thesis statement:

The economic, social, and political effects of the Civil War lasted for generations.

Concluding statement (summary):

In summary, the impact of the Civil War was felt for many years after the fighting ended.

EXAMPLE 2:

Thesis statement:

If climate change is not addressed worldwide, coastal cities will be in danger.

Concluding statement (solution or recommendation):

To conclude, nations must work together to prevent rising sea levels from causing widespread destruction.

EXAMPLE 3:

Thesis statement:

Theodore Roosevelt's presidency saw the development of the national parks.

Concluding statement:

One of Theodore Roosevelt's most important legacies was his approach to conservation.

Students do not need to write concluding sentences for each paragraph in a multiple-paragraph composition.

Using a Transition Outline to Write an Essay

Converting a TO into a draft should be an efficient process. Students will know what their topic is, the basics of what they want to say, and the order in which they want to say it. In the drafting and revising process, they can devote their mental energy to crafting clear, interesting, and varied sentences—including topic sentences for their body paragraphs—and using transitions to create a coherent and effective composition.

When students revise their drafts, the benefits of continuing to work on sentence-level activities alongside lengthier writing become clear. Those activities will continue to help students remember to apply strategies like varying their sentence structure and including information their intended audience might need. Students may also need to cite evidence from texts and incorporate quotations.

Using Transitions to Link Paragraphs

Transitions enhance coherence and flow in longer pieces of writing. When your students are converting TOs into drafts of compositions and revising them, remind them to use transitions to link one paragraph to the next. Virtually any of the transitions they've learned to connect sentences can also be used to connect paragraphs. See Appendix C, "Transition Words and Phrases."

RESOURCE

Transition Words and Phrases
Appendix C

For example, if a student is writing a compare-and-contrast composition about red and white blood cells and she has written one paragraph about red blood cells and the next about white blood cells, she can use a change-of-direction transition to create a link between the two paragraphs:

> *Red blood cells carry respiratory gases throughout the body. These cells lack a nucleus, which means that there is room inside each cell for more of a pigment called hemoglobin. Hemoglobin gives red blood cells their color and is responsible for carrying oxygen around the body. Red blood cells also transport carbon dioxide.*

> ***On the other hand**, white blood cells fight infection. These cells circulate throughout the bloodstream and tissues to attack unknown organisms that may cause an illness or injury. Unlike red blood cells, white blood cells have a nucleus.*

Incorporating Quotations

When students begin to write longer compositions, they are often encouraged not just to cite evidence from texts but also to quote from them directly. When students are creating outlines, they should be taught how to include the page number(s) and source(s) of the quotation(s) they plan to use. If they are using more than one source, they will need to include the author as well.

Too frequently, students will use a quotation without providing any context, introduction, or attribution. In addition, it's often not clear why students have chosen a particular quotation. They may assume its meaning and relevance are obvious, or they may not have fully understood the words themselves. At times it seems that students are inserting a quotation simply to prove they've read the text rather than to support the point they're making.

If you want your students to use quotations effectively, you have to show them how to be judicious about selecting the text they want to quote and how to incorporate that text smoothly into their own writing. They'll need to answer these questions:

What does the quotation mean?

Whose words are they?

How does the quotation support the point I'm making?

Understanding the Quotation

To ensure that students actually understand the words they're quoting, ask them to paraphrase the quotation for you. For example:

Quotation: *"Human suffering anywhere concerns men and women everywhere."*

Paraphrased quotation: *No matter where suffering happens and who is affected, it has an impact everywhere and on everyone.*

Once they've done that, students should make sure they know the source of the quotation and whether that source or speaker is reliable. Then they can ask themselves if the quotation belongs in the spot where they're intending to use it. If it does, they can include the source of the quotation and page number on an appropriate detail line of their TO.

Determining What's Noteworthy

It's helpful to explain to students that a longer quote isn't always a better quote. A succinct phrase may have more impact than a discussion that goes on for several lines.

Nor is it always necessary for students to include a direct quotation. Paraphrasing text often works just as well. However, even if a quotation is paraphrased, students should include an attribution to the text on which it's based.

Quotations should be reserved for instances when the author of the text has said something particularly noteworthy. Consider guiding your students in identifying those distinctive quotations before they attempt to select them independently.

Weaving In Quotations

Once they've settled on a quotation that is on point and worthy of inclusion, students will need to learn how to weave it into their own writing.

The book *They Say/I Say*[2] suggests introducing quotations using phrases like these:

Jones states, "_____."

As the author of the article argues, "_____."

According to Jones, "_____."

The authors also suggest following up the quotation with an explanation that paraphrases it. For example,

In other words, Jones is saying _____.

Therefore, according to the author, _____.

Jones's point is that _____.

Level 1 Example

According to Helen Keller, "The best and most beautiful things in the world cannot be seen or even touched. They must be felt with the heart." Her point was that even though she was blind and deaf, she was still able to experience the most meaningful parts of life.

Level 2 Example

More advanced students may be quoting from primary sources or historical documents, and this is when setting up and paraphrasing quotations is particularly important. It won't always be clear to a reader where the quotation is from and—especially if the language is complex or archaic—what it means.

The Declaration of Independence states, "But when a long train of abuses and usurpations, pursuing invariably the same Object evinces a design to reduce them under absolute Despotism, it is their right, it is their duty, to throw off such Government, and to provide new Guards for their future security." In other words, revolution is justified only when the government has carried out a sustained and deliberate campaign against the rights of the people.

TEACHER TIP

Emphasize to your students the importance of citations and attribution when they use quotations in their writing. Quotations should be set off by quotation marks or, if lengthy, be indented as a block quote. Older students can be introduced to the various ways to cite sources, such as footnotes, endnotes, and in-text. It's best to demonstrate just one form of documentation, preferably the MLA,[3] APA,[4] or Chicago/Turabian[5] formats.

The example in Exhibit 9.5 assumes students have learned about Susan B. Anthony and Elizabeth Cady Stanton.

Transition Outline (TO)

NAME: _Tyrell_   DATE: _____

TOPIC: _Women's Rights Activists_

THESIS STATEMENT: _Susan B. Anthony and Elizabeth Cady Stanton were_
the driving force behind the women's rights movement.

Main Idea	Details
Anthony ¶ 1 ↓ TS	on the ground organizer + strategist attended rallies across country focus = right to vote/Quote: pg. 1, S.B.A. Address created NAWSA = powerful org. → women's rts advocate
Stanton ¶ 2 ↓ TS	philosopher, thinker + commentator 1848/Seneca Falls wrote speeches, books + pamphlets pushed for lib. divorce laws + co-ed

CONCLUDING STATEMENT: _In closing, both Susan B. Anthony and_
Elizabeth Cady Stanton left important legacies for women's rights.

Exhibit 9.5

The MPO for Level 2 Students

If your Level 2 students have already had practice with the TO, most of the steps involved in creating the MPO will be familiar.

If they haven't had that practice, guide them through these activities, all of which are described in detail in the previous section:

OUTLINING
- Select a topic and identify the purpose.
- Develop a thesis statement.
- Fill in the Main Idea boxes.
- Fill in the Details boxes.
- Write a concluding statement.

DRAFTING AND REVISING
- Use transitions to link paragraphs.
- Incorporate quotations.

A significant difference between the TO and the MPO is that instead of writing a thesis statement as a stand-alone sentence, students will now create a multi-sentence introductory paragraph composed of a thesis statement as well as general and specific statements. The same is true for a concluding paragraph. This process often requires a good deal of guidance and practice.

Constructing an MPO involves six steps. The sequence of the steps corresponds to the numbers that appear on the sample MPO template in Exhibit 9.6. MPOs can have three, four, five, or more paragraphs. As we noted earlier, students don't have to start with three-paragraph MPOs and then progress to longer ones. The number of paragraphs assigned should depend on the topic and the content.

As with the SPO and TO, you should spend a lot of time developing MPOs with the whole class before expecting students to develop an MPO independently.

Multiple-Paragraph Outline (MPO)

NAME: _____   DATE: _____

1 TOPIC: _____

2 THESIS STATEMENT: _____

_____

Main Idea	Details
Introduction ¶ 1	5
¶ 2 3	4
¶ 3 3	4
Conclusion ¶ 4	6

Exhibit 9.6

THE STEPS FOR DEVELOPING AN MPO

1. Select a topic and identify the composition's purpose.

2. Develop the thesis statement as a complete sentence on the solid line at the top of the outline. Tell students that this is the only time they'll write a complete sentence on the MPO.

3. Write the main idea of each paragraph as a phrase or category in the Main Idea boxes on the left-hand side of the MPO and include T.S. as a reminder to create a topic sentence later when drafting.

4. Write the supporting details for each main idea in the Details boxes in the right-hand column of the MPO.

5. Indicate the structure of the introductory paragraph by writing the letters *G* (for *general* statement), *S* (for *specific* statement), and *T* (for *thesis* statement). The statements themselves should be created only after the outline is done.

6. For the concluding paragraph, invert the order of the introduction to *T*, *S*, and *G*.

Steps 1–4 have been described previously, but steps 5 and 6 are new and specific to the MPO. The next section will define GST and TSG and describe the process of using them as a guide to develop introductions and conclusions.

Using the MPO to Draft and Revise Compositions

Converting an MPO to a draft is more challenging than undertaking that process with a TO because students will need to create general and specific statements during the drafting process. They will need ample practice with the preparatory activities described in this section.

Don't forget that students should use transition words and phrases to connect their paragraphs and smoothly incorporate quotations, as discussed previously in this chapter.

Introductions: The GST Structure

Introductions set forth the topic of the composition and should engage the reader's interest. Writing introductory and concluding paragraphs requires the ability to summarize information and make generalizations at an even more sophisticated level than that required for writing only the thesis statement.

Both introductory and concluding paragraphs should consist of at least three sentences. In addition to the thesis statement, students will also need to learn how to construct general and specific statements that support their thesis. This process, which is described in *The St. Martin's Handbook,*[6] will result in coherent paragraphs that provide context for the thesis statement.

Some teachers may believe that the GST format makes students' introductions too formulaic. But the fact is that most developing writers actually need and appreciate a formula to help them structure coherent introductions and conclusions. We have seen this technique applied in sophisticated essays written by experienced writers.

According to the handbook, introductory paragraphs should unfold in this order:

1. First sentence: general statement (*G*)
   There are books that were written decades ago that are relevant today because of their timely themes.

2. Second sentence: specific statement (*S*)
   The Great Gatsby has fascinated readers over the years because of its focus on extreme wealth, unbridled materialism, and the decay of social and moral values.

3. Third sentence: thesis statement (*T*)
   Although the book was published in 1925, the characters, the setting, and the conflicts resonate with present-day readers.

Using the GST format can be challenging. Even students who have had experience crafting thesis statements may need support in coming up with general and specific statements. One way to provide that support is to model or guide them through the process.

GST: Classroom Example

Using the topic of Nelson Mandela, whom the class had been studying, Ms. Jackson began by asking her tenth graders to come up with a **thesis statement** about him. After some discussion, the class agreed on the following:

> _Nelson Mandela is remembered for his role in the abolition of apartheid and his election as South Africa's first Black president._

After completing the Main Idea and Details boxes for the composition with the whole class, Ms. Jackson asked the students what general category of individuals they thought Mandela belonged to. One student said, "freedom fighters"; another said, "civil rights activists"; and a third suggested "people who had a big effect on history." Ms. Jackson chose the third phrasing, and collectively the class wrote:

> _During the 20th century, certain individuals had a significant impact on history._

Ms. Jackson told the class that could be their **general statement**. Now, she said, it was time to narrow the focus to come up with a more **specific statement**, perhaps by placing Mandela in a particular place. The students came up with "South Africa." Ms. Jackson asked them to try writing a specific statement using an appositive. After comparing their different formulations, the class agreed on this one:

> _Nelson Mandela, a leader in the struggle for equal rights for all citizens, brought great change to South Africa._

The class then put all three sentences together to form an introductory paragraph using the GST format:

> _During the 20th century, certain individuals had a significant impact on history. Nelson Mandela, a leader in the struggle for equal rights for all citizens, brought great change to South Africa. Mandela is remembered for his role in the abolition of apartheid and his election as South Africa's first Black president._

Here are two additional examples of introductory paragraphs that follow the GST format. The words in bold indicate elements of the plans of development that are embedded in the thesis statements.

BOOK REPORT

[G] Only a few of the countless books published each year become classics. [S] William Golding's novel about a group of British schoolboys stranded on an island after a plane crash has been required reading in many schools for decades. [T] _Lord of the Flies_ has intrigued readers because of its **plot, characters,** and **the lessons** that can be learned from this compelling tale.

SIGNIFICANT EVENT

[G] All of the great presidents have a signature achievement that profoundly affected future generations. [S] The acquisition of the Louisiana Territory from France is considered by many to be Thomas Jefferson's outstanding accomplishment. [T] As a result of the Louisiana Purchase, he significantly **increased the size of the United States, extended its borders,** and **opened up new trade routes.**

Writing General, Specific, and Thesis Statements

The amount of time you spend teaching your students how to develop general, specific, and thesis statements will vary depending on their abilities and the complexity of the content they're studying.

The following kinds of activities should be modeled and practiced frequently with the entire class before you have students try them independently. The following activities are listed in the sequence in which they should be introduced.

1. Write a Thesis Statement (T) When Given a Topic

DIRECTIONS: Write a thesis statement (T) for the given topic.

TOPIC: Napoleon's impact

T: _Napoleon's impact on France had both positive and negative aspects._

2. Distinguish among General (G), Specific (S), and Thesis (T) Statements

DIRECTIONS: Identify the general statement, specific statement, and thesis statement by writing G, S, or T.

___S___ In 1936, an athlete impressed spectators at the Berlin Olympics with his skill and talent.

___T___ Jesse Owens, a formidable Black track and field star, is remembered for shattering world records.

___G___ Many Olympians have made a significant impact on their sport.

3. Write an S When Given a G and a T

If students are having trouble coming up with a specific statement, you can suggest that they try answering one or more of the question words (*who, what, when, where, why,* and *how*). Another good option is to include an appositive. The following example assumes students have read the book *Lyddie*.[7]

DIRECTIONS: Write a specific statement (S) for the given general statement (G) and thesis statement (T).

G: People often have different ideas of how to define "fairness."

S: *Diana and Lyddie, two characters in Katherine Paterson's novel Lyddie, have differing points of view.*

T: Although Diana is radical and tries to entice other factory workers to sign a petition, Lyddie does not agree with Diana's perspective until the very end of the novel.

---

4. Write a G and an S When Given a T

DIRECTIONS: Write a general statement (G) and a specific statement (S) for the given thesis statement (T).

G: *An invasive species is an organism that is not native to a particular area.*

S: *In the Florida everglades, the Burmese python has been wreaking havoc on native animal populations since it was first introduced to the area in 1994.*

T: Although these enormous reptiles continue to pose a problem for this once-thriving ecosystem, scientists in Florida are developing methods to reduce their numbers.

---

5. Adding Sentences to the Introductory Paragraph

As students become more proficient, there is no need to limit their introductions to three sentences. Typically, the fourth or fifth sentences are specific statements, often facts or statistics.

DIRECTIONS: Write an additional specific statement (S).

G: As the United States grew in industrial and economic power, two controversial figures emerged.

S: By the end of the 19th century, Andrew Carnegie controlled almost the entire steel industry and John Rockefeller's Standard Oil Company controlled 90% of the refining business.

S: _Both men made tremendous philanthropic contributions that made them heroic in the views of many._

T: However, there have been debates about whether these early builders of big business in America should be considered "robber barons" or "captains of industry."

Crafting Conclusions

As with the concluding statement in the TO, the function of the concluding paragraph in the MPO is to restate and reinforce the thesis statement of the composition. It should accomplish at least one of the same goals as the TO concluding statement, such as offering a summary, solution, or recommendation.

The structure of the concluding paragraph reverses the structure of the introductory one: instead of GST, the concluding paragraph follows a TSG pattern. The thesis statement should be rephrased and positioned as the first sentence instead of the last.

Consider these examples of an introduction and conclusion following the GST and TSG formats on the topic of the monarch butterfly.

INTRODUCTORY PARAGRAPH:

The migration of the monarch butterfly has always been fascinating to scientists. However, there are both habitat and environmental factors that pose threats to this favorite flying insect. Even though historically the monarch butterfly population has come back from challenges that have threatened its existence, recovering from the use of pesticides, climate change, and development may be more problematic.

CONCLUDING PARAGRAPH:

Although monarch butterflies have bounced back from past threats caused by nature, the hazards caused by people may be too monumental for this popular butterfly population to overcome. Concerns about the future of the monarch are valid and serious. It is imperative to address the dangers confronting this remarkable butterfly before it becomes extinct.

Remind students that the last words in a composition usually have the most impact on the reader; therefore, the concluding paragraph should contain its key points. After the first sentence, which will be the rephrased thesis statement, students should write specific and general statements that differ from the ones they used in their introductory paragraph. Both should expand on the S and G statements that appear there. If students are having trouble rephrasing the three types of statements in their conclusions, you can provide them with some sample introductory paragraphs and have them practice reconstructing them as concluding paragraphs.

Examples 9.7 and 9.8 show a completed MPO and the essay it outlines.

Multiple-Paragraph Outline (MPO)

NAME: _____   DATE: _____

TOPIC: _Primary Causes of American Revolution_____

THESIS STATEMENT: _The Intolerable Acts and the Stamp Act were crucial_

_in the decision to declare war on Great Britain._____

Main Idea	Details
Introduction ¶ 1	G .... S .... T ....
Intolerable ¶ 2 Acts ↓ TS	_1774: 4 laws/punish MA for Boston Tea Party_ .... _denied MA rt to govern itself_ .... _blockade Boston harbor/elim fair trials_ .... _unified colonists First Cont. Congress._ ....
Stamp Act ¶ 3 ↓ TS	_GB raises $$/tax for all printed paper_ _Sons of Liberty/Patrick Henry VA Resolves_ _Taxation w/o representation_ .... _repealed yr later_ ....
Conclusion ¶ 4	T .... S .... G ....

Exhibit 9.7

Title:
Two Primary Causes of the American Revolution

The factors that led to the American Revolution have been described by countless historians. There were multiple events that played a role in the colonists' rebellion, but two are especially important. The Intolerable Acts and the Stamp Act were crucial in the decision to declare war on Great Britain.

In 1774, the British wanted to make an example of Massachusetts after the Boston Tea Party. As a result, the Intolerable Acts, a group of four acts, were passed. They denied Massachusetts the right to govern itself. In addition, Boston Harbor was blockaded, and fair trials were prevented. Finally, the last act applied to all the colonies, not just Massachusetts. British troops were ordered to be stationed at more convenient locations and the expenses were to be paid by the colonies.

In 1765, the Stamp Act was intended to raise money from the colonists by taxing all printed paper, even playing cards, but it was enacted without the approval of their assemblies. The colonists believed they should have the same rights as the English. Patrick Henry's publication attacking the act, Virginia Resolves, was widely read. The phrase "taxation without representation" became popular.

The Intolerable Acts and the Stamp Act were primary reasons for the American Revolution. As a result of the burdens these acts placed on the colonists, their fury grew. Their anger eventually led to a strong desire for independence from Great Britain.

Exhibit 9.8

Differentiating TO and MPO Activities

Practice in any of the preceding activities can help students who are having difficulty with particular elements of the TO and MPO. Here are some further suggestions you can use for additional support:

- TO: Provide students with the thesis and concluding statement(s).

- TO and MPO: Provide students with the thesis statement and words and phrases for the Main Idea column to help them organize their paragraphs.

- TO and MPO: Provide students with both a main idea and details for the first body paragraph.

- MPO: Provide Level 2 students who are ready for the MPO with a thesis statement and/or the general or specific statements to use in their introduction and conclusion.

Adapting the TO and MPO:
The Pre-Transition Outline

For students, particularly those in elementary school, who are not ready for the TO or MPO formats, we suggest using a hybrid of an SPO and TO, the Pre-Transition Outline (PTO), to help them begin thinking about the requirements of MPOs and essays. As with the TO, for the PTO students select the topic first and then develop a thesis statement. In contrast to the TO, on the PTO students write out a full topic sentence for each paragraph as they would on an SPO; however, they do not need to add a concluding sentence for each paragraph. Instead, the PTO ends with a concluding statement that paraphrases the thesis statement.

It's best if the PTO is only two or three paragraphs long and has three or four details. The fourth detail is in parentheses to indicate that it is considered optional depending on the topic. See the following example of a completed PTO. (Also see Appendix J.)

RESOURCE

Pre-Transition
Outline (PTO)
Appendix J

When students have mastered completing the PTO and developing drafts based on it, move right on to the TO. It's preferable to have students become accustomed to the TO sooner rather than later because, together with the MPO, those formats will be more beneficial to students as they write longer essays about more complex and detailed topics.

Pre-Transition Outline (PTO)

NAME: _____ DATE: _____

TOPIC: _____

THESIS STATEMENT: *Susan B. Anthony and Elizabeth Cady Stanton were the driving forces behind the women's rights movement.*

T.S. *Susan B. Anthony, an activist in the women's suffrage movement, is considered a national icon.*

　1. *on the ground organizer + strategist*
　2. *attended rallies across country*
　3. *focus = right to vote / quote: pg. 1 S.B.A. Address*
　(4.) *created NAWSA = powerful org. → women's rts advocate*

T.S. *Elizabeth Cady Stanton, one of the first leaders to demand equal rights for women, was an influential suffragist.*

　1. *philosopher, thinker + commentator*
　2. *1848/Seneca Falls*
　3. *wrote speeches, books + pamphlets*
　(4.) *pushed for lib. divorce laws + co-ed*

CONCLUDING STATEMENT: *In closing, both Susan B. Anthony and Elizabeth Cady Stanton left important legacies for women's rights.*

Research Papers

Teaching students effective research skills is challenging but important. If students haven't learned how to research a topic, they may find themselves investing a lot of effort in a project that relies on information that is questionable or just plain wrong.

It's all too easy for students to stumble on a website that looks reliable but is riddled with misinformation. Students may also mistake personal opinions they find online for fact or become overwhelmed by the amount of information available.

Make sure your students are staying on track over the days or weeks that they're working on their projects. Once students have their topics, it's best to set up a detailed schedule listing due dates for each stage of the process: gathering material, developing a thesis, coming up with a bibliography, taking and organizing notes, and so on. We suggest that you require students to get your approval for each section before moving on to the next step.

A full discussion of how to help your students do research online is beyond the scope of this book, but we can offer a few suggestions. We also recommend consulting the article "The Challenge That's Bigger than Fake News: Civic Reasoning in a Social Media Environment," published in *American Educator* magazine and authored by a group of researchers at Stanford University.[8]

Surfing the Internet—with Guardrails

Model the process of searching online for the class, just as you model TWR strategies and activities. Tell students that when they look for information and evidence on the internet, it's important to be aware of the following guidelines and search suggestions, which are drawn from the aforementioned *American Educator* article as well as an article in *Education Week* on teaching online research skills:[9]

- Use precise keywords in online searches. Typing *Kennedy assassination* might return results about the assassinations of both John F. Kennedy and Robert Kennedy instead of just one of them.

- Use certain words and symbols to refine online searches.

  ▶ Use quotation marks around search terms to get the exact wording.

  ▶ Insert "AND" between search terms to produce results that focus on both subjects.

  ▶ Include a space followed by a minus sign to eliminate a particular meaning of a term (for example, a student searching for information about the Australian Outback could type *Outback -car* to eliminate results relating to the Outback vehicle).

- Check whether a website's URL ends in *.com*, *.gov*, or *.edu*. Websites connected with a government agency (*.gov*) or university (*.edu*) are generally more trustworthy than someone's personal website. But warn students that *.org*, previously associated with mission-driven organizations, is no longer a sign of reliability; practically any organization can now obtain that designation.

- Evaluate websites with a critical eye. Students should be asking questions such as: Who wrote this? What is his or her perspective? Who is sponsoring this site? Are there links and references to other sources that corroborate the information? Asking these questions while on the site itself may not be enough. It can be more useful to leave the site and see what other sources say about it.

- Don't click on the first result that comes up after a Google search. It's best to go down the list and examine URLs and the sentences that accompany each result for clues to reliability.

- Use Wikipedia wisely. Although many educators warn students away from the site, it can be useful if you know how to use it. Students should learn to investigate Wikipedia's "Talk" pages, where they'll find debates on controversial issues, and to use the references at the end of each article as resources for lateral reading.

Ms. Hamilton was right: her fifth graders didn't do well on their written responses for the state test. But the following year, she tried a different approach. She taught her students sentence-level strategies as well as how to create the SPO and TO.

In the spring, as in previous years, she wanted to do what she could to prepare her students for the writing prompts they would see on the state test. They would probably still have to deal with unfamiliar content in the reading passages. But, she hoped, at least they would now have writing skills that would help them produce coherent responses.

The day before testing began, she gave them a text to read about space exploration—a topic they hadn't learned about in class. "Based on this article," she wrote on the board, "what are the most significant challenges to exploring outer space?" Then she handed out blank sheets of paper.

Almost all of her students got right to work. But they didn't just start writing. First, they created outlines without a template, identifying the topic and writing a thesis statement below it, using the prompt on the board as a guide.

Most wrote some version of "There are several significant challenges to exploring outer space," but some outlined a plan of development. A boy named Malik, for example, wrote, "The most significant challenges to exploring outer space are radiation, the lack of gravity, and the distance from Earth."

Then students drew boxes for main ideas and details and began filling them in. Once they had their concluding statements at the bottom, they were off and running, converting their outlines into drafts.

Ms. Hamilton felt a wave of relief wash over her. This year, when her students saw a writing prompt on the test, she was pretty sure they wouldn't just flail or freeze. They would know what to do.

To Sum Up

- Before trying to create TOs, students need ample experience developing topic sentences, writing supporting details in note form, and constructing coherent paragraphs.

- Level 1 and less advanced Level 2 students should initially use these skills to create simple three- or four-paragraph TOs for book reports, biographies, and compositions on scientific or geographic topics.

- Introduce students to the TO or MPO by modeling the process of creating one.

- When students are still learning to create TOs and MPOs, you should assign the topics; for more experienced students, you should provide guidance in selecting a topic.

- Provide students with models of thesis statements that fit the type of TO or MPO they're constructing, and, when appropriate, have them include a plan of development that maps out the structure of the composition.

- Have students fill in the Main Idea and corresponding Details boxes for each paragraph of the TO and MPO in note form.

- To prepare Level 2 students to write introductory paragraphs for the MPO, introduce them to the GST formula—incorporating general, specific, and thesis statements—and have them practice distinguishing among the three types of statements and then creating them.

- Have students reverse the formula to TSG for the conclusion.

- Have students convert their completed TOs and MPOs to drafts and then revise them by varying sentence structure, incorporating quotations (if any), and using transitions to link paragraphs and sentences.

- If Level 2 students' MPOs require independent research, have students commit to a schedule with deadlines for each step of the process.

BOOK DISCUSSION QUESTIONS:

1. Why is outlining an essential step before writing an essay?

2. What are the important skills a student should have before writing at length?

3. What are the steps for developing a TO?

4. What is a plan of development within a thesis statement?

5. What are good topics for beginning instruction in developing TOs and MPOs?

6. What activities can help ensure that a) students understand the quotation and b) the quotation reinforces a point in the essay?

7. Describe the GST structure for an introductory paragraph.

8. Using the topic of cell phones, write a G, S, and T.

9. Enumerate the activities you would use to teach students how to develop general, specific, and thesis statements.

10. What are the similarities and differences between the introductory paragraph and the concluding paragraph in a composition developed from an MPO?

Notes

1. Iowa Department of Education, "Iowa Academic Standards" (n.d.), https://educateiowa.gov /iowa-academic-standards.

2. C. Birkenstein and G. Graff, *They Say/I Say*, 4th ed. (New York: W.W. Norton, 2018).

3. Purdue University Online Writing Lab, "MLA Formatting and Style Guide" (n.d.), https:// owl.purdue.edu/owl/research_and_citation /mla_style/mla_formatting_and_style_guide /mla_formatting_and_style_guide.html.

4. Purdue University Online Writing Lab, "General Format" (n.d.), https://owl.purdue.edu/owl /research_and_citation/apa_style/apa_formatting _and_style_guide/general_format.html.

5. Purdue University Online Writing Lab, "Chicago Manual of Style, 17th ed." (n.d.), https://owl .purdue.edu/owl/research_and_citation/chicago _manual_17th_edition/cmos_formatting_and _style_guide/chicago_manual_of_style_17th _edition.html.

6. A. Lunsford and R. Connors, *The St. Martin's Handbook*, 8th ed. (New York: St. Martin's Press, 1995), p. 112.

7. K. Paterson, *Lyddie* (Waterville, ME: Thorndike Press, 2019).

8. S. McGrew, T. Ortega, J. Breakstone, and S. Wineburg, "The Challenge That's Bigger than Fake News: Civic Reasoning in a Social Media Environment," *American Educator* (2017, Fall), https://www.aft.org/ae/fall2017/mcgrew _ortega_breakstone_wineburg.

9. L. H. O'Hanlon, "Teaching Students Better Online Research Skills," *Education Week* (22 May 2013), www.edweek.org/ew/articles/2013/05/22/32el -studentresearch.h32.html.

CHAPTER 10

Taking a Stand

Writing Opinion, Pro/Con, and Argumentative Essays

Ms. Giannelli was familiar with the state writing standards that applied to her seventh graders. She knew they needed to be able to write arguments in which they supported their claims with clear reasons and relevant evidence, while acknowledging another point of view.

After searching online for argumentative writing prompts, Ms. Giannelli found a wealth of ideas for middle schoolers. She decided to give her class a choice of just three topics:

- Should cell phones be allowed at school?
- Should students have homework on weekends?
- Should exotic animals be kept in captivity?

Ms. Giannelli knew her students had lots of opinions on the first two questions, and she suspected the third one would appeal to the animal lovers in the class. To help them get started on a topic they might not know much about, she provided the two sentences that had accompanied the prompt online: "Many exotic animals live longer in captivity. However, many people argue that it's not a good way of life for them."

Ms. Giannelli was pleased to see that as students chose their topics, there was a buzz of excitement in the air. After about half an hour, she decided to check their progress.

Some students seemed to have gotten stuck after the first sentence or two—especially those who had chosen to write about animals in captivity. Most were against the idea, but they had trouble coming up with reasons beyond their conviction that the animals would be unhappy.

Students who chose one of the other topics had produced more prose, but it wasn't what Ms. Giannelli had hoped for. Ari's essay was pretty typical. She took a strong stand against homework on weekends. But her reasons were entirely personal. She explained how tired she was after school on Fridays and listed all the activities she would like to engage in during a typical weekend. Ms. Giannelli didn't think these reasons counted as "evidence." Nor did Ari acknowledge that anyone else might think homework on weekends was a good idea, let alone raise the arguments such a person might make and try to rebut them.

The standards were clear, and it was equally clear Ms. Giannelli's students weren't equipped to meet them. What wasn't clear was what she could do about that.

Teachers frequently assign opinion and argumentative essays to satisfy the requirements of state writing standards. Children as young as third grade are expected to present their claims and convince a reader of their point of view. By sixth grade, they're supposed to be supporting their claims with evidence, and by seventh grade they should be acknowledging arguments on the other side. As we have discovered, even older students often struggle to write these kinds of essays if they haven't learned the appropriate language and structures.

When you have students practice the skills leading up to argumentative writing, choose a topic that has two debatable sides. Whenever possible, the topic should be embedded in the content students are studying. Often opinion or argumentative writing is treated as a separate category that can be addressed only by having students take and defend positions on topics beyond the school curriculum—such as the pros and cons of school uniforms. However, choosing a topic they've been studying is an ideal way to build and deepen their knowledge of content. Stay alert for topics in the curriculum, at whatever grade level you're teaching, that lend themselves to pro/con writing. For example, students can write about the pros and cons of traveling west in covered wagons, the strengths and weaknesses or flaws in a particular book or character, or arguments for and against using atomic bombs to attack Japan in World War II.

If you've been using TWR's method, your students have already been building the skills they'll need to craft effective arguments:

- Completing sentence stems using *because*, *but*, and *so* develops students' ability to connect a **claim** to evidence, introduce a **counterclaim,** and describe cause/effect relationships.

- Using subordinating conjunctions such as *while* and *although* and transitions such as *however* and *on the other hand* to begin sentences enables students to acknowledge or make a claim while simultaneously bringing in an opposing claim.

- Sentence expansion using a kernel that takes a position develops students' ability to state a claim.

- Transitions present and evaluate reasons, evidence, and claims.

- Creating topic sentences and thesis statements enables students to identify the main points they want to make in an argument.

- Summarizing develops students' ability to succinctly describe claims on both sides.

- Creating Single-Paragraph Outlines (SPOs that are either pro or con), Transition Outlines (TOs), and Multiple-Paragraph Outlines (MPOs) helps students logically organize claims and evidence.

- Incorporating quotations and paraphrases during the revision process teaches students how to cite evidence for claims in an effective way.

As we emphasize throughout this book, however, these strategies will help students write well only if they have knowledge of what they're writing about. That applies to argumentative writing as much as to any other genre.

Preparing for Argumentative Writing

Often students approach argumentative writing by progressing along three types of paragraphs and compositions:

- **Opinion:** Author tries to convince a reader to adopt a certain point of view; opinion writing is the easiest and is generally assigned to elementary students.

- **Pro/con:** Author lays out two sides of an issue and presents the evidence to support each side but doesn't take a position.

- **Argumentative:** Author presents the evidence for both sides but also decides which position has more merit and defends the one he supports.

Opinion and pro/con writing assignments constitute a scaffold leading to the argumentative essay—the most challenging of these three types of writing. In writing opinion pieces, younger students get practice listing reasons that support a claim. When crafting body paragraphs of a pro/con essay, students learn to state opposing positions and present evidence that supports each one. If they actually agree with one side rather than the other, they get practice suspending their own opinions and putting themselves in the shoes of someone on the other side—a skill that will serve them well when they turn to argumentative writing and need to summarize an opposing viewpoint fairly.

WHY PRACTICE WRITING OPINION, PRO/CON, AND ARGUMENTATIVE PIECES?

- Develops analytical and logical thinking skills
- Helps students distinguish reliable sources from unreliable ones
- Improves organizational skills
- Teaches students to cite textual evidence effectively
- Develops the ability to assess and rank stronger and weaker arguments
- Reinforces academic knowledge and vocabulary

Planning and outlining before writing a draft of any of these essay types deepens and reinforces students' understanding of content. Moreover, as with other outline strategies, these benefits will accrue whether or not students create a finished product.

Sentence-Level Activities: Laying the Foundation for Arguments

To prepare your students for the challenges of writing argumentative essays, you can give them sentence-level activities that will introduce some of the techniques they'll ultimately use for that type of writing. The conjunction, transition, and sentence expansion activities that follow will also deepen students' comprehension of the curriculum content in which they're embedded and spur them to think analytically about what they've learned.

Using Conjunctions to Present a Position

The following examples illustrate how conjunction activities can introduce students to the idea of identifying evidence that supports claims.

When students use *because*, they need to find evidence that supports the proposition given in the sentence stem. When they use *so*, they need to consider what action people should take as a result of that evidence. As always, using the conjunction *but* may be more challenging because students need to come up with opposing evidence—laying the foundation for pro/con, and, eventually, argumentative writing.

Level 1 Example

DIRECTIONS: Complete the following sentence stems.

Weather forecasts can be helpful because *people need to prepare for different conditions.*

Weather forecasts can be helpful, but *they are not always accurate.*

Weather forecasts can be helpful, so *it is important to check them regularly.*

Level 2 Example

DIRECTIONS: Complete the following sentence stems.

Genetically Modified Organisms (GMOs) should be used in agriculture because *they can be engineered to resist pests, tolerate harsh conditions, and increase crop yields.*

Genetically Modified Organisms (GMOs) should be used in agriculture, but *there are concerns about their impact on biodiversity, their potential health risks, and the ethics of genetic manipulation.*

Genetically Modified Organisms (GMOs) should be used in agriculture, so *it's important to conduct ongoing research and establish regulations to ensure their safe and responsible use.*

Using Transitions to Introduce and Support Claims

A transition may begin a sentence, thus creating a link between that sentence and the one that precedes it, or link thoughts within a sentence. When used at the beginning or end of a paragraph, transitions can underscore a theme or idea that knits the paragraph's various sentences together. And, of course, transitions can and should be used judiciously to connect the paragraphs in a multiple-paragraph essay. These functions are explained in more detail in Chapter 9.

RESOURCE

Transition Words and Phrases
Appendix C

All five categories of transition words and phrases can be helpful in presenting and evaluating reasons, evidence, and claims (see Appendix C). Students can learn to use the following types of transitions:

- **Time-and-sequence** transitions such as *in addition*, *moreover*, and *finally* to list reasons and claims on each side

- **Illustration** transitions such as *for example* and *specifically* to provide examples of a general claim or introduce evidence

- **Emphasis** transitions such as *most important*, *moreover*, or *certainly* to highlight the most important claims or underscore an argument

- **Change-of-direction** transitions such as *however*, *although*, and *in contrast* to introduce or acknowledge opposing claims

- **Conclusion** transitions such as *thus* or *in the end* to signal that they're wrapping up an argument

Change-of-direction transitions are particularly useful for introducing a contrasting point, example, or argument. They can come in the middle of sentences, as with *but*, or at the beginning of a new sentence, as with *however*. When one paragraph is devoted to a claim and the next to a counterclaim, tell your students they can introduce the second paragraph with a change-of-direction transition such as *on the other hand*.

Another type of change-of-direction transition—the subordinating conjunction—is particularly useful for thesis statements in pro/con or argumentative essays. If students begin their thesis statements with words such as *although* and *while*, they'll be able to acknowledge two opposing claims. They'll also be able to avoid using the first person (*I believe*), which can detract from the authority of their argument.

Using Sentence Expansion to Build Argumentative Skills

Another sentence-level activity that can be adapted to build argumentative skills is sentence expansion. Remember that sentence expansion involves giving students a kernel sentence—a simple, active, declarative sentence with only one verb—along with the question words to help them expand it. To make sentence expansion into an argumentative activity, make the kernel sentence you give students one that takes a position. This example is embedded in content from the book *Flowers for Algernon*:[1]

DIRECTIONS: Expand the kernel sentence.

His life greatly improved.

Who?   *Charlie*

When?   *after experimental surgery*

Why?   *intelligence ↑*

EXPANDED SENTENCE: *After the experimental surgery, Charlie's life greatly improved because his intelligence increased.*

Then you might also give them a kernel that takes the opposite position. For example:

DIRECTIONS: Expand the kernel sentence.

His quality of life declined.

Who?   *Charlie* ....

When? *after experimental surgery* ....

Why?   *lost friends → lonely* ....

EXPANDED SENTENCE: *After the experimental surgery, Charlie's quality of life declined because he lost his friends and became lonely.*

Using Sentence-Level Activities Together

Level 1 Example

Ms. Cole's second-grade class had been reading about the advantages and disadvantages of keeping animals in zoos as opposed to their natural habitats. To help students understand the debate and work on their writing skills, Ms. Cole gave them sentence stems that required them to supply a logical or evidence-based reason to support the pro-zoo side and explain what followed from that position:

Zoos are good for animals because *they protect endangered species from extinction.*

Zoos are good for animals, so *people should continue to support them.*

Since many zoos educate visitors about conservation, *people learn to respect the environment.*

Then she made the activity more challenging by asking them to consider arguments on the other side:

Zoos are not good for animals because *animals should not be removed from their native habitats.*

Zoos are not good for animals, so *they should not be supported by the public.*

Since many zoos keep animals in unsafe conditions, *animals develop health problems.*

Finally, Ms. Cole asked her students to summarize both positions without taking a side:

Although some people believe that zoos help certain species survive, ___ *others argue that animals should not be held captive.*

Next Ms. Cole wanted her students to practice using transition words between sentences. Although the students weren't yet ready to write pro/con paragraphs about zoos, she wanted them to have experience creating the kinds of connections between thoughts that they would need to use during the drafting and revising stages.

Ms. Cole gave her students pairs of sentences that had no transition words connecting them. The students needed to choose an appropriate transition word for each pair and write it in the blank. To provide additional support, Ms. Cole provided a word bank of transition words for her students to choose from. Initially, she gave them sentences that only required them to take one side, either pro or con, like this:

If zoos are closed, many animal species may become extinct. *For example,* the numbers of wild gorillas and elephants have decreased because of poachers.

Zoos have improved over the years. *As a result,* animals live longer in them and are healthier.

Then she introduced transitions that required students to offer contrasting evidence, laying the groundwork for pro/con and argumentative writing:

> Some people believe zoos can be good for animals. On the other hand, *critics say that animals have better lives in the wild.*

Level 2 Example

When his Level 2 history class was studying the presidency of Theodore Roosevelt, Mr. Hidalgo gave them the following sentence stems to develop their argumentative writing skills:

> Theodore Roosevelt has many admirers because *he established national parks and expanded national forests.*

Mr. Hidalgo then made the activity more challenging by introducing stems that required students to consider both pro and con considerations, such as this one:

> Although Theodore Roosevelt moved the United States toward becoming a world power, *critics argue that Roosevelt had imperialistic tendencies, particularly in his approach to foreign affairs.*

He also had students complete stems in a way that took a position to help them distinguish between pro/con writing and argumentative writing, and to prepare them for the latter:

> While critics of Theodore Roosevelt point to his use of military interventions and limited action on civil rights, *his accomplishments in conservation, foreign affairs, and support of workers' rights are outstanding legacies.*

Mr. Hidalgo had students supply transition words to link sentences about Roosevelt's administration. But because his Level 2 students were more experienced writers, he had them come up with their own transition words rather than giving them a word bank to choose from:

> Theodore Roosevelt supported a rebellion in Panama against Colombia. *Consequently,* he was criticized for interfering in the internal affairs of another country.

Alternatively, Mr. Hidalgo could have given students the transition and had them complete the sentence:

> Theodore Roosevelt supported a rebellion in Panama against Colombia. Consequently, *he was criticized for interfering in the internal affairs of another country.*

Opinion Writing

Opinion writing is the least demanding type of writing in this genre because students can present one point of view without bringing in arguments on the other side. For Level 1 writers, an opinion piece can consist of just one paragraph. However, they must do more than simply state their opinions. They need to back up their opinions with reasons, although their reasons can be based on personal experience rather than evidence.

For example, a student might write an opinion piece arguing that dogs make better pets than cats. She might talk about how loyal, affectionate, and obedient her own dog is. She wouldn't need to bring in and evaluate arguments against dogs (they need to be walked) or in favor of cats (they keep themselves clean).

Fact versus Opinion: Introducing the Distinction

It's important for students to develop an understanding of the difference between opinion and fact because opinions won't be enough to support their arguments later on when they're writing pro/con or argumentative essays. They'll need evidence.

You can start introducing students to the fact/opinion distinction in the early elementary grades. In one of our partner schools, for example, a first-grade teacher had her class collectively plan an opinion paragraph explaining why a lot of children love summer. As they came up with a topic sentence and details for the body, the teacher listed the latter in note form on a whiteboard.

Then she guided them through the process of coming up with a concluding sentence, producing an outline that looked something like this:

T.S. *A lot of students love summer.*

_____

1. *no school or homework* ....

2. *swimming* ....

3. *more time outside* ....

4. *longer days* ....

C.S. *Summer is the best time of the year!*

_____

During this kind of activity, a teacher can point out that the concluding sentence is an opinion, and the details on the numbered lines are facts that support it.

Some topics don't lend themselves to reasons beyond the author's personal experience. If you ask your students to write an opinion piece about what the best holiday is, they're probably going to list the reasons *they* like Christmas or Thanksgiving. To help your students develop the skills that will help them write argumentative essays, you'll need to choose topics that lend themselves to reasoned debate, based on facts. **Your students will need to have factual information they can draw on to support their opinions.**

Pro/Con Writing

Level 2 students may be able to go straight to pro/con compositions, which are a significant step up from opinion pieces. Each body paragraph in the essay presents one side of an issue and the evidence that supports it. A student might write a pro paragraph explaining that the ambition of Alexander the Great was a positive trait because he brought the benefits of Greek civilization to other lands. Then the student could write a con paragraph that it was a negative trait because Alexander's conquest of foreign lands caused so much suffering.

A pro/con essay has an introduction and a conclusion, but—unlike in an argumentative essay—students take a neutral stance, simply presenting the claims and evidence on each side.

Using Pro or Con SPOs and Paragraphs as Stepping Stones

Before asking your students to undertake an entire argumentative essay—which would raise two points of view and present evidence for and evaluate each—first give them ample practice planning a single paragraph that summarizes the arguments for a position on one side, backed by evidence. Next, they can practice planning another single paragraph that summarizes the opposing view—again, backed by evidence. These activities will prepare them to write a pro/con essay that neutrally presents two points of view. The activities will also equip students for the more challenging task of deciding which position is stronger and why, which they'll confront when they write argumentative essays.

It's important to include language like "some argue," and "others say" in a pro/con essay. If the second half of the sentence just says, "it led him to take actions that caused a great deal of suffering," the author is making an argument rather than neutrally summarizing claims on both sides—and that kind of writing belongs in an argumentative essay, not a pro/con one.

Matching Opposing Topic Sentences with Details

A great way to introduce the skill of constructing arguments on two sides is to provide two SPOs, one pro and one con, that have only the topic sentences filled in. At the top, provide a list of details, in note form, and ask students to match each detail to the appropriate topic sentence. As always, when first introducing students to this activity, model it by guiding the whole class through it orally.

Level 1 Example

Ms. Cole gave her class the following activity on zoos. One topic sentence took a pro-zoo position and the other an anti-zoo one. Students had to look at the list of details provided and copy them onto the appropriate dotted lines.

DIRECTIONS: Write each detail under the appropriate topic sentence.

provide food + water + shelter

captivity → animals distressed

care for injured + abandoned animals

educate visitors/conservation

small exhibits/little room to roam (e.g., elephants)

no socializing w/ others → bored

protect endangered species → ↓ animals extinct

visitors tease animals

T.S. Zoos are harmful to animals and should be abolished.

1. small exhibits/little room to roam (e.g., elephants)
2. captivity → animals distressed
3. no socializing w/ others → bored
4. visitors tease animals

T.S. Zoos provide benefits to both animals and people.

1. provide food + water + shelter
2. care for injured + abandoned animals
3. protect endangered species → ↓ animals extinct
4. educate visitors/conservation

Level 2 Example

Mr. Hidalgo gave his history class the following activity about the presidency of Theodore Roosevelt.

DIRECTIONS: Write each detail under the appropriate topic sentence.

conservation

not enough progress/civil rts

over-regulated business

treatment of Nat. Amer.

PR + Philippines → expansion + aggression

constructed Panama Canal

supported workers

consumer rts.

T.S. Theodore Roosevelt's presidency was flawed.

1. *PR + Philippines → expansion + aggression*
2. *not enough progress/civil rts.*
3. *over-regulated business*
4. *treatment of Nat. Amer.*

T.S. Theodore Roosevelt left a great legacy.

1. *conservation*
2. *supported workers*
3. *constructed Panama Canal*
4. *consumer rts*

By providing details, you're essentially doing the research for your students so they can focus on deciding which evidence supports which claim. When embedded in the content of the curriculum, this activity will also encourage your students to engage in close reading of texts. They'll need to think carefully to decide which details from the text go with which topic sentence.

Tell your students they should list the strongest reason or evidence last, where it will have the most impact on the reader. That means they'll need to decide which detail provides the strongest argument in support of each claim. This practice evaluating the strength of claims will also prepare students for deciding which position they want to take when it's time to write argumentative essays.

Creating Pro/Con SPOs from Scratch

Once students have become familiar with matching details to the appropriate topic sentence and evaluating their strength, they can start creating their own SPOs. Tell them to write a topic sentence and a concluding sentence for each paragraph—pro and con—and write supporting details in note form on the dotted lines of each outline.

Level 1 Example

Ms. Cole decided her class was now ready to build on their previous activities by creating their own SPOs on the subject of zoos—one summarizing the pro arguments and the other summarizing the opposing view. To do this, they would need to create topic and concluding sentences.

Since her students were second graders, they hadn't yet been introduced to all three strategies for creating effective topic and concluding sentences—using one of the sentence types, using an appositive, and using a subordinating conjunction. Ms. Cole had taught them only the first strategy, using one of the four sentence types: a command, a question, an exclamation, or a statement. She reminded them of each type before they began filling out their SPOs.

The following are examples of the SPOs students produced:

T.S. Zoos benefit animals in many ways. _____

_____

1. provide food + water + shelter ....
2. care for injured + abandoned animals ....
3. protect endangered species → ↓ animals extinct ......
4. educate visitors/conservation ....

C.S. Zoos keep animals safe and help them survive. _____

_____

T.S. It is cruel to keep animals in zoos. _____

_____

1. small exhibits/little place to roam (e.g., elephants) ...
2. captivity → animals distressed ....
3. could never survive in the wild ....
4. visitors tease animals ....

C.S. Boycott zoos! _____

_____

Level 2 Example

Mr. Hidalgo also had his history students plan their own pro/con SPOs on Theodore Roosevelt. He required his students to come up with different topic sentences than the ones he had supplied for the matching activity, and he reminded them of the three strategies to create one.

Similarly, he required students to come up with some different details than the ones he had provided. He reminded them to include the sources for the details in note form so that they would be able to provide citations or incorporate quotations from the text if and when they turned their SPOs into paragraphs.

T.S. _Theodore Roosevelt's presidency had shortcomings._

1. _used force to achieve foreign policy_
2. _over-regulated business_
3. _not enough progress/civil rts_
4. _treatment of Nat. Americans_

C.S. _Although Theodore Roosevelt accomplished a great deal, his presidency was flawed._

T.S. *Theodore Roosevelt, the 26th president, had a positive impact on the United States.*

1. *nat'l parks + exp. forests*
2. *labor unions*
3. *constructed Panama Canal*
4. *consumer rts/Food and Drug Administration*

C.S. *In conclusion, Theodore Roosevelt left an impressive record of accomplishments.*

TOs and MPOs for Pro/Con Compositions

The next phase in developing the skills necessary for the argumentative essay is to have students create a TO or MPO that considers both sides but doesn't take a position. To do that, they can build on their existing pro and con SPOs or use a new topic.

As we discussed in Chapter 9, the first steps in creating TOs and MPOs are for you to select a topic and lead the students in developing a thesis statement. If students are choosing a new topic at this point, make sure that it's both debatable and manageable—neither too broad nor too narrow. Ask yourself if students will be able to handle the amount of evidence or research required.

A TO or MPO for a pro/con essay might look something like the ones in Exhibits 10.1 and 10.2:

Transition Outline (TO)

NAME: _____   DATE: _____

TOPIC: *Alexander the Great*

THESIS STATEMENT: *Although some argue that Alexander's ambition was a positive trait, others say it led him to take actions that caused a great deal of suffering.*

Main Idea	Details
Pro ¶ 1 ↓ T.S.	....
Con ¶ 2 ↓ T.S.	....

CONCLUDING STATEMENT: _____

_____

Exhibit 10.1

Multiple-Paragraph Outline (MPO)

NAME: _____   DATE: _____

TOPIC: _Alexander the Great_

THESIS STATEMENT: _Although some argue that Alexander's ambition was a positive trait, others say it led him to take actions that caused a great deal of suffering._

Main Idea	Details
Introduction ¶ 1	G .... S .... T ....
Pro ¶ 2 ↓ T.S.	....
Con ¶ 3 ↓ T.S.	....
Conclusion ¶ 4	T .... S .... G ....

Exhibit 10.2

As always, the TO and the MPO will differ in what they require of students. In a pro/con TO, students will write thesis and concluding statements that consist of one sentence acknowledging that there are arguments on both sides. A thesis statement might be:

> *There are arguments for and against increasing the minimum wage.*

Alternatively, students can construct a thesis or concluding statement for a pro/con essay that makes use of a subordinating conjunction:

> *Although some argue that increasing the minimum wage would have a negative impact on many small businesses, others claim that an increased wage would be beneficial to many households.*

Remember that if students leave out a phrase like "others claim that," they're constructing a thesis statement for an *argumentative* essay, not a pro/con essay. A thesis statement for an argumentative essay would read like this:

> *Although some argue that increasing the minimum wage would have a negative impact on the U.S. economy, an increased wage would be beneficial to many households.*

This thesis statement signals that the author has considered the evidence on both sides, has come to a conclusion about which side makes more sense, and is prepared to defend that conclusion with evidence. You can introduce your students to the distinction between pro/con and argumentative thesis statements at this point, but if they haven't had sufficient practice with pro/con essays, they may not be ready to move on to argumentative writing.

If students are developing an MPO rather than a TO, they'll need to construct a thesis statement but not a concluding statement. When they write their draft, they'll create general and specific statements for their introductory and concluding paragraphs, along with a reworded thesis statement to use in the latter.

The Argumentative Essay

An argumentative essay has to be both persuasive and fair. Students will need to convince the reader that their own position is the stronger one but, at the same time, present the opposing point of view accurately. Their experience writing neutral pro/con essays will help them with the latter task.

Composing argumentative essays will enhance skills that your students will generally find useful in later life, in the workplace, and personally.

Of all the writing genres, argumentative writing will be the most effective at sharpening students' analytical faculties. Learning to construct and defend an argument will enable them to think logically and critically.

Using an MPO to Plan an Argumentative Essay

Before your students can start creating an MPO for an argumentative essay, they have to decide which position they're taking. To do that, they'll need to understand the facts and evidence on both sides. Be sure that the class has spent ample time studying and discussing the topic first.

Students need to know that when creating a thesis statement for an argumentative essay, they should put the argument they're making last. For example, if a student wants to argue that the Industrial Revolution was essentially a positive development, they would *not* write:

> Although the Industrial Revolution brought many benefits, its drawbacks cannot be ignored.

Instead, they would end the sentence with the point that the Industrial Revolution brought benefits, as in this sentence:

> Although the Industrial Revolution had its drawbacks, the many benefits it brought cannot be ignored.

In addition to the introductory and concluding paragraphs—which will use the GST and TSG structures—the essay will have three or more body paragraphs (see Exhibit 10.3).

- **1st paragraph.** Introduction GST
- **2nd paragraph.** Lays out the background of the issue accurately, but presents evidence in a way that tends to support the author's position.
- **3rd paragraph.** Presents the counterclaim and the evidence to support it.
- **4th paragraph.** Provides the strongest evidence for the author's point of view.
- **5th paragraph.** Conclusion TSG

Multiple-Paragraph Outline (MPO)

NAME: _____   DATE: _____

TOPIC: _____

THESIS STATEMENT: _____

_____

Main Idea	Details
Introduction ¶ 1	....
background ¶ 2 ↓ T.S.	....
counterclaims ¶ 3 ↓ T.S.	....
claims ¶ 4 ↓ T.S.	....
Conclusion ¶ 5	....

Exhibit 10.3

The standard argumentative essay often consists of five or more paragraphs, although this is not always a requirement. However, when your students begin to write these essays, you may decide to limit them to four paragraphs. They will omit the paragraph right after the introduction that lays out the problem and introduces their own argument. Instead they'll have only two body paragraphs: the first presenting the counterclaim and evidence and the second presenting their own claim and evidence.

Students should not attempt to raise a claim and rebut it in the same paragraph. In our experience, that approach often leads to a fragmented and confusing presentation of the information.

Incorporating Evidence and Quotations

Since students are unlikely to be experts in the topics they're writing about, they'll need to introduce citations, paraphrases, and quotations. Although they should cite authorities supporting both sides, they'll need to show why those who support their own side are more convincing.

At the MPO stage, your students won't actually be incorporating complete citations and quotations, but they will be making notations on their outlines referring to them. Later, they'll integrate that evidence as footnotes and references when they convert their MPOs into drafts and final copies. To prepare your students for that task, have them practice introducing quotations and other evidence in a way that supports a claim (see Chapter 9).

Certain words are particularly well suited to framing quotations or paraphrases in argumentative writing. When introducing a quotation or summary that supports their claim, students should characterize the source in a way that indicates its authority and uses stronger verbs than *says* or even *believes* to introduce the statement. More powerful verbs include *endorses, asserts, emphasizes, reminds us,* and *affirms.*

For example, a student seeking authority in arguing against harsh forms of juvenile justice could simply write the following:

> Professor Clarke said, "Programs like boot camps have been shown to be ineffective in preventing juvenile delinquency."

Think how much more mileage the student could get out of that quotation by framing it with an appositive that indicates the speaker's authority and using a verb that links the speaker's ideas to the student's own point of views, such as:

> Professor Clarke, a nationally recognized expert on juvenile justice reform, endorses this view when she writes, "Programs like boot camps have been shown to be ineffective in preventing juvenile delinquency."

Illustration transitions are also effective ways to introduce textual evidence and quotations, as shown here:

> Experts in the field of juvenile justice reform agree that harsh measures don't work. **For example,** Professor Clarke has written that boot camps "have been shown to be ineffective in preventing juvenile delinquency."

Level 2 Example

Mr. Hidalgo felt that his students were now ready not only to summarize the arguments on both sides of the debate, but also to take a position and evaluate claims on the other side. He asked his students to think carefully about the arguments on each side and then choose the position they personally felt was stronger. Their next task was to craft a thesis statement that stated their position and acknowledged a counterclaim.

He also wanted his students to start citing sources for their evidence and quotations, so he told them to be sure to note them on the details lines of their MPOs. Exhibit 10.4 shows the MPO that one of his students produced.

Multiple-Paragraph Outline (MPO)

NAME: _____   DATE: _____

TOPIC: _President Theodore Roosevelt_

THESIS STATEMENT: _Although Theodore Roosevelt had detractors, his_
legacy had a lasting positive impact in many areas.

Main Idea	Details
Introduction ¶ 1	G S T
background ¶ 2 ↓ T.S.	trust buster Square Deal = equality for all Consumer rts + protection Roosevelt Corollary
counterclaims ¶ 3 ↓ T.S.	little progress on civil rts P.R. aggression + expansion poor treatment of Nat. Amer
claims ¶ 4 ↓ T.S.	conservation = 150 nat'l forests Global power (Lacayo, Time mag) Panama Canal negotiated end Russo-Japanese War
Conclusion ¶ 5	T S G

Differentiating Argumentative Assignments

Level 1 students are not yet experienced enough to plan and write argumentative essays. Therefore, they should keep practicing opinion and pro/con pieces until they've developed the skills necessary for tasks like writing general, specific, and thesis statements; engaging in research; and distinguishing between stronger and weaker arguments.

However, you may be teaching a class where some Level 2 students are ready to plan argumentative essays using the MPO and others should instead use the TO. Those using the TO will not need to create general and specific statements, and they may not dive as deeply into the evidence, but they will be acquiring skills that will enable them to write more fully fleshed-out argumentative essays in the future.

Argumentative Terms

As students move to more sophisticated expository and argumentative writing, consider giving them lists of words that are geared to those types of writing. For example, topic sentences using words such as *although* or *while* work particularly well for both pro/con and argumentative writing.

This would be a good point to introduce your students to words that will come in handy in presenting arguments that are made by others. For example, they can describe those on one side as *proponents* and those on the other as *naysayers*. Instead of simply using the verb *said*, they can use verbs such as *argue* and *maintain*.

EXAMPLES:

Defenders of Theodore Roosevelt argue....

Critics of Theodore Roosevelt assert....

Exhibit 10.5 provides a list of terms to help students craft their pro/con and argumentative TO and MPO thesis statements.

Argumentative Nouns and Verbs

NOUNS

advocates	naysayers
adversaries	opponents
challengers	proponents
critics	supporters
defenders	detractors

VERBS

acknowledge	defend
advocate	dispute
argue	interpret
assert	object
believe	observe
claim	oppose
concur	propose
criticize	state
debate	support

Exhibit 10.5

Review: Argumentative Writing Activities

If you're a middle or high school teacher, the following scaffolds will help you guide your students through the activities that lead to the crafting of an argumentative essay. These activities will enable students to organize their material more effectively, think more analytically, and write more coherently as they prepare to tackle argumentative assignments.

If you're an elementary teacher, your students are probably not yet ready to create argumentative essays. However, if you use the activities leading up to pro/con essays, you'll be laying the foundation for their ability to write argumentative essays at higher grade levels.

SENTENCE-LEVEL STRATEGIES

- Use *because-but-so* activities to present students with a sentence stem that takes a position and have them:

  ▶ Connect a claim to evidence (*because*), introduce a counterclaim (*but*), and describe cause/effect relationships (*so*).

- Use subordinating conjunctions (*while*, *although*, and *even though*) to write sentences that acknowledge a counterclaim and state a claim.

- Use sentence-expansion activities to present students with a kernel sentence that takes a position.

- Use transition activities to present and evaluate reasons, evidence, and claims.

SINGLE-PARAGRAPH OUTLINE

- Practice writing topic sentences for paragraphs that summarize a position on one side of an issue, using the three strategies for creating them:

  ▶ Sentence type (a statement expressing the position of advocates)
  ▶ Subordinating conjunction
  ▶ Appositive

- Match topic sentences taking opposing positions with appropriate details.

- Use an SPO to plan a paragraph that summarizes a position, backed by evidence.

- Use an SPO to plan a paragraph that summarizes an opposing view, also backed by evidence.

TO AND MPO: PRO/CON

- Practice writing a pro/con thesis statement that presents two sides of an argument without taking a position for a TO (e.g., "Although there are many who argue that an extended school year will benefit students, opponents believe that additional time will not produce meaningful results").

- Write a complete pro/con TO or MPO that presents the evidence for two sides of an argument without taking a position.

MPO: ARGUMENT (FOR MIDDLE AND HIGH SCHOOL LEVEL 2 STUDENTS)

Some students in a class might be ready for the argumentative essay but not yet ready for the MPO, in which case they should use the TO.

- Practice writing an argumentative thesis statement that presents two sides of an argument and takes a position, placing the author's position at the end of the thesis statement (e.g., "Although extending the school year has many drawbacks, its benefits outweigh them").

- Develop a four- or five-paragraph MPO that lays out two sides of an argument and takes a position.

  ▶ **1st paragraph.** Introduction: Write only "GST" in the Details box. The thesis statement should be written as a complete sentence on the solid line above the outline.

  ▶ **2nd paragraph.** Lay out the background of the issue accurately, but in a way that tends to support the author's position. (When students are first being introduced to the argumentative MPO, they may omit this paragraph.)

  ▶ **3rd paragraph.** Present the counterclaim and the evidence to support it.

  ▶ **4th paragraph.** Provide the strongest evidence for the author's point of view.

  ▶ **5th paragraph.** Conclusion: Write only "TSG."

DRAFTING AND REVISING

- Generate general and specific statements.

- Practice using transition words and phrases to present and evaluate reasons and claims:

  ▶ Time and sequence: List reasons and claims on each side.

  ▶ Illustration: Provide examples of a general claim or introduce evidence.

  ▶ Emphasis: Highlight important claims or underscore an argument.

  ▶ Change of direction: Introduce or acknowledge opposing claims.

  ▶ Conclusion: Signal wrapping up an argument.

- Practice activities that introduce and explain a quotation in a way that supports a claim.

To Sum Up

To be able to plan and write an effective argumentative essay, your students will need to be able to do the following:

- Understand the difference between fact and opinion.

- Use nouns and verbs that are well suited to argumentative writing (see Exhibit 10.5).

- Integrate quotations with appropriate introductions and explanations.

- Use the SPO to plan two separate paragraphs presenting opposing points of view and evidence to support them.

- Use the TO to plan pro/con essays that present two points of view and supporting evidence in a neutral manner.

- Use the MPO (or TO) to plan four- or five-paragraph argumentative essays that take a position backed by evidence.

- Determine which piece(s) of evidence is (are) the strongest and therefore should be mentioned last.

1. Discuss the major differences among opinion, pro/con, and argumentative writing.

2. What six important skills do students develop when writing opinion, pro/con, and argumentative pieces?

3. How can sentence activities with *because*, *but*, and *so* help students learn to present contrasting points of view?

4. Explain how transition words and phrases are useful in presenting a position or evidence.

5. Choose a topic with two sides (e.g., banning books, keeping animals in zoos, lowering the voting age from 18 to 16) and create a sentence activity for it.

6. Describe how learning to create separate SPOs for opposing points of view can help prepare students for the pro/con essay.

7. Why should students place their strongest claim *last* when writing an argumentative essay?

Notes

1. D. Keyes, *Flowers for Algernon* (New York: HarperCollins, 2007).

How to Assess Writing and Adapt the Hochman Method to Your Classroom

CHAPTER 11

A Gauge and a Guide

Assessing Students' Writing

Mya was a third grader at a school with a high-poverty population. Over 75% of students came from socioeconomically disadvantaged families, and Mya was one of them.

At the beginning of the year, Mya's teacher, Mr. Corwin, gave his students a prompt to gauge their writing skills. Exhibit 11.1 shows what Mya wrote.

Beginning of the Year Writing Assessment

Directions: Please write a paragraph about what you think will be interesting about 3rd grade.

I think that learning new fundation sounds transitioning from classroom to classroom trying new challenges taking new test and making new friends will be interesting about 3rd grade.

Exhibit 11.1

The paragraph had no particular structure. In fact, it was just one long run-on sentence. It sounded just like Mya did when she spoke in class.

Mya's school was partnering with The Writing Revolution organization, and Mr. Corwin got training in the Hochman Method from the organization's faculty. Over the course of the year, he was able to teach his students how to construct sentences and outline paragraphs.

At the end of the year, Mr. Corwin gave Mya and her classmates another prompt, to see how their writing skills had progressed. Mya's SPO and paragraph are shown in Exhibits 11.2 and 11.3.

Directions: Use the following Single-Paragraph Outline to plan a paragraph about what you liked most about the school year.

T.S. In school I liked the trip to the science barge most.

1. s.h first field trip in 3rd grade
2. power vacuum with bicycle
3. goose with eggs on board
4. plant plants.

C.S. In conclusion, this is why I like the trip to the science barge the most.

Exhibit 11.2

Directions: Please write a paragraph about what you liked most about the school year.

In school I liked the trip to the science barge most. The science barge was the first feild trip we went on in 3rd grade. We had to behave in school to go on it. On board we got to power a vacuum with a bicycle. I've always wanted to try that. Although I didn't get to ride it I was happy for my friends that did. In the area with the bicycle there was a goose with eggs!! In order to keep the eggs warm she picked out some of her feathers and moved it around. Also she would get up and turn to look somewhere else and when she did you could see the tiny eggs underneath her. At the end of the trip we got to plant plants. First, we put dirt made of coconut husk into a mixture of salt and sand (spun very fast) with the plant inside into the dirt. The salt and sand holds water for the plant! We had to mix plant food with water and give that to the plant because the sail we gave it doesn't have the nutrients it needs to survive. In conclusion, this is why I like the trip to the science barge the most.

Exhibit 11.3

Mr. Corwin realized that Mya still had a few things to learn about writing. But when he looked back at her beginning-of-the-year writing sample, he was struck by the differences he saw. Her paragraph now had a clear structure, with a topic and concluding sentence and supporting details. Her sentences were complete and didn't run on indefinitely. She was able to use transitions to connect her thoughts. And she had learned how to use subordinating conjunctions.

Mya's response to a writing prompt at the beginning of the year had provided her teacher with guidance on what skills she already had and what she needed to learn. And her end-of-year response revealed—to her and to Mr. Corwin—how far she had come in just one school year.

Don't Guess—Assess!

WHY ASSESS YOUR STUDENTS' WRITING?

- Enables you to pinpoint skills individual students have or need to acquire
- Provides information about the skills you need to focus on for your class as a whole
- Helps you set goals for individual students and your class
- Tracks the progress your students make over the course of the year

Using Writing to Monitor Learning

The strategies and activities you have read about in this book teach students writing skills and guide them to acquire knowledge on a daily basis. As you have probably noticed, they also have great value in revealing how much students are learning, not only about writing skills, but also about the material they are studying. In other words, these activities serve as **formative assessments**. They will help you to monitor your students' comprehension of material that has been taught, determine your next instructional steps, and enable you to provide explicit, effective feedback that will move students forward.

In many schools, particularly at the elementary level, students' progress in literacy is measured by periodic "benchmark" assessments designed to evaluate general comprehension skills like "finding the main idea" of a text. Studies have found that such tests are highly unreliable. In one study, about a thousand children took four different standardized measures of comprehension. Researchers found that the odds of any two tests identifying the same student as a poor reader or a high-achieving one were less than half.[1]

And because the reading passages on the tests are unrelated to topics in the curriculum, the tests also don't even attempt to assess what students have learned about any content they may have been taught. Writing activities like those described in this book can be a far more reliable and accurate measure of learning—for students, their parents, and their teachers.

Formative assessments have other advantages as well. When students get prompt and regular feedback, they have a clearer sense of what they've accomplished and what they still need to work on.

In addition, research has shown that when formative assessment is done frequently, it's one of the most effective ways to enable students to transfer information to long-term memory—a key step in learning.[2]

Here is an example of formative assessment if your class has read *Night*.[3]

DIRECTIONS: Complete the following sentence stems.

The prisoners are forced on a death march because **they have to evacuate the concentration camp.**

The prisoners are forced on a death march, but **Eliezer manages to survive.**

The prisoners are forced on a death march, so **most die from fatigue, disease, and the bitter cold weather.**

Summative assessments, which occur at the end of a unit of study, measure what learning students have gained over a period of time—at least in theory. When standardized state reading tests are used as summative assessments, they rarely serve that purpose. They usually do not measure the writing skills you have taught, and, as with standardized benchmark assessments, the content of the passages is unlikely to align to the content of the curriculum you're using. In any event, the results are generally not available until months after the tests have been administered. It makes far more sense to use summative assessments, including those that require written responses, grounded in content that has actually been taught.

Periodic Assessments to Monitor Writing Progress

In addition to using TWR activities to monitor your students' progress in learning content you have taught, you should also give periodic assessments specifically aimed at measuring their progress in acquiring writing skills.

For these kinds of assessments, provide prompts on generic topics that give you a sense of where your students are in relation to each other, what their general strengths and weaknesses are, and what your goals for writing instruction should be.

At the beginning, middle, and end of the school year, it's important to assess:

- What skills have been transferred to independent writing
- What skills your students need to acquire

You should give your students a simple prompt without providing guidance or assistance. Be sure the topic is one that your students know well enough to write about coherently. All your students should have the same prompt so that it will be easier for you to analyze their strengths and weaknesses.

A prompt can consist of a single word or a brief phrase. Some prompts we have found to be useful are:

Friends (or friendship or how to make/keep friends)

Hopes for the future

Role model

Special gift or possession

Personal goals

Favorite season

Favorite pastime

Why do we study the past?*

*For older students.

One of the skills you are evaluating is a student's ability to write a topic sentence, so avoid prompts that provide a "sentence starter." If the prompt is "a great school trip," for example, many students will start the assignment with those four words. Simple phrases such as "school trip" or "role model" make better prompts.

Alternatively, you can provide more explanation. For example, rather than simply asking students to write about "a role model," you could give them the following paragraph:

> *A role model is someone you admire for having qualities you would like to have. A role model is a person whose behavior or achievements you respect. Think about someone you consider a role model, and write about why that person is special to you. You may choose someone you know or someone you have read about. You may choose someone who is alive today or someone who is no longer here but has made a lasting impression on you.*

Another word of caution: try to avoid prompts that are apt to yield lists, such as "winning the lottery" or "my favorite things."

Many other subjects could work well as prompts, and you, as the teacher, are the best judge of what your particular students are likely to be able to write about.

You may not want to use the same prompt for all three writing assessments at the beginning, middle, and end of the school year. However, it can provide a clearer basis for comparison if you stay with the same general topic. For example:

Beginning of the year:
Write a paragraph about the best or more interesting parts of [previous grade level]. Describe at least two.

Middle of the year:
Write a paragraph about which subject is your favorite and why. Give two or three reasons.

End of the year:
Write a paragraph about the best or most interesting parts of [ending grade level]. Describe at least two.

How to Administer Beginning-, Middle-, and End-of-Year Writing Assessments

When you are administering the assessment, the first step is to **explain the purpose of the activity**. Let your students know that the assessment will help you understand where they need help to further develop their writing skills. Remind them to do their best work so you'll be able to see what they already know how to do and what they still need help with.

To get an accurate picture of what students can do independently, try not to give them any help during the assessment. If a student has difficulty spelling a word, for example, ask him to make his best guess and provide the correct spelling only if he's unable to continue. If a student just can't get started, you might have to provide her with a general suggestion or a topic sentence. **If you do need to provide students with help, be sure to note on the assessment exactly what was done with teacher support.**

Your **instructions must be explicit**. First, make it clear that students should keep their writing samples brief. If you're teaching first graders, you may want to tell them that it's fine to write just a sentence or two. Even with older Level 1 and some Level 2 students, it's best to limit the samples to a single paragraph. You'll be asking them to revise and edit their work later, and that may feel overwhelming if they've written at length.

If students have learned how to develop an SPO, be sure to remind them to complete one before writing so that you can assess their outlining skills. If Level 2 students have been taught to develop Multiple-Paragraph Outlines (TOs and MPOs), you might allow them to write up to three paragraphs—after completing an outline, of course. Be sure that students' outlines are attached to their writing samples.

Typically, these assessments will take no more than one class period to complete, but some students may take less time. **Return the assessment samples to students in the next day or two and ask them to revise and edit their work.** Tell them that the best writers often find ways to improve and correct their work and that it's important for you to see what they would like to change in their writing.

It's not necessary to have students make final copies of the assessment, unless the revised and edited version is illegible.

When the allotted time for revision and editing is up, collect the students' samples and date them. After assessing a student's work, put it in a dedicated folder so you can monitor individual progress.

How to Evaluate Beginning-, Middle-, and End-of-Year Writing Assessments

As we noted in Chapter 6, the following four criteria are generally used to assess writing quality.

STRUCTURE

- Are the sentences in the paragraph, or the paragraphs in a longer composition, arranged appropriately?

COHERENCE

- Are the sentences (and paragraphs) logically related to one another?

UNITY

- Does every sentence support the main idea of the paragraph?
- Does every paragraph support the main idea of the composition?

WELL-CONSTRUCTED SENTENCES

- Are the sentences grammatically correct and clear?
- Are there compound and complex sentences in addition to simple, active ones?
- Do the sentences begin in a variety of ways?

Judging the quality of student writing may be one of the most difficult tasks in all of educational assessment. Some aspects of writing are easy to quantify—total number of words or sentences, sentence length, spelling, or proper grammar and usage—but others are highly subjective.

Even experts have disagreed on the best way to go about measuring writing quality. "Over the years," one team of experts has written, "writing assessment research and practice has suffered from dissension at every point, on almost every feature of stimulating, producing, evaluating, and teaching writing."[4]

Several factors can interfere with the accuracy of writing assessments:

- **Decoding.** When students are asked to write in response to a written prompt, some may have difficulty decoding it.

- **Background information.** Lack of knowledge about the topic causes some students to have trouble understanding the prompt and/or producing a response.

- **Computers.** If students write their responses on computers, those who are comfortable using computers will have an advantage over those who aren't.

- **Mechanical errors.** There are questions about how much weight to give to errors in capitalization, punctuation, spelling, and grammar. Although students need to master these aspects of writing, technical mistakes can be distracting and lead teachers to overlook the progress students may have made in organizing their ideas or using complex sentence structures.

- **Handwriting.** Poor handwriting often has a negative influence on the evaluator. We'll address the subject of handwriting in more detail later in this chapter.

The **Writing Assessment Checklists** (Appendix F) can't entirely eliminate the difficulties involved in evaluating writing, but they can provide guidelines for more accurate judgments, grounded in strategies you have taught. They will tell you where each student stands and can be filled out fairly quickly.

RESOURCE

Writing Assessment Checklists
Appendix F

ASK THE EXPERTS

Although there's been disagreement among experts about the best way to evaluate students' writing, one meta-analysis of 136 studies of writing assessment came up with some recommendations.[5] They make the most sense when applied to students above third grade, when most have already acquired the basic mechanics of writing.

- Use assessments to provide students with feedback about the effectiveness of their writing.

- Teach students how to evaluate the effectiveness of their own writing.

- Monitor students' progress in writing on an ongoing basis.

The report also listed six best practices in writing assessment:

- **Allow students to use either paper or computers to write—or have them use the medium you know they're used to.** Studies have shown that students who use computers score better than those who write by hand—unless they have little experience using a computer to write, in which case they score worse.

- **Try not to judge a writing sample on the basis of the student's handwriting.**

- **Mask the students' identities when scoring papers.** Teachers may subconsciously give a student a higher or lower score depending on the quality of her previous work or her race, gender, or ethnicity. One easy way to guard against implicit bias is to have students put their names on the back of a paper rather than the front.

- **Put students' papers in random order before scoring them.** Some studies have suggested that raters' scores will vary depending on the quality of the essays they've just read. If a rater has just read a series of high-quality essays, she's more likely to give the next piece of writing she reads a lower score—and vice versa.

- **Collect multiple samples of each student's work.** The quality of a student's writing often varies with the type of composition. Some are better at writing narratives, and others may excel at argumentative or informational essays.

- **Try to ensure the reliability of your scoring.** Much of what goes into scoring a piece of writing is subjective. To control for that, schools can offer training for teachers on how to assess writing. Administrators can provide benchmark descriptions or examples for each point on a scale, have multiple teachers score each paper, and base scores on more than one writing task.

Comparative Judgment: Another Way of Assessing Writing Quality

An interesting approach to evaluating writing offers hope that the task will become easier. This method, offered through a British organization called No More Marking, is both more efficient and more reliable than standard methods. The method, called *comparative judgment*, involves having readers compare two pieces of student writing and decide which one is better. Studies have shown that when many such gut-level comparisons are aggregated, the judgments are highly consistent.[6]

At TWR partner schools, teachers may use comparative judgment to assess writing progress. Usually the judging is done within a single grade level by teachers of that grade. Student names are not visible, and judging can be done anonymously.

After judging the writing samples, teachers discuss trends they are noticing across the grade, which informs their next steps for instruction. For example, if teachers notice that many students are not beginning their paragraphs with topic sentences, they can practice using the SPO and the scaffolding activities as a whole class to reinforce this skill.

Since assessment using comparative judgment takes far less time than other methods of evaluating student writing, teachers have the opportunity to see the writing of a broader range of students than is typical with other rating methods, enabling them to gain perspective that is both deeper and wider on strengths and areas that need improvement.

No More Marking provides lots of valuable data about how students are doing. Once teachers have that data, the Hochman Method provides the specific strategies that teachers can use to address the weaknesses in student writing that it identifies.

Having Students Write in Response to What They've Read

Many teachers have their students write in response to a specific passage rather than the general prompts we have recommended. There are some benefits, but also potential pitfalls to this approach.

The Pros and the Cons

Having students write about a passage they're given simulates more closely the kind of writing students will be asked to do on state assessments toward the end of the school year. Generally, state literacy tests give students a passage to read and ask them to write in response to it, citing evidence from the text. The tests may also ask students to read two different texts and compare them.

It's important to understand that using texts as a basis for writing assessments brings its own potential problems. Students may have trouble decoding the texts, or they may lack the background knowledge that would enable them to understand them—especially if the texts don't relate to content covered in the curriculum. If that's the case, the assessment will not be accurately measuring your students' writing skills.

Handwriting Matters

One significant problem as students draft and revise their paragraphs and compositions or take tests is the poor quality of their handwriting. Although research hasn't established that using cursive confers cognitive benefits, it's clear there are other reasons to teach students how to use it. Good handwriting—including well-formed cursive—can influence a reader's evaluation of the quality of a piece of writing. In addition, students who have never learned or don't use cursive are often unable to read documents, letters, and notes written in cursive. This can prove to be a disadvantage in reading certain text and in communicating with others.[7]

Studies do indicate that it's important for children to have handwriting instruction of some kind as opposed to only learning to touch type on a computer. When students engage in the physical activity of carefully shaping letters, it increases their ability to recognize letters, promotes their recall of words, and improves their spelling accuracy.[8]

Many schools no longer focus on handwriting instruction, whether cursive or printing. That has led to random acts of capitalization as well as to the failure on the part of many students to leave enough space between words.

Maintaining Student Portfolios

It's a good idea to keep a folder or portfolio of samples of each student's work and assessments throughout the year. This collection of a student's writing can provide a dramatic reminder of the progress a student has made—progress that otherwise might be overlooked. It also provides valuable information for the teacher who has the student the following year.

To Sum Up

- When assessing student writing, be aware of the factors that can interfere with an accurate picture—such as a student's difficulty decoding or understanding the text used as a prompt and the frequency of mechanical errors.

- Administer writing assessments in response to a prompt or a text three times a year to measure students' independent writing ability.

- Assess students' ability to develop outlines.

- Assess students' ability to revise and edit their work by allowing them to do so a day or two after the assessment is administered.

- Use the Writing Assessment Checklists to record individual students' progress and that of the class as a whole.

- Use data from assessments to help set your objectives for the class as a whole and differentiate instruction to meet students' individual needs.

- Maintain a folder or portfolio of each student's work to track progress made over the year.

BOOK DISCUSSION QUESTIONS

1. What vital information is provided by assessing a student's writing?

2. Discuss the differences between formative assessments and summative assessments.

3. Enumerate the key steps for administering beginning-, middle-, and end-of-year writing assessments.

4. How can teachers be as objective as possible when evaluating writing samples?

5. Explain why handwriting instruction is important.

6. What purposes are served by keeping a portfolio or samples of each student's work and assessments?

Notes

1. J. Keenan and C. Meenan, "Test Differences in Diagnosing Reading Comprehension Deficits," *Journal of Learning Disabilities* (2014), 47(2): 125–135.

2. D. Wiliam, *Embedded Formative Assessment*, 2nd ed. (Bloomington, IN: Solution Tree Press, 2017).

3. E. Wiesel and M. Wiesel, *Night* (New York: Penguin Classics, 2004).

4. S. Graham, K. Harris, and M. Hebert, "Informing Writing: The Benefits of Formative Assessment. A Carnegie Corporation Time to Act Report" (Washington, DC: Alliance for Excellent Education, 2011), Foreword.

5. Graham et al., "Informing Writing."

6. M. Lesterhuis, R. Bouwer, T. van Daal, V. Donche, and S. De Maeyer, "Validity of Comparative Judgment Scores: How Assessors Evaluate Aspects of Text Quality When Comparing Argumentative Texts," *Frontiers in Education* 7 (13 May 2022), https://www.frontiersin.org /articles/10.3389/feduc.2022.823895/full#h8.

7. S. Randazzo, "Cursive Comes Back, Now That Kids Can't Read Grandma's Letters," *Wall Street Journal* (27 November 2023), https://www.wsj .com/us-news/education/cursive-writing-letters -school-98fe7bfa.

8. R.W. Wiley and B. Rapp, "The Effects of Handwriting Experience on Literacy Learning," *Psychological Science* (2021), 32(7): 1086–1103.

CHAPTER 12

Revolutionizing Learning

Embedding Writing Activities into Content

Throughout this book we've given you reminders that unless you're introducing a new TWR strategy, writing activities and assignments should be embedded in the content you're teaching. If you're teaching about the Aztec Empire, for example, your writing activities, including sentence-level work, should be about the Aztec Empire. When you adapt TWR strategies to your particular content, you will be drawing on and reinforcing knowledge of the material your students have been reading and discussing.

It's also far more effective to weave writing into regular instruction and embed it in curricular content than to teach it in a separate writing block. Rather than having to transfer skills they've acquired while writing about something that has nothing to do with the curriculum—a transfer that often doesn't happen—your students will be developing skills and content knowledge simultaneously. **Writing isn't just a skill. Writing instruction can also be a powerful tool for teaching content.**

Keep in mind that the *content* of TWR activities is what drives their rigor: the same strategy can challenge students at different grade levels, depending on the content. For example, if you've been teaching kindergarteners about butterflies, you might have them do a *because-but-so* activity orally on caterpillars and cocoons. If you're teaching an AP American History class, you can also give your high school students a *because-but-so* activity—but you'll have them do it in written form and focus on the effectiveness of the New Deal. The format of the exercise is the same, but the latter activity is obviously far more rigorous.

Similarly, the principles of organizing and planning Single-Paragraph Outlines (SPOs), Transition Outlines (TOs), and Multiple-Paragraph Outlines (MPOs) don't differ significantly from one grade level or ability level to another. It's the content that makes the task more challenging.

Using Strategies Concurrently

One way to have students keep practicing strategies you've already taught is to bring in several different strategies while teaching a single book or topic. This is, in fact, the optimal way to use the strategies once your students have become familiar with several of them.

The following examples illustrate how to use this approach with Level 1 and Level 2 students. In both cases, the strategies help students develop their writing or prewriting skills while simultaneously deepening their understanding of content.

Level 1 Examples

If your class has read *Henry's Freedom Box*,[1] consider the following activity:

Henry didn't know his birthday because *no one kept records of enslaved people's birthdays.*

Henry got married and had three children, but *his family was separated and sold.*

Henry survived his journey in the small crate for 27 hours. As a result, *he arrived in Philadelphia where he finally could be free.*

You could also have students develop a Single-Paragraph Outline:

T.S. _Henry's Freedom Box, a true story, has won many awards._

    1. _Richmond VA / sep from mother/ worked in factory_

    2. _marries → 3 children / family sold_

    3. _mails himself in small crate / 27 hrs._

    4. _in Philadelphia Henry a free man_

C.S. _Henry was brave and determined in spite of terrible struggles._

Level 2 Examples

If your class has been studying Sumer, Babylon, and Hammurabi, you might give them the following *because-but-so* activity—shown with possible student responses:

Hammurabi created a written code of laws because _he wanted to impose order on Babylon._

Hammurabi created a written code of laws, but _many Babylonians couldn't read them._

Hammurabi created a written code of laws, so _there was a decrease in crime._

You could also have students develop test questions about the content using expository terms:

> 1. _Explain the purpose of a written code of laws._
>
> 2. _Enumerate the reasons for creating a code of laws._
>
> 3. _Describe how social class influenced punishments._

Next, you could give your students sentence stems beginning with subordinating conjunctions and have them develop complete sentences, as in the following examples:

> If Hammurabi had not developed a written code of laws, _he would have failed to unite Babylonia._
>
> Although Sumer's city-states were defeated, _the Babylonian Empire adopted many of their ideas and practices._

If students have been introduced to SPOs, have them complete an SPO. More able students can go on to convert the outline into a paragraph.

> T.S. _Sumer, an ancient Mesopotamian civilization, is lauded for the lasting impact of its innovations._
>
> 1. _cuneiform = system of writing/maps & sci info_
> 2. _# system → basis today for measuring time_
> 3. _architectural structures (arches, columns, ramps)_
> 4. _written code of laws_
>
> C.S. _The contributions of Sumer had a major influence on later civilizations._

Using TWR Strategies to "Revolutionize" Your Materials

Most textbooks and other instructional materials provide end-of-chapter or end-of-unit comprehension questions that don't reflect TWR strategies. Usually, you'll be able to draw on your knowledge of TWR's method to make those activities more powerful and reinforce the writing instruction you've been providing. Here are some Level 1 and 2 examples.

Level 1 Examples

If your class has read *The Cricket in Times Square*,[2] they may have been asked to complete an activity like this one:

Original Activity

DIRECTIONS: Answer the following questions.

1. Why was Chester worried about being in New York City? _____

   _____

2. What did Tucker do to make him feel better? _____

   _____

3. Where did Tucker take Chester? _____

   _____

Instead, students can be asked to complete the following revolutionized activity:

Revolutionized Activity

DIRECTIONS: Complete the sentences using *because*, *but*, and *so*.

Chester was worried about being in New York City because _____

_____

Chester was worried about being in New York City, but _____

_____

Chester was worried about being in New York City, so _____

_____

If your class has been learning about rainforest animals and plants, they may have been asked to complete an activity like this one:

Original Activity

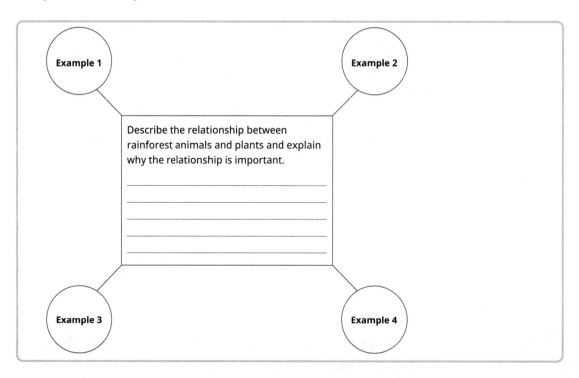

Instead, students can be asked to complete the following revolutionized activity:

Revolutionized Activity

DIRECTIONS: Using key words and phrases, write details for the given topic sentence.

T.S. *Rainforest animals and plants interact in many ways that are important for maintaining a balanced ecosystem.*

1. ....

2. ....

3. ....

4. ....

Level 2 Example

After studying different types of subatomic particles, students were asked the following questions:

DIRECTIONS: Answer the following questions.

1. What types of subatomic particles does an atom contain?_____

   _____

2. Why are electrons attracted to positive objects? _____

   _____

3. How do protons behave? _____

   _____

4. What does neutral mean? _____

   _____

The teacher "revolutionized" the questions in the following way:

DIRECTIONS: Complete the second sentence following the transition word.

1. An atom contains three types of subatomic particles. Specifically, _____

   _____

2. Electrons have a negative charge. As a result, _____

   _____

3. Protons repel each other. However, _____

   _____

4. The neutron is neutral. In other words, _____

   _____

How to Use TWR to Differentiate Your Instruction

Most classrooms encompass a range of student ability—sometimes a wide range. One of the most challenging aspects of teaching is accommodating all of those levels without going over some students' heads while boring others.

Keep an Eye Out for Struggling Students

As we've demonstrated throughout this book, TWR activities easily lend themselves to differentiation. It's not necessary to come up with a completely different version of the activities or use different content for students of varying abilities—in fact, that approach risks leaving struggling students permanently behind. What's important is that you have a clear idea of what students are supposed to be learning and activities that will give you a good sense of whether all students have mastered it.[3]

Modify the Same Strategy for Students at Different Levels

We've described throughout this book how you can differentiate many of the strategies as we've introduced them. But to recap, here are some examples:

- **Sentence expansion.** Ask fewer question words of students who are having difficulty. For example, give all students a kernel such as "They rebelled," but ask some students *who*, *when*, *why*, and *where* while asking others only *who* and *when*.

- **Because-but-so.** Give all students the same stem—for example, "The British invaded the colonies"—but ask some students to provide complete sentences for all three conjunctions while asking others to write a sentence for only one or two conjunctions.

- **Appositives.** Ask all students to supply an appositive to describe a person, place, or thing, but give some students a list of words and phrases to choose from.

- **Sentence-combining.** Give all students a group of short sentences to combine into one longer one, but provide some students with fewer sentences to combine.

- **Unelaborated paragraph revision.** Give all students the same bare-bones paragraph, but give some students fewer instructions on how to revise it. For example, you might give some students a list of six things to do and limit others to only one or two, such as "Improve T.S. and C.S."

- **SPOs.** Have all students complete an SPO, but provide some students with the topic or the concluding sentence while asking others to come up with those sentences independently. You might also require some students to use only key words and phrases for their notes on the dotted lines, while others use abbreviations and symbols as well.

- **TOs or MPOs.** Have all students complete a TO or MPO, but provide some students with the categories they'll need to organize their paragraphs while having others come up with their own categories.

- **MPOs.** When students are converting an MPO into a draft, you can also provide some students with the general or specific statements to include in their introduction and conclusion.

To Sum Up

- By weaving TWR activities into regular instruction and embedding them in curricular content, you'll be able to use writing instruction as a powerful teaching tool.

- Use several strategies concurrently while teaching any topic.

- Differentiate TWR activities for students who are struggling or are racing ahead, without altering the basic form of the activity or using different content.

- Transform open-ended questions in your instructional materials into more focused activities using strategies from The Writing Revolution.

BOOK DISCUSSION QUESTIONS

1. Choose a topic (e.g., a science topic, book chapter, current event) and devise activities on that topic for your grade level using: *because*, *but*, and *so*; sentence expansion; subordinating conjunctions; and an SPO, TO, or MPO.

2. Why do the TWR strategies assess student comprehension more accurately than typical end-of-unit textbook questions?

Notes

1. E. Levine, *Henry's Freedom Box* (New York: Scholastic Press, 2007).

2. G. Selden, *The Cricket in Times Square* (New York: Farrar, Straus and Cudahy, 1960).

3. K. Marshall, "Rethinking Differentiation—Using Teachers' Time Most Effectively," *Kappan* (2016, September): 8–13.

CHAPTER 13

Putting the Method into Practice

Leave No Strategy Behind

Throughout this book, we present TWR strategies in a linear fashion. But in practice, you should **not** aim to get all students to master a particular strategy and then move on, leaving that strategy behind. Since content and writing skills are so interconnected, "mastery" will depend as much on the content you're teaching as on any particular strategy. In addition, bringing back strategies you've already covered will help remind students to use them in their writing.

As a result, it's best to keep moving through your curricular sequence, continuously bringing previously taught strategies into your instruction and using them alongside others that you're introducing. As you move along, you can always modify strategies for students who are struggling.

Laying a Strong Foundation: Sentence-Level Activities

As we pointed out in Chapter 2, sentences are the foundation for all writing. If students haven't learned to write a clear, coherent sentence, they'll never be able to write a clear, coherent paragraph or essay. And sentence-level activities can be just as challenging for students as lengthier writing assignments—sometimes even more challenging. Whether students are writing a sentence, paragraph, or composition, the content drives the rigor.

All students, regardless of their grade or ability level, need to practice crafting various kinds of sentences. Throughout this book, you've seen multiple examples of TWR sentence activities for all levels and in all subjects.

If you're teaching beginning writers, English language learners, students with learning disabilities, or the many students who write the way they speak, the first step is to make sure they understand what a sentence is. As we noted in Chapter 1, simply getting them to repeat an abstract definition, such as "a sentence has a subject and predicate and expressses a complete thought," is unlikely to be enough. They will need ample practice in distinguishing between complete sentences and fragments—and turning fragments into complete sentences. They'll also need practice in correcting run-on sentences.

Even if your students are more proficient writers, it is still important to introduce them to the whole range of TWR sentence strategies. The difference is that your pace can be faster. Level 2 students can do much of their sentence-level work in the context of expanding unelaborated paragraphs and improving their own writing in response to your specific feedback as they draft, revise, and edit. These students will also benefit from sentence activities used as comprehension checks on tests, quizzes, and exit slips.

Generally, all students, regardless of grade level, should practice at least some sentence activities daily, orally and in writing, whether through the kinds of checks we just listed or through do-now activities, stop-and-jots, turn-and-talks, or homework. When students are ready to develop outlines, continue to include regular practice with sentences in your lessons. As students start converting their outlines into drafts, they will need to use what they've learned from the sentence activities as tools for revision.

Breaking Down the Writing Process

To make writing manageable for your students, break down the process into four basic steps—outlining, drafting, revising and editing, and final copy—as shown here.

1. Outlining ★   3. Revising/editing ★
2. Drafting   4. Final copy

Most instructional time should be spent on Steps 1 and 3 (hence the red stars), outlining and revising and editing the draft. Lessons can end after Steps 1 or 3—but not after Step 2.

Always have your students revise and edit a draft, whether or not they go on to turn it into a final copy.

The outlining and revising/editing stages need to be broken down into a number of smaller components—first in the context of paragraphs, and later in the context of compositions.

Don't skip any of the scaffolding steps; just speed up your rate for more proficient students. Make sure that all students have had practice identifying and constructing topic sentences before you ask them to create one for an SPO.

It's important to provide your students with plenty of demonstrations and practice to get them to the point where they'll be able to craft varied sentences; outline and write cohesive, coherent paragraphs and compositions; and revise their writing effectively. You may be tempted to let your students just plunge into a piece of writing without going through all these steps. After all, don't experienced writers do that? The answer is that some do and many don't. Especially for more analytical and longer forms of writing—books, for example—many accomplished writers find outlining to be essential, and **all** professional writers take time to revise.

Beyond that, experienced, competent writers are able to juggle numerous factors simultaneously so that composing becomes a recursive process. They may fine-tune their sentences as they go, replacing a word here and omitting a comma there. They may repeatedly shift the order of paragraphs and ideas. But these writers can draw on ample writing experience as well as deep knowledge of both written language and their topic. They may be equipped to draft, revise, and even plan their writing more or less simultaneously.

The great majority of the students we work with, however, lack both that kind of experience and that level of knowledge. They need to approach the task one step at a time, while continuing to practice previously learned strategies, in order to produce an effective piece of writing. As with sentence activities, even after your students have become experienced at creating outlines and revising drafts, it's important to keep practicing the scaffolding activities that helped them arrive at that point.

Pacing the Strategies: Using Your Judgment

Teachers often ask questions like: "How long should we keep teaching fragments?" "When can we start the Single-Paragraph Outline?" "Should I stay with sentence expansion until I think the students have mastered it?" "How do we know when to start writing introductions?"

We understand that teachers want clear guidelines about the pacing of the strategies and at what point they should move on to the next one. We wish we could provide them with straightforward answers, but writing instruction doesn't work like that. There's no one-size-fits-all approach. You will need to determine where your students are at the outset, what they need, and how fast they are able to move through the sequence of strategies. The beginning-of-the-year writing assessment we discussed in Chapter 11 will help you determine your instructional priorities and objectives, and later formative assessments will guide you to modify them.

When deciding how long to spend on any one TWR strategy or activity, you have to exercise your own judgment about your students' oral and written language abilities. Among the factors to consider are the following:

- Performance on beginning- and middle-of-year assessments
- The grade level at which they were introduced to TWR strategies
- Their familiarity with the conventions of English grammar
- Their sense of what they need to include, omit, or revise in their writing so that it's understandable to a reader

In addition—as we noted previously—writing, more than any other task, taxes a student's working memory and executive functions. Remember that there's a limit to how many things we can hold in our working memory. If your students are still struggling with the mechanics of writing—handwriting, spelling, usage, and so on—they won't have the space in working memory to simultaneously think about higher-level aspects such as purpose, meaning, audience, word choice, and syntax. Before they can address those considerations in depth and without guidance, their lower-level skills will need to have reached a point where the mechanics are not absorbing most of their attention.

Sequence of Activities through the Grades

The sequence on the following pages assumes that students are being introduced to the Hochman Method in the given grade level(s). If that's not the case for your students, you'll need to adjust accordingly. However, don't assume that simply because students are in ninth or tenth grade, they already understand the concept of a sentence or how to plan and construct an effective paragraph. We know from our experience that many high school students have yet to acquire these skills.

All students who are being introduced to the method for the first time, no matter their grade level, should begin with sentence-level strategies and activities and proceed through the sequence in order.

It is not necessary for students to demonstrate mastery of every sentence strategy before moving on. Once they have been introduced to a few basic strategies, they can learn how to develop simple Single-Paragraph Outlines. They can also use those strategies to convert the words and phrases they've written on their outlines into sentences in a paragraph.

The sequence is recursive. The activities for each of the following grades incorporate those introduced in all previous grades. They should be a regular part of instruction for middle and high school students, including both those who are familiar with the strategies and those who are new to the method. Always remember that when they're embedded in the content of the curriculum, these activities not only teach writing, but also are a powerful method of teaching subject matter.

Although this book is primarily a resource for grades 3–12, we thought it would be helpful to include what a K–2 sequence would look like as a foundation for the grades that follow.

Grades K–2

Grade Level	Sentences	Note-Taking	SPO and Paragraph	Revising and Editing	Summaries	TO, MPO, and Compositions
K	All of these activities should be practiced orally. Practice sentence expansion (*when, where, why*). Use the basic conjunctions *because* and *but*. Identify sentence types (statements and questions). Change fragments to sentences. Use correct capitalization and end punctuation. Complete sentence stems beginning with the subordinating conjunctions *after* and *before*.			All of these activities should be practiced orally. Brainstorm more vivid or specific vocabulary for vague or overused words (e.g., *fun, good*).		

Grade Level	Sentences	Note-Taking	SPO and Paragraph	Revising and Editing	Summaries	TO, MPO, and Compositions
1	**Include grade K activities plus:** Practice sentence expansion (*who*).* Identify sentence types (commands, exclamations). Develop questions.* Add the subordinating conjunctions *if* and *when*.* ***Initially, practice these activities orally.**		Practice creating SPOs and paragraphs as a whole class.	**Continue grade K activities.**		

Grade Level	Sentences	Note-Taking	SPO and Paragraph	Revising and Editing	Summaries	TO, MPO, and Compositions
2	Include all grade K and 1 activities plus: Practice sentence expansion with all question words. Use the basic conjunctions *because, but,* and *so.* Correct run-ons. Unscramble sentences with five or six words. Add the subordinating conjunctions *Even though, Whenever,* and *Although.* Complete a sentence beginning with an illustration transition that follows a statement (e.g., *Dogs make good pets. For example _____.*) Combine two to three sentences.		Include all grade 1 activities plus: Create a narrative SPO as a whole class using time and sequence transitions. Brainstorm details (written as key words and phrases) for a given topic sentence and fill in an SPO as a whole class (narrative and expository text structures). Distinguish topic sentences from detail sentences. Generate a topic sentence from given detail sentences using the sentence types. Select relevant details from a list to support a given topic sentence.	Include all grade K and 1 activities plus: Revise an unelaborated paragraph with the entire class using explicit directions.		

Grade Level	Sentences	Note-Taking	SPO and Paragraph	Revising and Editing	Summaries	TO, MPO, and Compositions
3	Change fragments to sentences. Unscramble sentences. Use correct capitalization and punctuation. Differentiate between sentence types. Practice sentence expansion. Develop questions about content. Correct run-ons. Use the basic conjunctions *because, but,* and *so.* Use the subordinating conjunctions *After, Before, If, When, Even though, Whenever, Although,* and *Since.* Combine two or three sentences. Apply transitions: time and sequence 1A, conclusion, and illustration. Practice appositives (introduce at the middle or toward the end of the year).	Write key words, phrases, and common abbreviations on dotted lines. Mid-year: introduce symbols (/, =, →, +).	Create SPOs for the following text structures as a whole class: • narrative • opinion • expository Use SPO scaffolding activities: • Create an SPO with the whole class. • Distinguish a T.S. from details. • Identify the T.S. and sequence details. • Given a T.S., select relevant details and eliminate irrelevant detail(s) from a list or SPO. • Given a T.S., generate details. • Practice the two ways (or three if introduced to appositives) of writing a T.S. or C.S. • Given topic/prompt, generate a T.S. • Given a T.S. and details, generate a C.S. • Given a topic/prompt, construct an SPO independently. Draft a paragraph based on an SPO.	Brainstorm more vivid or specific vocabulary for vague or overused words. Brainstorm more specific replacements for vague words. Improve given topic and concluding sentences. Revise unelaborated paragraphs (first as a class and then in pairs or small groups) given explicit instructions. Revise a draft given explicit feedback. Proofread and edit for commas, capitalization, punctuation, fragments, run-ons, and spelling errors.		

Grade Level	Sentences	Note-Taking	SPO and Paragraph	Revising and Editing	Summaries	TO, MPO, and Compositions
4	Include grade 3 activities plus: Add the subordinating conjunctions *While* and *Unless*. Combine three or four sentences. Add transitions: time and sequence 1B, change of direction, and emphases.	Include grade 3 activities plus: Introduce other symbols.	Include grade 3 activities plus: Create SPOs for the following text structures: • problem/solution • cause/effect Create pro SPOs and con SPOs.	Include grade 3 activities plus: Revise unelaborated paragraphs independently given explicit directions. Check for verb tense and number agreement. Use sentence strategies when revising (transitions, appositives, subordinating conjunctions, sentence expansion, etc.). Use Revise and Edit Checklist for drafts.	Summary Sentence SPO Summary	Introduce a TO as a whole class. Develop a thesis statement about the topic as a whole class for a TO. Develop a concluding statement as a whole class for a TO. Draft a composition from a TO. Revise and edit a composition.

Grade Level	Sentences	Note-Taking	SPO and Paragraph	Revising and Editing	Summaries	TO, MPO, and Compositions
5	Include all grade 3 and 4 activities.	Include all grade 3 and 4 activities.	Include all grade 3 and 4 activities.	Include all grade 3 and 4 activities plus: Cite evidence from text using illustration transitions and direct or paraphrased quotations. Revise unelaborated paragraphs independently given general directions.	Include all grade 4 activities.	Include all grade 4 activities plus: Develop a neutral pro/con three-paragraph TO and composition. Create TOs for these text structures: • narrative • problem/solution • compare and contrast • cause/effect

Grades 6–8

Grade Level	Sentences	Note-Taking	SPO and Paragraph	Revising and Editing	Summaries	TO, MPO, and Compositions
6	Use the following strategies: • Change fragments to sentences. • Unscramble sentences. • Differentiate between sentence types. • Practice sentence expansion. • Develop questions. • Use the basic conjunctions *because, but,* and *so.* • Use the subordinating conjunctions *After, Before, If, When, Even though, Whenever, Although, Since, While,* and *Unless.* • Combine three to five sentences. • Use transitions. • Use appositives.	Write key words, phrases, common abbreviations, and symbols on dotted lines.	Create SPOs for the following text structures: • narrative • opinion • problem/solution • cause/effect Create separate pro SPOs and con SPOs. Use SPO scaffolding activities: • Create an SPO as a whole class. • Distinguish a T.S. from details. • Identify T.S. and sequence details. • Given a T.S., select relevant details from a list. • Eliminate irrelevant detail(s) from a list or SPO. • Given a T.S., generate details. • Practice the three strategies for writing a T.S. or C.S. • Given a topic/prompt, generate a T.S. • Given a T.S. and details, generate a C.S. • Given a topic/prompt, construct an SPO independently. Draft a paragraph based on an SPO.	Use specific and varied vocabulary for overused or vague words. Improve a given topic and concluding sentences using the three strategies. Revise unelaborated paragraphs when given explicit instructions, and later, general instructions. Revise a draft when given explicit instructions, and later, general instructions. Proofread and edit for commas, capitalization, punctuation, fragments, run-ons, and spelling errors. Check for verb tense and number agreement. Use sentence strategies when revising (e.g., transitions, appositives, basic and subordinating conjunctions, sentence expansion). Cite evidence from text using illustration transitions and direct or paraphrased quotations. Use Revise and Edit Checklist to check drafts.	Summary Sentence SPO Summary	Develop a thesis statement for TO as a whole class. Create a TO as a whole class. Given a thesis statement, fill in Main Idea boxes. Given a thesis statement, fill in Details boxes in note form. Develop a draft from a TO. Revise and edit a draft based on a TO. Create a TO independently. Create TOs for the following text structures: • narrative • problem/solution • compare and contrast • cause/effect Develop a neutral pro/con three- or four-paragraph TO and composition.

Grades 7 and 8

Students should continue to practice all the sentence, note-taking, paragraph (SPO), revision, and summary activities introduced in grade 6.

Students should be introduced to the MPO and the activities that follow. Students who are not ready for the MPO can continue to use the TO but with the same topic as the rest of the class.

- Create an MPO as a whole class.

- Introduce the general, specific, and thesis statement format for introductions for MPOs.

- Introduce the thesis, specific, and general statement format for conclusions for MPOs.

- Practice writing a plan of development for some MPOs.

- Develop a draft from an MPO.

- Write introductions and conclusions independently for compositions from an MPO.

- Revise and edit drafts based on MPOs.

- Create MPOs for the following text structures:

  ▶ narrative
  ▶ problem/solution
  ▶ compare and contrast
  ▶ cause/effect
  ▶ pro/con

- Given a debatable topic, research both sides and develop a thesis statement for a pro/con essay.

- Sequence claims and counterclaims for a pro/con composition.

- Draft, revise, and edit a pro/con composition from an MPO.

Grades 9–12

Grade Level	Sentences	Note-Taking	SPO and Paragraph	Revising and Editing	Summaries	MPO and Compositions
9 and 10	Change fragments to sentences.	Write key words, phrases, common abbreviat ons, and symbols on dotted lines.	Create SPOs for these text structures: • narrative • problem/solution • cause/effect	Brainstorm more vivid or specific vocabulary for overused or vague words.	Summary Sentence SPO Summary	*Use the TO for students not ready for the MPO.*
	Unscramble sentences.		Create separate pro SPOs and con SPOs.	Improve given topic and concluding sentences.		Create an MPO as a whole class.
	Use correct capitalization and punctuation.		Use SPO scaffolding activities:	Revise unelaborated paragraphs when given explicit and general instructions.		Introduce the general, specific, and thesis statement format for introductions for MPOs.
	Differentiate between sentence types.		• Create an SPO as a whole class. • Distinguish a T.S. from details.	Revise a draft when given explicit and general instructions.		Introduce the thesis, specific, and general statement format for conclusions for MPOs.
	Practice sentence expansion.		• Identify a T.S. and sequence details.	Proofread and edit for correct capitalization and punctuation.		Write introductions and conclusions independently for compositions from an MPO.
	Develop questions.		• Given a T.S., select relevant details from a list.	Check for verb tense and number agreement.		Develop a composition from an MPO.
	Correct run-ons.		• Eliminate irrelevant detail(s) from a list or SPO.	Use sentence strategies when revising (e.g., transitions, appositives, subordinating conjunctions, sentence expansion).		Create MPOs for these text structures:
	Use the basic conjunctions *because, but,* and *so.*		• Given a T.S., generate details.			• narrative • problem/solution • compare and contrast • cause/effect
	Use the subordinating conjunctions *After, Before, If, When, Even though, Whenever, Although, Since, While,* and *Unless.*		• Practice the three strategies for writing a T.S. or C.S. • Given a topic/prompt, generate a T.S. • Given a T.S. and details, generate C.S.	Cite evidence from text using illustration transitions and direct or paraphrased quotations.		Given a debatable topic, research both sides and develop a thesis statement for an argumentative essay.
	Combine three to five sentences.		• Given a topic/prompt, construct an SPO independently.	Use the Revise and Edit Checklist to check drafts.		Sequence claims and counterclaims for an argumentative composition.
	Use transitions. Use appositives.		Develop a paragraph based on an SPO.			Develop an argumentative composition from an

Grades 11 and 12

Students should continue to practice all the sentence, note-taking, paragraph (SPO), revision, summary, and composition (MPO) activities introduced in grades 9 and 10. Remember that the rigor of the activities is driven by the content.

In addition, students should be introduced to the research paper activities that follow.

The entire process for creating a research paper should first be modeled by the teacher and practiced as a whole class. Begin with a biographical model.

PART 1: BACKGROUND ARTICLE, SOURCES, AND RESEARCH PLAN

- Read and annotate background article.
- Gather primary and secondary sources from academic databases.
- Underline key words and phrases in sources.
- Develop Works Cited page.
- Develop research plan and thesis statement.
- Take notes based on sources on index cards.
- Sequence index cards based on research plan.

PART 2: PREPARE EXPANDED MPO ACCORDING TO RESEARCH PLAN

- Use notes from index cards to develop details for MPO.
- Draft research paper introduction.
- Convert the MPO into a research paper.

Practice the research paper process for the following models:

1. Biographical
2. Significant event
3. Problem or issue
4. Argumentative
5. Compare and contrast

Pacing Guides

Pacing guides displaying the preceding activities in the context of an academic year can be found on the Book Resources website.

TWR pacing guides are meant to be fluid. Sometimes you'll quicken the pace and at other times you'll need to backtrack. Bear in mind that your pace will be determined by your students' skill level, not their grade level. If you're teaching at the middle or high school level, you may be able to proceed through the sequence of strategies more rapidly than a teacher whose students are in the early elementary grades. But that may not be the case if your students are still learning English, have language-based learning disabilities, or face other challenges.

More than a Writing Method: Using TWR to Advance Your Students' Thinking

TWR isn't just a method of teaching writing—it's a method of teaching. It may be different from what you're used to, and it may take some adjustment. But teachers have told us that they quickly become comfortable with the method. Soon they are able to integrate it into all of their instruction: presenting information, asking questions, checking comprehension, and setting goals. They use it routinely because they see it's producing dramatic improvements not only in their students' writing but also in students' mastery of content, analytical abilities, reading comprehension, and speaking skills.

You're more likely to see these results if other teachers in your school are implementing the Hochman Method at the same time and in as many subjects as possible. Ideally, you'll be collaborating with these other teachers, coordinating your pacing, and sharing observations and ideas.

But even if you're just working on your own, you can have a significant impact on your students' writing skills and their learning in general. If you provide your students with step-by-step strategies that improve their writing and thinking and expand their knowledge—and have them practice the strategies frequently and consistently—you'll be providing them with a precious gift that could well change the trajectory of their lives.

To Sum Up

- Continue using TWR strategies that you have already taught alongside new ones that you are introducing.

- All students, regardless of grade or ability level, should begin with TWR sentence-level activities and practice all of the scaffolding steps that lead to creating outlines.

- To decide how long to spend on a particular TWR strategy or set of activities, use your own judgment about your particular students' needs and abilities.

- Use TWR's pacing guides, in combination with beginning-of-the-year assessments, to determine goals for the year.

- Note that the pacing guide for each grade incorporates all TWR activities described as having been introduced in previous grades.

Appendixes

As a reminder, you'll also find additional resources, including customizable templates, sample activities, posters, and sample pacing guides, at www.thewritingrevolution.org/resources/book-resources.

A. Expository Writing Terms

B. Abbreviations and Symbols

C. Transition Words and Phrases

D. Proofreading Symbols

E. Student Revise and Edit Checklist

F. Writing Assessment Checklists

G. Single-Paragraph Outline

H. Single-Paragraph Outline (Book Report)

I. Summary Sentence

J. Pre-Transition Outline (2 Paragraphs)

K. Pre-Transition Outline (3 Paragraphs)

L. Transition Outline (3 Paragraphs)

M. Transition Outline (4 Paragraphs)

N. Transition Outline (5 Paragraphs)

O. Multiple-Paragraph Outline (3 Paragraphs)

P. Multiple-Paragraph Outline (4 Paragraphs)

Q. Multiple-Paragraph Outline (5 Paragraphs)

R. Multiple-Paragraph Outline (Book Report)

A. Expository Writing Terms

ANALYZE
Tell about the main ideas or specific points, how they are related, and why they are important.

COMMENT
Discuss, criticize, or explain the subject.

COMPARE
Describe how things are alike.

CONTRAST
Describe how things are different.

CRITICIZE
Evaluate on the basis of strengths and weaknesses.

DEFINE
Give the meaning of a word or concept.

DESCRIBE
Present a word picture of a thing, person, situation, or series of events. Use details that include the five senses: seeing, hearing, smelling, touching, and tasting.

DISCUSS
Present ideas or opinions about or consider from various points of view.

ENUMERATE
Name or list specified points, such as main ideas or steps in a sequence, one by one.

EVALUATE
Give your own judgment or expert opinion of how important an idea is; explain strengths and weaknesses, advantages, and limitations.

EXPLAIN
Make clear; interpret.

ILLUSTRATE
Explain by giving examples.

INTERPRET
Give the meaning by using examples, ideas, or opinions.

JUSTIFY
Present good reasons why you think an idea is important; present facts to support a position.

RELATE
Describe how things are connected or how one thing can cause another.

STATE
Describe as clearly as possible.

SUMMARIZE
Sum up; present main points briefly.

TRACE
Follow the progress or history of an idea.

B. Abbreviations and Symbols

Abbreviations

am or pm	before or after noon	lg	large
amt	amount	max	maximum
asap	as soon as possible	min	minimum
b/4	before	nat'l	national
b/c	because	p., pp.	page, pages
C.S.	concluding sentence	re:	regarding
ch	chapter	S	specific statement
cont'd	continued	sm	small
e.g. or ex.	for example	T	thesis statement
esp.	especially	T.S.	topic sentence
etc.	et cetera: and so forth	vs.	versus
G	general statement	w/	with
gov't	government	w/in	within
i.e.	in other words	w/o	without

addresses	(Ave., St.)	numbers	(four = 4)
days	(Mon., Tue., Wed., etc.)	states or countries	(NY, US)
measurements	(qt., ft., lb. tsp.)	titles	(Ms., Mrs., Mr., Dr.)
months	(Jan., Feb., Mar., etc.)		

Symbols

/	comma or period	< or >	less than or more than
=	means that	%	percent
+ or &	and	@	at
→	results in	$	money
*	important	↑ or ↓	increase or decrease
#	number	¶	paragraph

C. Transition Words and Phrases

1A: Time and Sequence	1B: Time and Sequence	2: Conclusion
first	initially	in conclusion
second	previously	to conclude
last	soon	in closing
then	later on	in summary
next	at last	clearly
finally	additionally	as a result*
also	currently	consequently*
in addition	earlier	finally
before**	meanwhile	therefore*
later	during**	thus*
after	simultaneously	in the end
	furthermore	ultimately

3. Illustration	4. Change of Direction	5. Emphasis
for example	but	in addition
for instance	however	in particular
such as	even though**	certainly
specifically	in contrast	obviously
as an illustration	otherwise	above all
to illustrate	on the other hand	most important
in particular	although**	primarily
particularly	yet	particularly
	instead	moreover
	on the contrary	notably
		keep in mind

*Examples of cause/effect transitions; see the section "Conclusion Transitions" for more information.

**These transitions need to be followed by a phrase or begin a dependent clause.

D. Proofreading Symbols

Symbol	Meaning
⋀	Insert
⊙	Insert period
⋀	Insert comma
⋁	Insert apostrophe
#	Insert space
¶	New paragraph
no ¶	No new paragraph
◯	Close up the space
b cap	Capitalize
Bℓc	Make lowercase (small letter)
ℓ	Delete
rwd.	Reword
⟵	Move according to arrow direction
ei̯tr	Transpose
[	Move to the left
]	Move to the right
⋀	Add a letter

E. Student Revise and Edit Checklist

DOES YOUR DRAFT FOLLOW YOUR OUTLINE?

1. Is your topic sentence (or thesis statement) clearly stated? _____

2. Did you use one of the three strategies for your topic sentence? _____

3. Are the supporting details in the best sequence? _____

4. Do the supporting details support your topic sentence? _____

5. Is your concluding sentence (or conclusion paragraph) too close to repeating your topic sentence (or introductory paragraph?) _____

6. TO AND MPO: Do all Main Idea boxes support your thesis statement? _____

CAN YOU IMPROVE YOUR SENTENCES?

1. Did you use different types of sentences? _____

2. Did you use subordinating conjunctions? _____

3. Did you use *but*, *because*, or *so*? _____

4. Are there sentences that should be combined? _____

5. Are there sentences that should be expanded? _____

6. Did you use transitions? _____

7. Are your word choices vivid? _____

8. Are your word choices accurate? _____

DOES YOUR DRAFT CONTAIN ERRORS?

1. Are there run-on sentences? _____

2. Are there sentence fragments? _____

3. Are there spelling errors? _____

4. Is your punctuation correct? _____

5. Have you capitalized words correctly? _____

6. Have you checked tense and number agreement? _____

7. Are any of your words, phrases, or ideas repetitive? _____

8. Are any of your words, phrases, or ideas irrelevant? _____

F. Writing Assessment Checklists

Writing Assessment Checklist

Single-Paragraph Outline (SPO)

Student: _____ Date: _____

Grade: _____

Criteria	Yes	Developing	No	Comments
Developed topic sentence using one of the three strategies (check strategy used): ☐ sentence type ☐ subordinating conjunction ☐ appositive				
Wrote details in note form				
Sequenced details correctly				
Included 3–4 supporting details				
Wrote concluding sentence using one of the three strategies (check strategy used): ☐ sentence type ☐ subordinating conjunction ☐ appositive				

Writing Assessment Checklist

Paragraph (From SPO)

Student: _____ Date: _____

Grade: _____

Criteria	Yes	Developing	No	Comments
Paragraph follows outline				
Paragraph has a topic sentence				
Each sentence supports topic sentence				
Used sentence strategies (check appropriate boxes): ☐ sentence expansion ☐ because, but, so ☐ subordinating conjunctions ☐ appositives ☐ transitions				
Paragraph has a concluding sentence				
Edited for (check appropriate boxes): ☐ fragments/run-ons ☐ spelling ☐ capitalization ☐ tense agreement ☐ number agreement ☐ repetition ☐ irrelevant information				
Paragraph includes concluding sentence				

Writing Assessment Checklist

Transition Outline (TO)

Student: _____ Date: _____

Grade: _____

Criteria	Yes	Developing	No	Comments
Developed thesis statement				
Wrote categories for main idea column				
Wrote details in note form				
Sequenced details correctly				
Included at least 3 supporting details				
Developed a concluding statement				

Writing Assessment Checklist

Composition (From TO)

Student: _____   Date: _____

Grade: _____

Criteria	Yes	Developing	No	Comments
Composition follows outline				
Composition includes thesis statement				
Each paragraph has a topic sentence				
Each paragraph supports thesis statement				
Used a variety of sentence strategies including: ☐ sentence expansion ☐ basic and subordinating conjunctions ☐ appositives				
Used transitions correctly				
Composition includes concluding statement				
Edited for: ☐ fragments/run-ons ☐ spelling ☐ capitalization ☐ tense agreement ☐ number agreement ☐ repetition ☐ irrelevant information				

Writing Assessment Checklist

Multiple-Paragraph Outline (MPO)

Student: _____   Date: _____

Grade: _____

Criteria	Yes	Developing	No	Comments
Developed thesis statement				
Wrote G, S, T and T, S, G for intro and conclusion				
Developed categories for main idea column				
Sequenced categories correctly				
Wrote details in note form				
Sequenced details correctly				
Included at least 3–4 supporting details				

Writing Assessment Checklist

Composition (From MPO)

Student: _____   Date: _____

Grade: _____

Criteria	Yes	Developing	No	Comments
Composition follows outline				
Each paragraph has a topic sentence				
Each paragraph supports thesis statement				
Used sentence strategies (check appropriate boxes): ☐ sentence expansion ☐ basic and subordinating conjunctions ☐ appositives				
Used transitions correctly				
Composed effective introduction: ☐ general statement ☐ specific statement ☐ thesis statement				
Composed effective conclusion: ☐ rephrased thesis statement ☐ specific statement ☐ general statement				
Edited for (check appropriate boxes): ☐ fragments ☐ run-ons ☐ spelling ☐ capitalization ☐ tense agreement ☐ number agreement ☐ repetition				

THE WRITING REVOLUTION®

G. Single-Paragraph Outline

NAME: _____ DATE: _____

T.S. _____

_____

_____

1. ....

2. ....

3. ....

4. ....

C.S. _____

_____

_____

H. Single-Paragraph Outline

(Book Report)

NAME: _____ DATE: _____

T.S. (INCLUDE TITLE AND AUTHOR): _____

_____

_____

BOOK SUMMARY:

1. ....

2. ....

3. ....

4. ....

C.S. (OPINION AND RECOMMENDED AUDIENCE): _____

_____

_____

THE WRITING REVOLUTION

I. Summary Sentence

NAME: _____ DATE: _____

WHO/WHAT? ....

(DID/WILL DO) WHAT? ....

WHEN? ....

WHERE? ....

WHY? ....

HOW? ....

SUMMARY SENTENCE

_____

_____

_____

J. Pre-Transition Outline (PTO)

(2 Paragraphs)

NAME: _____ DATE: _____

TOPIC: _____

THESIS STATEMENT: _____

_____

T.S. _____

_____

    1. ....

    2. ....

    3. ....

    (4.) ....

T.S. _____

_____

    1. ....

    2. ....

    3. ....

    (4.) ....

CONCLUDING STATEMENT: _____

_____

K. Pre-Transition Outline (PTO)

(3 Paragraphs)

NAME: _____ DATE: _____

TOPIC: _____

THESIS STATEMENT: _____

_____

T.S. _____

_____

    1. ....

    2. ....

    3. ....

    (4.) ....

T.S. _____

_____

    1. ....

    2. ....

    3. ....

    (4.) ....

T.S. _____

_____

    1. ....

    2. ....

    3. ....

    (4.) ....

CONCLUDING STATEMENT: _____

_____

L. Transition Outline (TO)

(3 Paragraphs)

NAME: _____ DATE: _____

TOPIC: _____

THESIS STATEMENT: _____

_____

Main Idea	Details
¶ 1	....
¶ 2	....
¶ 3	....

CONCLUDING STATEMENT: _____

_____

Copyright © 2024 The Writing Revolution

M. Transition Outline (TO)
(4 Paragraphs)

NAME: _____ DATE: _____

TOPIC: _____

THESIS STATEMENT: _____

_____

Main Idea	Details
¶ 1	....
¶ 2	....
¶ 3	....
¶ 4	....

CONCLUDING STATEMENT: _____

_____

N. Transition Outline (TO)

(5 Paragraphs)

NAME: _____ DATE: _____

TOPIC: _____

THESIS STATEMENT: _____

_____

Main Idea	Details
¶ 1	....
¶ 2	....
¶ 3	....
¶ 4	....
¶ 5	....

CONCLUDING STATEMENT: _____

_____

THE WRITING REVOLUTION®

O. Multiple-Paragraph Outline (MPO)
(3 Paragraphs)

NAME: _____ DATE: _____

TOPIC: _____

THESIS STATEMENT: _____

_____

Main Idea	Details
Introduction ¶ 1	....
¶ 2	....
Conclusion ¶ 3	....

P. Multiple-Paragraph Outline (MPO)

(4 Paragraphs)

NAME: _____ DATE: _____

TOPIC: _____

THESIS STATEMENT: _____

_____

Main Idea	Details
Introduction ¶ 1	....
¶ 2	....
¶ 3	....
Conclusion ¶ 4	....

Q. Multiple-Paragraph Outline (MPO)

(5 Paragraphs)

NAME: _____ DATE: _____

TOPIC: _____

THESIS STATEMENT: _____

_____

Main Idea	Details
Introduction ¶ 1	....
¶ 2	....
¶ 3	....
¶ 4	....
Conclusion ¶ 5	....

R. Multiple-Paragraph Outline (MPO)

(Book Report)

NAME: _____   DATE: _____

TOPIC: _____

THESIS STATEMENT: _____

_____

Main Idea	Details
Introduction ¶ 1	....
Book Summary ¶ 2	....
Opinion ¶ 3	....

THE WRITING REVOLUTION®

Glossary

ADJECTIVES
Words that modify a noun or pronoun, making its meaning more exact.

> Sarah is a <u>fine young</u> lady.

APPOSITIVE
A second noun, or a phrase or clause equivalent to a noun, that is placed beside another noun to explain it more fully.

> George Washington, <u>a great general,</u> was the first president of the United States.

ARGUMENTATIVE WRITING
Writing that presents a claim (or claims) and supports it (or them) with evidence and examples, usually citing sources; it acknowledges and sometimes rebuts opposing views or counterclaims.

CAUSE/EFFECT
A text structure that shows a relationship between the cause (why something happened) and the effect (what happened).

CLAIM
The writer's thesis; a statement of the writer's argument.

CLAUSES
Groups of words that contain a subject and a predicate and are part of a sentence.

> Jim saw the bird <u>as it fell from the sky</u>.

COGNITIVE LOAD

The burden on working memory that occurs when individuals process new information. Excessive cognitive load can interfere with learning, but some cognitive load is necessary for learning to take place.

COHERENCE

The quality of writing in which sentences and paragraphs are logically related to each other.

COMPARE AND CONTRAST

A text structure that shows how two or more things are alike and/or how they are different.

COMPLEX SENTENCE

A sentence that consists of a main clause and one or more subordinate clauses.

> Since it was raining, we decided to stay home.

> Rachel decided to stay home even though Seth went out.

COMPOSITION (ESSAY)

A series of paragraphs united by a common theme.

CONCLUDING SENTENCE

A concluding sentence is the last sentence of a paragraph and restates the topic sentence or summarizes the supporting information presented in the paragraph. Depending on the topic, it might be a call to action.

CONJUNCTIONS

Words that join other words, phrases, and clauses to one another. They help make writing clear and linguistically rich. *See also* coordinating conjunctions *and* subordinating conjunction.

COORDINATING CONJUNCTIONS

Conjunctions that join two or more independent clauses, such as *and, but, or, yet, nor, for,* and *so.*

> Terrell ate quickly, yet he was still late.

COUNTERCLAIM

An opposing point of view; the position(s) refuting the claim.

DECLARATIVE SENTENCE (STATEMENT)
A sentence that states a fact or opinion and ends with a period.

> The show starts at eight o'clock.

DELIBERATE PRACTICE
The systematic practice of breaking down a complex learning process into manageable chunks, under the guidance of and with targeted feedback from a teacher or coach.

DEPENDENT (SUBORDINATE) CLAUSE
A clause that does not express a complete thought and cannot stand alone as a sentence.

> As soon as Carlita left, it began to rain.

DESCRIPTIVE
A text structure that describes a topic, idea, person, place, or thing by its features, characteristics, or examples.

DO-NOW ACTIVITIES
Brief activities that students do at the beginning of or during class.

EDITING
Correcting the mechanics of writing, including punctuation, capitalization, spelling, grammar, and usage.

ESSAY
A series of paragraphs united by a common theme.

EXCLAMATORY SENTENCE (EXCLAMATION)
A sentence that expresses strong or sudden feeling. It ends with an exclamation point.

> I need help this minute!

EXECUTIVE FUNCTIONS
Cognitive processes that affect all aspects of memory, attention, and language; they have a great impact on writing.

EXIT SLIPS (OR TICKETS)
Brief writing tasks to be completed by students at the end of a class, using a specific sentence activity or one of the scaffolding activities leading to a paragraph or composition. They reflect the content studied during the class period and assess comprehension.

EXPOSITORY TERMS

Words that require an explanatory or informative response, such as *discuss*, *justify*, or *describe*.

EXPOSITORY WRITING

The kind of writing that aims to explain, describe, or inform.

FRAGMENT

A group of words that is not a grammatically complete sentence. Usually a fragment lacks a subject, verb, or both or is a dependent clause that is not connected to an independent clause.

> Before I left the house

FORMATIVE ASSESSMENTS

An evaluation method that involves regularly monitoring students' comprehension of what they have been taught and then determining next instructional steps.

IMPERATIVE SENTENCE (COMMAND)

A sentence that tells someone to do something; the subject is not always explicitly stated.

> Come here immediately.

INDEPENDENT (MAIN) CLAUSE

A clause that expresses a complete thought and could stand alone as a sentence.

> Although Lisa has a Toyota, <u>Kevin has a Ford.</u>

INDEPENDENT WRITING SAMPLE

Assessment given at the beginning, middle, and end of the school year, designed to provide an overall picture of students' independent writing, measure their progress, and highlight areas where they need more support.

INTERROGATIVE SENTENCE (QUESTION)

A sentence that asks a question. It ends with a question mark.

> Is Eli coming?

KERNEL SENTENCES

Simple, active, declarative sentences containing no modifiers or connectives. They may be used as the basis for constructing more elaborate sentences.

The children ran.

Rob threw the ball.

LONG-TERM MEMORY

The store of accumulated information transferred from short-term or working memory. Long-term memory can hold an unlimited amount of information for an indefinite period of time.

MAIN CLAUSE

See independent (main) clause.

MULTIPLE-PARAGRAPH OUTLINE (MPO)

A plan for developing an essay.

NARRATIVE

A text structure that describes items or events in order or relates the steps necessary to do or make something.

NOUN

A word that names a person, place, thing, quality, action, or idea. *See also* proper noun.

Susan has lovely eyes.

Hatred is a destructive emotion.

NUMBER AGREEMENT

A singular subject must have a singular verb.

This apple is very crisp.

A plural subject must have a plural verb.

These apples are very crisp.

OPINION WRITING

Writing that presents the author's opinion, giving reasons in support of it, but does not raise or rebut counterarguments. The reasons offered may be based on the author's personal experience rather than objective evidence.

OUTLINES

Plans that help the writer identify the main points of a paragraph or essay and organize details in a way that effectively conveys information to a reader.

PARAGRAPH

A group of sentences that includes details supporting a specific point.

PHRASE

A group of related words that does not contain both a verb and its subject.

> without her shoes

> Despite Jae's directions

PLAN OF DEVELOPMENT

A summary of the main points the writer will discuss in an essay. It is often embedded in the thesis statement.

> The outcome of the Civil War had profound social, economic, and political effects.

PRE-TRANSITION OUTLINE

A hybrid of an SPO and TO for students who are not yet ready for the TO or MPO formats. *See also* Transition Outline (TO).

PREDICATE

One or more words, including a verb, that says something about the subject of a sentence.

> Samantha danced for hours.

> The volcano erupted.

PROBLEM/SOLUTION

A text structure that describes a problem, sometimes explains why the problem exists, and then gives one or more possible solutions.

PRO/CON ESSAY

A multiple-paragraph composition that presents two sides of an issue but does not take a position.

PRONOUN

A word used in place of a noun. The noun a pronoun replaces is called its *antecedent*.

> Akira went to the store because it was open all night.

PROPER NOUN

A specific person, place, or thing; it begins with a capital letter.

> Simon, New York, Monday

REBUT

To refute an opposing point of view or counterclaim in an argumentative essay.

RELATIVE CLAUSE

A dependent clause that has a subject and a verb but cannot stand on its own as a complete sentence.

> <u>Although I took an umbrella</u>, I still got wet.

RETRIEVAL PRACTICE

The strategy of recalling information that is stored in long-term memory and needs to be remembered in order to enhance learning. Such practice helps ensure that individuals will be able to retrieve that information easily when they need it.

REVISING

Improving the content, organization, sentence structures, or word choice of a piece of writing.

RUN-ON SENTENCES

Written sequences of two or more main clauses that are not separated by a period or any other punctuation or joined by a conjunction.

> Rose defrosted the refrigerator the ice was an inch thick.

SENTENCE

A set of words that expresses a complete thought, typically containing a subject and predicate and conveying a statement, question, exclamation, or command. Sentences generally consist of a main clause and sometimes one or more subordinate clauses. *See also* complex sentence, declarative sentence (statement), exclamatory sentence (exclamation), interrogative sentence (question), *and* imperative sentence (command).

SENTENCE STEM

An independent or a dependent clause beginning a sentence that the writer is expected to complete.

> Although the colonists settled near rivers, _____.

> The colonists settled near rivers, but _____.

SINGLE-PARAGRAPH OUTLINE (SPO)
A plan for one paragraph.

STOP-AND-JOT
A brief writing task, usually a sentence activity, that is assigned during a lesson and may be shared with the class. It serves as a comprehension check and can be a scaffolding activity for a paragraph.

SUBJECT
The part of a sentence that states who or what the sentence is about.

> The <u>plant</u> grew rapidly.

> <u>Joe</u> caught the ball.

SUBORDINATE CLAUSE
See dependent clause.

SUBORDINATING CONJUNCTIONS
A word or phrase that links a dependent clause to an independent clause. It indicates that a clause adds information relating to the sentence's main idea, signaling a cause/effect relationship or a shift in time and place between the two clauses.

SUMMARY
A brief, concise restatement (not a retelling) of the main idea of a composition, lecture, or reading selection.

SUMMARY SENTENCE
A single sentence summarizing a specific text or event that could serve as the topic sentence of a paragraph.

SUMMATIVE ASSESSMENTS
An evaluation that takes place at the end of a unit of study to measure what students have learned over a period of time.

SYNTAX
The specific ways in which words are ordered to create logical, meaningful phrases, clauses, and sentences.

TENSE AGREEMENT

Consistency in verb tenses within one sentence and from one sentence to the next.

> Last Tuesday, as I <u>was driving</u> to school, a child <u>ran</u> in front of my car. I <u>swerved</u> to avoid hitting her.

TEXT STRUCTURES

The organization of a paragraph or essay. *See also* cause/effect, compare and contrast, narrative, and problem/solution.

THESIS STATEMENT

A sentence stating the main theme of a composition. It is usually included as the last sentence in the introductory paragraph and rephrased as the first sentence in the conclusion.

TOPIC SENTENCE

A statement of the main idea of a paragraph.

TRANSITIONS

Words and phrases that provide connections between ideas, sentences, and paragraphs and improve the flow and clarity of writing.

TRANSITION OUTLINE (TO) An intermediate step, if needed, for students who are comfortable creating an SPO but not yet ready for the MPO. It can be used to plan a multiple-paragraph essay.

TURN-AND-TALK

In-class activity in which students turn to a partner to discuss a specific topic. This enables students to formulate and share ideas with their peers instead of always answering a teacher's questions.

UNELABORATED PARAGRAPH

Four to six related sentences that have no mechanical errors but are extremely simple and need to be revised. Initially, specific instructions are given for revision. Later, students decide with each other and then on their own what revisions are needed to make the paragraph better.

VERB

A word or group of words used to express physical or mental action, condition, or being.

WORKING MEMORY

The aspect of cognition that enables us to take in and comprehend new information. Generally, individuals can hold only about four or five items of new information in working memory for about twenty seconds.

Index

C

capitalization
    editing for, 159
    practice of, with fragments, 37
    sentence-level work with, 104–105

cause/effect, 126, 152, 199, 201

change-of-direction transitions, 88, 89, 93, 166, 232, 312

citations, 206, 251, 303

claims, 228, 229, 232–233, 242, 249, 251

clarity, 172

clauses, 78, 97

cognitive load
    for argumentative essays, 122
    and free-writing, 114
    literacy and, 32–33
    and note-taking, 62
    planning to reduce, 115–117
    of writing at length, 188

coherence, 127, 189, 271

combining sentences, 102–104

commands
    excluded from sentence-level work, 38, 39, 48, 57
    in four basic sentence types, 70, 71
    as topic sentence, 143

comparative judgment, 273–274

compare-and-contrast assignments, 153

comparisons, 76, 200, 201, 309

complex sentences, 7, 11, 68 69

compositions. *See* essay/long-form writing

comprehension
    assessments of, 15, 265–266
    because-but-so activity for, 79
    of cited quotations, 204–205
    of complex sentences, 68–69
    gaps in, 4
    note-taking for, 59
    sentence-level, 290

    unelaborated paragraphs for, 169
    via question writing, 74–75

computer work, 271, 273, 275

concluding sentence (C.S.)
    practice developing, 130
    revising, 162–163
    for Single-Paragraph Outlines, 129–149
    three strategies for, 143–144

conclusions
    via appositives, 98
    for argumentative writing, 122
    concluding sentences, 85, 98
    concluding transitions, 88, 89, 91–92, 232, 312
    tips for writing, 201–202
    transitioning to, 166
    in Transition Outlines, 190, 197
    TSG structure for, 216–218

conjunctions
    argument built via, 231
    because-but-so activity for, 78–83
    in complex sentences, 7, 77–78
    and sentence-combining, 102–103
    subordinating, 69, 84–87
    testing knowledge via, 15–17
    and word choice, 165

content knowledge
    for because-but-so activity, 79
    via note-taking, 62, 63
    sentence instruction within, 35, 42, 51–54, 105
    writing as testing, 14, 15–17, 289

conventions, English language, 104–105, 174

counterclaims, 228, 229, 249

creativity, 114

curriculum
    assessments related to, 267
    Hochman Method across, 22
    mastery of, 289
    topics related to core, 118, 123, 228

TWR improvements to, 283–286
writing based on, 13–15, 279–280
cursive, 275

D

daily instruction, 106–107
declarative sentences, 70, 71
deliberate practice, 9–10
dependent (subordinate) clauses, 78
descriptive writing, 24, 151
details
    developed in outlines, 201
    for pro/con writing, 239, 242
    in Single-Paragraph Outlines, 137–142
    in topic/concluding sentences, 145–148
development plan, 197
diagramming sentences, 18
differentiating instruction, 20, 23, 286–287
distractions, 116
do-now activities, 15, 106, 182
drafting
    of argumentative essays, 258
    via Multiple-Paragraph Outline, 208, 210–221
    outlines for, 193
    from Single-Paragraph Outline, 154
    in writing process, 18–20, 290–291

E

editing
    of assessments, 270
    checklist for, 314
    revising vs., 158–160
    tips for, 174–175
    in writing process, 18, 290–291
elementary school. See also Level 1 (elementary) instruction
    content knowledge in, 14–15
    instructional sequence for, 293–299
    long-form writing in, 188
    Pre-Transition Outline in, 220–221

TWR across curriculum, 22
writing instruction in, 3, 11–12
emphasis transitions, 88, 89, 94, 166, 232, 312
enumeration, 76
error checks, 272, 314
essay/long-form writing
    argumentative, 248–258
    average high school, 1
    characteristics of, 189
    cognitive load of, 115–117, 187–188
    four types of, 24, 196
    incorporating quotations in, 204–207
    introductions to, 211–216
    Multiple-Paragraph Outline for, 208–221
    outlines for, 19, 189–190
    of research papers, 222–223
    vs. sentence instruction, 33
    skills needed for, 193–194
    step-by-step approach to, 3
    strategies for, 24
    three types of, 121–123
    topic, audience, and purpose of, 117–121
    from Transition Outlines, 203
evaluations. See assessments
evidence, argumentative, 251–252
exclamatory sentences, 70, 71, 143
executive functions, 115
exit tickets, 15
experience, personal, 118
explicit instruction
    for assessments, 269
    feedback with, 172–173
    in writing process, 6, 10–12
expository writing
    early-grade instruction in, 13
    in four writing types, 24
    importance of, 2
    overview of, 121–122
    planning for, 114
    terms for, 76–77, 309–310

F

facts vs. opinions, 237–238
feedback
    prompt, 22
    for revisions, 172–173
fiction, 122
formality, 119
formative assessments, 265, 266
fragments, sentence
    how to fix, 34–39
    transitions and, 94
free-writing, 114

G

general statements, 211–218
Google searches, 222–223
grammar
    editing for, 159
    sentence-level teaching of, 104–105
    taught in writing context, 17–18, 174
graphic organizers, 126
group work
    on Multiple-Paragraph Outline, 208
    to outline paragraphs, 117
    on Single-Paragraph Outline, 131–136
    on unelaborated paragraphs, 168, 171
GST structure, 211–216, 218

H

handwriting, 172, 272, 273, 275
Harvard Outline, 126
higher-level cognitive functions, 74
high school. *See* Level 2 (secondary-level)
    instruction
Hochman, Judith, 6
Hochman Method. *See* The Writing
    Revolution (TWR)

I

illustration transitions, 88, 89, 92–93, 166,
    232, 252, 312

images, responding to, 75–76
imperative sentences, 70, 71
independent (main) clauses, 78
internet research, 222
interpretations, 200
interrogative sentences, 70, 71
introductory paragraph, 208, 211–216, 217

J

judgment, personal, 199

K

kernel sentences
    as complete thoughts, 65
    creating, 48, 65
    expanding, 23, 46–48, 57, 229,
        233–234
    vs. fragments, 38
knowledge
    assessments of, 266
    background, 118, 271
    and cognitive load, 32–33
    essays based on, 194
    gaps in, 189
    in middle school, 14–15
    note-taking to reinforce, 59
    outlines to reinforce, 154
    verbal delivery of, 118–119
    writing to reinforce, 279

L

learning
    boosting, 5, 304
    embedded in writing, 20
    via note-taking, 58, 59, 62
    reviews in, 106
    summarizing for, 179
    via question writing, 74–76
    via sentence-combining, 104
    via sentence expansion, 46
    via writing, 13–15, 279

Jewish Holidays
Cookbook

Jewish Holidays Cookbook

Festive meals for celebrating the year

by Jill Colella Bloomfield

Rabbi Janet Ozur Bass, consultant
photography by Angela Coppola

DK Publishing

LONDON, NEW YORK, MELBOURNE,
MUNICH, AND DELHI

Editor Nancy Ellwood
Designer Bill Miller
Managing Art Editor Michelle Baxter
Art Director Dirk Kaufman
DTP Coordinator Kathy Farias
Production Manager Ivor Parker
Publishing Director Beth Sutinis

Photography by Angela Coppola

First Edition, 2008
08 09 10 11 12 10 9 8 7 6 5 4 3 2

Published in the United States
by DK Publishing
375 Hudson Street, New York, New York 10014

Copyright © 2008 DK Publishing

DK books are available at special discounts
for bulk purchases for sales promotions, premiums,
fund-raising, or educational use.
For details, contact:
DK Publishing Special Markets,
375 Hudson Street, New York, NY 10014
SpecialSales@dk.com

A catalog record for this book is available from
the Library of Congress.

ISBN 978-0-7566-4080-7

Color Reproduction by Colourscan, Singapore
Printed and bound in China by Leo Paper Products Ltd.

Discover more at
www.dk.com

contents

foreWord

The Jewish holidays teach us that there are many ways and many places to celebrate Jewish tradition. As a rabbi I meet many people who think that the synagogue is the center of Jewish life, and it is indeed a very important place for the Jewish community to gather. However, as a mother and a daughter, I know that the home—and table—is the centerpiece where families can find, create, and pass down tradition.

Cooking with people we care about allows us a way to share memories and create new ones. Most people can remember the smell of their favorite food from childhood, or a kind word that was passed along with a great taste. Both the word and the taste enhance each other.

My mother taught me many important lessons in the kitchen. She taught me that Friday night is a sacred time for family, and always added a little more love to her Shabbat recipes. And she taught me that food is an important way to remember the people we love when she showed me how her mother made the foods that she loved while growing up.

My memories of our Jewish kitchen are filled with the hilarious laughter and beautiful music of my mother, my sisters, and all the wonderful people who came into our lives. The food, while it tasted terrific on the table, somehow tasted like magic when we were all together in the kitchen preparing it. We created our "sister assembly lines" to make Purim hamantaschen, Shabbat challah, and matzoh balls. Whether I was rolling, cutting, kneading, filling, or pinching, my sisters and I were side by side celebrating what it means to be Jewish.

We should all grab a pot, a pan, some ingredients, and this idea: We can teach valuable Jewish lessons in our kitchens and at our dining room tables. We can teach someone that cooking is about using our resources wisely, being generous, and taking only what we need. We can teach the mitzvah of hospitality by graciously opening our hearts and homes to old friends and family, and extend that mitzvah to new friends who might have no other holiday table at which to celebrate.

When we put care and love into the food we create for the Jewish holidays, we, too, can become a part of the amazing legacy of the Jewish tradition.

Janet J. Bass

how to use this book

Welcome to *Jewish Holidays Cookbook*! Inside you'll not only learn to cook traditional Jewish foods, but you'll learn about why those foods are important to Jewish culture, and why people eat them for certain holidays. There is a lot of information coming your way, so here's a look at what the pages ahead mean.

PESACH

Pesach brings families together to the seder table in celebration of their history and traditions. It is a time to remember the struggles of the Israelites, and to eat and enjoy matzoh, haroset, meringues, and other treats from the Old World.

Pesach, or Passover, celebrates the trials and triumphs of the Israelite people in Egypt.

Pharaoh kept the Israelites as slaves, and treated them cruelly for many years. When he finally decided to let the Israelites follow Moses out of Egypt, the Israelites left in a hurry because they feared that Pharaoh would change his mind. He did change his mind, and sent his army after them. So the Israelites fled into the desert.

Because they left Egypt so quickly, the Israelites did not have time to let their bread dough rise before baking it. So instead of having leavened bread, they had flat matzoh. To remember the escape of Israelite ancestors, many Jews do not eat leavened foods during Pesach. Some families completely remove anything that contains flour or leavening agents (called "*chametz*") from their homes during Pesach.

Seder plate

"The Torah teaches that the first seder was held the night before the Israelites left Egypt. They ate Passover lamb and talked about the miracles that were happening all around them."

–Rabbi Ozur Bass

During the first two nights of Pesach, a seder is held, at which the Haggadah is read aloud. *Haggadah* means "the telling," and it tells the story of the Israelites' flight from Egypt.

Everything on the seder table is used to help tell the story, especially the items placed on the special seder plate. The symbolic foods on the seder plate are: a roasted shank bone, a roasted egg, horseradish, romaine lettuce (or parsley), celery, and haroset.

After the Haggadah is read, families celebrate with a delicious, festive meal. Many of the dishes traditionally served hearken back to ancient times, and are based on the foods available to the Israelites as they continued their journey through the desert.

Meringue cookies are perfect for Pesach.

the chapters

Each major holiday has its own chapter in the book. Each chapter starts with an introduction that tells you a bit about that holiday, its history and traditions, and how food plays a role.

the recipes

Rabbi Ozur Bass tells us about her cooking experiences throughout the years.

This color bar will tell you in which season each holiday takes place. (This one's fall)

These food tips give you a little more info on the recipe itself.

This tells you how many people each recipe serves.

Learn a bit about the recipe and the holiday.

Some recipes have variations that you can try.

Here's a list of the foods you'll need to make the recipe.

These are the instructions that tell you how to make the recipe.

This tells you which holiday you're cooking for.

Step-by-step photos will help you along.

Look here for extra tips and information.

Want to know if a recipe is dairy, meat, or pareve? Find it here.

Final pictures show you how the recipe should look when it's complete.

cooking tools

When you go to school you need notebooks and pencils and folders. When you cook, you need similar tools of the trade. Chances are you've got everything you need right in your kitchen. See below for a list of kitchen tools and appliances that will come in handy when preparing your recipes.

Baking sheet

Also called a cookie sheet. This is a flat baking pan with no raised edges. Baking sheets should be used only for cookies and breads that will not spread very much when they bake.

Colander

Used to drain water from ingredients such as pasta or egg noodles. Colanders are also perfect for rinsing off fresh fruits and vegetables.

Cookie cutters

These forms are used to cut dough, sandwiches, or any soft food into fun shapes. Cookie cutters come in thousands of sizes and styles.

Cutting board

A surface upon which all ingredients should be cut. Some cutting boards are made of wood, others of plastic. It's a good idea to have separate cutting boards for raw meats, raw fish, and fresh fruits and vegetables.

Deep-frying thermometer

Used to measure the temperature of oil for frying.

Electric mixer

Used to mix just about anything. Electric mixers can be standing (such as this one), or handheld, and have different attachments for mixing different types of ingredients.

Frying pan

Also called a skillet. This is a large, flat pan on which foods cook evenly because they can be spread out into one layer.

Grater

This is used to shred ingredients such as cheese, potatoes, onions, and carrots.

Jelly roll pan

A flat baking pan with raised edges so that batter will stay in the pan. Often used to make thin, flat cakes.

Measuring cups

Used to measure out the exact amount of each ingredient.

Meat thermometer

…sed to measure the internal temperature of meats …ch as beef, chicken, and lamb.

Microplane

…his is a very fine grater, used to scrape the zest off … oranges, lemons, and limes.

Oven mitts

…hese protect your hands from hot …ots and pans. Be sure they're clean …nd dry when you use them.

Parchment paper

…his paper is often used to line baking …heets or cake pans to prevent food …om sticking to the pan. It is also …sed to create packets in which …od is steamed (called "en papillote").

Rolling pin

…sed to roll out dough for cookies and …es. Can also be used to crush crackers, …ookies, or cornflakes into crumbs.

Saucepan

… deep pot used to cook liquids and stews, and … boil pasta, noodles, rice, and couscous.

Skewers

…sed to make kebabs. Skewers are often …ade of bamboo or metal. Bamboo skewers …ork best if they are soaked in cold water …r about an hour before you use them …his prevents them from catching …re while on a grill).

Spatula

There are two types of spatulas: rubber spatulas help scrape food and batter from bowls. Flat spatulas are used to scoop food up off a pan or cooking surface.

Springform pan

A metal baking pan whose sides are removable. They can be expanded by opening the metal latch and then lifted away while delicate cakes (such as cheesecake) remain on the metal base.

Tongs

Used to grab large ingredients while they're cooking. You can use tongs to turn food in a pan.

Whisk

Used to whip food to a light, airy consistency.

Wooden spoons

Used to stir just about anything. Wooden spoons are great because they don't get hot like metals spoons do.

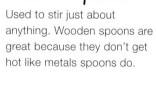

cooking tools ✳

11

kitchen safety

Working in the kitchen is an enjoyable experience, especially if you follow some important guidelines: Be sure to closely review your recipe before you start. Make sure you have the proper tools. And be safe! Clear off your work space, take your time, be careful, and always ask an adult for help when you need it. Here are some more guidelines to follow as you whip your recipes into shape:

● **Permission, please**

Always ask an adult's permission before you begin to cook. Know—and follow—the rules of your kitchen, and if you need help, ask for it.

● **Avoid accidents**

To avoid kitchen mishaps, get ready for cooking before you begin. Roll up long sleeves. Tie back long hair. Know how to use a kitchen fire extinguisher. Clean up spills as soon as they occur so no one slips and falls. For dangerous accidents like broken glass, ask an adult for help.

● **Hot pots**

Be careful of hot pots and pans. Be sure to have plenty of clean, dry pot holders and oven mitts to protect your hands. Don't substitute a dish towel for a pot holder.

● **Wash up and keep clean**

Always wash your hands before handling food. Once your hands are clean, avoid touching your hair and face. Any time you sneeze, use the bathroom, or touch raw meats, go ahead and wash your hands again.

● **Handling food wisely**

Be sure to use clean utensils and cutting boards. Wash fruit and vegetables carefully to remove dirt and sand. Always wash your hands immediately after handling raw meat, chicken, fish, and eggs. If any juices from raw meat spill, wipe them up right away. It's a good idea to use different cutting boards for raw meats, raw fish, and fruits and veggies.

● **Knife know-how**

Always ask an adult for help when using sharp knives. Use the smallest knife you need to do the job. Be sure to keep your fingers away from sharp blades. Never leave a knife hanging off the edge of the counter. And never put a knife in a place where someone can't see it, like in a sink filled with soapy water.

Don't lick your fingers while you cook.

Wash your hands after handling raw eggs.

Keeping Kosher

The word *kosher* means "fit or proper for use." Kosher cooking involves foods—and the utensils used to cook the foods—that are prepared a certain way, and deemed fit and proper for eating. The laws that govern this are called the laws of kashrut.

The laws of kashrut come from two main sources: the Torah and rabbinic law. The Torah gives many laws about which animals Jews can eat, and which they cannot. Some of these laws state that Jews can eat only land mammals that chew their cud and have true, split hooves (like cows), or sea animals that have both fins and scales (like most fish). Animals forbidden by the Torah include pigs, snakes and reptiles, some birds, and sea animals that have hard shells (like lobsters and crabs).

Rabbinic law is the second source of kosher rules, and often expands on laws introduced in the Torah. Where the Torah says that a goat may not be cooked in its mother's milk, rabbinic law states that no meat product of any kind may be cooked, prepared, or eaten with any dairy product. Rabbinic law also teaches that for an animal to be kosher it must be slaughtered and prepared in a particular way.

Besides being meat or dairy, kosher foods can also be pareve (pronounced PARV). Pareve foods have neither meat nor dairy in them, and therefore can be eaten with both. Fruits, vegetables, eggs, fish, and grains are all pareve.

The laws of kashrut may seem complicated, but it is not that difficult to keep a kosher kitchen. Most people will separate utensils, dishes, and cooking areas in which to prepare meat and dairy foods. Mass-produced foods (like cereals and snacks that you buy at the store) are marked with special symbols to indicate that they are kosher.

Neither the Torah nor rabbinic law explain *why* kosher rules were given, although throughout history many people have tried to come up with explanations.

Most people follow the laws of kashrut because they believe that keeping these rules is an important part of being Jewish, and because they believe this is what God would like them to do. Even so, the decision to keep kosher is a very personal one, often handed down through families from generation to generation.

No matter whether it's kosher or not, food plays an important role in Jewish culture. The recipes in this cookbook are based on many traditional foods cooked throughout the world, some with a modern twist. There are many more recipes still out there to be explored! Please note that none of the recipes here are specifically kosher, but they are labeled "meat," "dairy," or "pareve." Simple variations are offered so that you can maintain a kosher meal.

introduction

Food is a very important part of our lives. We need it to survive, of course, but we also use it to express our cultural identity. What we eat at home is a statement about where we are raised, what foods are available, and what flavors our parents hand down to us. And every year we have many opportunities to celebrate our culture and our history through food, especially during our holidays!

What we decide to eat depends on many factors—what foods are in season, what foods are familiar to us, and what holiday we're celebrating. Beginning with recipes for Shabbat such as challah, roasted chicken, and matzoh balls, this book explores Jewish holidays and festivals through delicious recipes.

Different festivals and holidays have special foods associated with them. The Jewish year begins at Rosh Hashanah, and recipes to welcome a sweet new year include sweet-and-sour gefilte fish, soda pop brisket, and honey cake. At Yom Kippur, after a meaningful fast, try recipes for kugel and smoked salmon frittata at your family's break-the-fast party.

Because Hanukkah is a time to remember the miracle of oil, its traditional foods are fried, like crispy potato latkes and *sofganiyot*. After Hanukkah, celebrate Tu B'Shevat—the festival of trees—by cooking with fruits and nuts. Fig spread and Tu B'Shevat granola are fun to eat in the shade of a beautiful old tree.

Purim can be made merry with hamantaschen and other recipes. The Achashverosh crown sandwich is easy (and tasty) to eat when hurrying to a Purim carnival.

Pesach, or Passover, is a time when cooks must be innovative as they avoid using leavening ingredients such as flour. Recipes like an Israeli meat pie called *mina* are easy to make. And flourless meringues are a great dessert at a seder.

Middle Eastern flavors influence Yom Ha'Atzmaut recipes like Israeli salad, falafel, and hummus, which are festive treats for celebrating independence.

Lag B'Omer is for picnics, bonfires, and recipes for lamb shish kebab, watermelon salad, and pomegranate lemonade. Shavuot is a holiday that celebrates the bounty of the spring harvest and receiving the Torah. Rich dairy foods like blintzes and cheesecake make Shavuot delicious to observe.

At the end you'll find pages on which you can take notes about the recipes. Record any variations or special touches that you've made to your dishes.

No matter if you're a beginning chef or already a pro in the kitchen, cooking new recipes is a wonderful way to celebrate the holidays. And if your dishes don't turn out perfectly, don't worry. Experimenting and trying again are all part of the cooking adventure. So invite your family and friends—Jewish and non-Jewish—into the kitchen to experience with you the delicious and diverse Jewish year!

Jill Bloomfield

How many ways can you cook with matzoh?

SHABBAT

How wonderfully special it is to be Jewish! Each week has its own joyful celebration. Every Friday at sundown Shabbat begins. Special candles are lit and a prayer is said. Parents bless their children and each other.

Shabbat is a holy day that celebrates God's day of rest after creating the world. On Shabbat, we, too, have the chance to sit back and celebrate all that we have created during the week. It is a special time to share with family and friends, attend services, and relax at home. Shabbat ends on Saturday evening after sundown.

Food is an important part of celebrating Shabbat. Some people say that eating three full meals on Shabbat is a mitzvah. Some people define mitzvahs (or mitzvot) as commandments, meaning that they are something that the Jewish people have to do because God told them to. Other people define mitzvot as traditions that have been kept in the Jewish community for many years. Still others define mitzvot as good deeds, because they believe that God wants them to make the world a better place. However you define mitzvot, they help people understand how we should act toward ourselves, one another, and God. Shabbat is a weekly reminder of the importance of mitzvot.

kiddush cup

"The Jewish faith is one not only of belief, but also of action. We try to act a certain way in this world because of our belief in what it means to be Jewish. Mitzvot help us understand that."

—Rabbi Ozur Bass

Some people make Shabbat a time to focus on family, their friends, and their relationship with God. Because of this they do not drive, watch television, or do homework on Shabbat. Instead, Shabbat is a time to play outside, go to the synagogue to sing and pray, hang out with people you enjoy, or read books just for pleasure.

For some Jews, certain types of work are not allowed on Shabbat, so food must be cooked in advance. Some foods are even left to cook overnight and then eaten the next day. These recipes can become part of your own family traditions.

The motzi is said over the challah at Shabbat dinner.

challah

Challah is traditionally served at the beginning of Shabbat dinner. A prayer is said over the freshly baked bread before dinner begins. Here's a recipe for your very own special Shabbat challah. This recipe makes two loaves.

get cooking...

1 Pour water into bottom of large mixing bowl. Add yeast, and allow to sit for 1 minute.

2 Add honey, oil, eggs, sugar, and salt to yeast mixture. Stir to combine.

3 Scoop spoonfuls of flour into the wet mixture, combining well each time. As you continue adding flour, the mixture will thicken. You can use your hands to mix in the flour.

4 After all of the flour is mixed in, knead the dough in the bowl until it is smooth. Add up to ½ cup of additional flour if your dough is sticky. Allow dough to rise for 1 hour in a warm place. The dough should double in size.

5 Turn the dough out onto a floured surface like a cutting board. Deflate risen dough by punching it. Divide dough into 2 equal pieces and knead each piece for 3 minutes. If dough is sticky, add a little bit of flour as you knead.

6 Grease 2 large baking sheets with margarine, and set them aside. Preheat the oven to 375°F (190°C).

7 Divide each loaf into 3 equal pieces. Roll each piece into a long rope about 1½ inches (4 cm) in diameter. These will be the 3 strands of your braid. Bring the ends of the strands together and begin braiding. After it is fully braided, tuck the beginning and end of your braid under the loaf. Repeat for the other loaf, and place each on a prepared baking sheet. Cover each loaf with a slightly damp towel and allow the loaves to rise once more, for 45 minutes.

ingredients...

- 2½ cups warm water
- 1 tablespoon active dry yeast
- ½ cup honey
- 6 tablespoons vegetable oil
- 2 eggs
- 1 tablespoon sugar
- 1 tablespoon salt
- 8 cups all-purpose flour
- 1 egg, beaten
- 2 tablespoons sesame seeds

8 After the loaves have risen, use a pastry brush to spread beaten egg over each one. Sprinkle the tops of the loaves with sesame seeds.

9 Bake on a low rack for about 35 to 45 minutes. The fully baked bread should be a deep golden color and should sound hollow when tapped.

Keep a bowl of flour handy.

Your challah is ready!

Try sprinkling your challah with poppy seeds.

This recipe is pareve. For a kosher meal, you can serve this with either dairy or meat foods.

The plural of challah is "challot."

roasted chicken with vegetables

serves
6

Celebrate with a classic Shabbat dinner of roasted chicken and hearty vegetables. Be sure to check that your chicken is fully cooked before serving.

ingredients...

1 whole chicken, about 4 lbs (1.8 kg)

1 tablespoon olive oil

1 teaspoon salt

1 teaspoon pepper

4 cups potato, cut into 2-inch (5-cm) chunks

1 cup onion, chopped

2 cups carrot, cut into 2-inch (5-cm) chunks

1 cup celery, cut into 1-inch (2.5-cm) chunks

1 cup chicken broth

1 teaspoon garlic powder

This recipe is a meat recipe. For a kosher meal, serve only with meat or pareve foods.

get cooking...

1 Preheat oven to 350°F (180°C). Rinse chicken and pat dry.

2 Rub chicken with olive oil, then sprinkle with salt and pepper. Put in a large roasting pan.

3 Place potatoes under the chicken and arrange other vegetables around the chicken.

4 Add chicken broth to roasting pan, making sure that all vegetables are moistened.

5 Sprinkle vegetables with garlic powder.

6 Cover the chicken and roasting pan tightly with aluminum foil.

7 Roast chicken for 90 minutes, basting occasionally. Then remove foil and roast for 20 minutes at 450°F (230°C) to crisp the skin. The chicken is done when its juices are clear.

Mom or dad can carve the chicken.

"Growing up, my sisters and I could count on the same delicious Shabbat dinner every week. To this day, every time I smell roasting chicken, I think of sharing Shabbat dinner with my family."   -Rabbi Ozur Bass

On a meat thermometer, the breast of a whole, fully cooked chicken should register 175°F (80°C).

"The best part about chicken soup for Shabbat is dunking the challah in it!" —Rabbi Ozur Bass

Always taste your soup as you cook so you can add salt or pepper as needed.

If you like your soup thicker, add more noodles.

chicken noodle soup

serves **6**

Soup is delicious at Shabbat dinner. This recipe is quick to prepare because it uses already-cooked chicken. You can buy cooked chickens at the store or use leftovers.

get cooking...

1 Melt butter or margarine in a large saucepan over medium heat. Add onion and cook for 1 minute, then add celery and carrots. Cook vegetables until slightly translucent, about 4 more minutes.

2 Add cooked chicken, and stir in with vegetables for 2 minutes, so flavors mix together.

3 Add all broth and oregano, basil, bay leaves, and garlic powder.

4 Allow soup to simmer for 20 minutes at medium heat. Ten minutes prior to serving, adjust heat to medium-high and bring soup to a boil. Add uncooked noodles and cook for 10 minutes or according to package instructions.

ingredients...

1 tablespoon butter or margarine

½ cup chopped yellow onion

½ cup chopped celery

1 cup carrot, cut 1-inch (2.5-cm) thick

8 oz (225 g) cooked chicken meat, roughly pulled

3 14½-oz (430-ml) cans chicken broth

2 14½-oz (430-ml) cans vegetable broth

½ teaspoon dried oregano

½ teaspoon dried basil

2 bay leaves

¼ teaspoon garlic powder

6 oz (170 g) egg noodles, uncooked

Have a soup potluck party. Your friends can bring soups, salad, or bread, and you can serve them your chicken noodle soup.

This recipe is meat. For a kosher meal, use margarine, vegetable oil, or olive oil.

shabbat

matzoh balls

Matzoh balls are a delicious treat. The key to making fluffy, light matzoh balls is to pack them loosely. You want them to float when they cook. Matzoh balls almost double in size when they cook, so be sure not to make yours too big.

get cooking...

1 Separate 2 eggs and put the egg whites in a medium-sized mixing bowl. Set the yolks aside because you will add them later. Whisk the egg whites until they are light and fluffy.

2 Crack the last egg and combine with the yolks you set aside. Using a fork, beat together. Gently fold the yolks into your fluffy egg whites.

3 Add matzoh meal, vegetable oil, 2 tablespoons of chicken broth, water, salt, white pepper, and garlic powder, again folding it carefully into your mixture.

4 Place bowl in refrigerator for 1 hour, until the mixture is chilled and firm to the touch.

5 Place two quarts chicken broth in a large pot. Bring to a boil over medium-high heat.

6 Remove matzoh mixture from the refrigerator. Using your hands, scoop out a small bit of mixture and gently roll it in your hands to form a ball, about 1 inch (2.5 cm) in diameter. (Rinse your hands with cold water if the dough is sticking to your fingers.)

7 Using a slotted spoon, place matzoh balls into the chicken stock 1 at a time. Reduce heat so mixture is at a low simmer. Cover pot and allow matzoh balls to cook gently for about 45 minutes until they are cooked through.

8 Serve your matzoh balls in the broth they cooked in, or as a substitute for the noodles in chicken noodle soup.

ingredients...

3 eggs

1 cup matzoh meal

4 tablespoons vegetable oil

2 quarts plus 2 tablespoons chicken broth

½ cup cold water

1 teaspoon salt

½ teaspoon white pepper

½ teaspoon garlic powder

Knaidlach is the Yiddish word for "matzoh ball."

This recipe is meat. For a kosher meal, serve only with other meat or pareve foods.

Roll your matzoh balls gently.

shabbat

24

"Most Jewish cooks have their own secrets as to how to make the best matzoh balls. One secret to light and fluffy balls is to substitute plain seltzer for the water."   —Rabbi Ozur Bass

This recipe can be made vegetarian; just substitute vegetable broth for chicken broth.

This recipe is pareve and can be eaten with either meat or dairy meals.

If you use dried beans, soak and prepare them the night before.

vegetable cholent

Cholent is a great lunch for Shabbat because traditionally it cooks overnight, and is ready for the Saturday midday meal. Most cultures have similar long-cooking stew or bean dishes, such as French cassoulet or American baked beans. Cholent almost always features beans, barley, and hearty vegetables.

get cooking...

1   Heat vegetable oil in a large saucepan over medium-high heat. Add onion and cook until tender.

2   Add garlic, stirring often so it does not burn. Add mushrooms and continue to stir for 2 to 3 minutes or until mushrooms shrink down a bit. Reduce heat to medium.

3   Add beans, stirring gently. Add barley, carrots, and potatoes. Add salt and pepper, then vinegar, hot water, and broth. Be sure all vegetables are covered with liquid.

4   Turn heat to low and cover tightly. Traditionally, cholent is allowed to cook overnight. However, if left over medium heat, the cholent will be done in about 60 minutes.

ingredients...

⅓ cup vegetable oil

1 medium onion, cut into small chunks

2 cloves garlic, finely minced

1 cup baby portobella mushrooms, sliced

1 15-oz (425-g) can dark red kidney beans, rinsed

1 15-oz (425-g) can pinto beans, rinsed

½ cup whole barley, uncooked

4 carrots, cut into small chunks

5 medium potatoes, peeled and quartered

½ teaspoon salt, plus more if desired

1 teaspoon ground black pepper

⅓ cup red wine vinegar

1 cup very hot water

2 cups vegetable broth

"The word *cholent* is from the French meaning 'warm and slow cooking.' Because the pot is sealed and left to finish cooking overnight, it was one of the foods that was invented so Jewish people could follow the laws of Shabbat. Some villages had big ovens in the middle of the town where every family would bring their pots on Friday afternoon and leave them there until Saturday lunch."
—Rabbi Ozur Bass

shabbat

27

chickpea and couscous salad

This refreshing and colorful salad is perfect for *Seudah Shlishit* (pronounced *seh-ooh-DAH shlee-SHEET*), a Shabbat meal eaten in the afternoon on Saturday. Eating three meals on Shabbat is considered a mitzvah, and *Seudah Shlishit* is the third meal.

This recipe is pareve and can be served with dairy or meat meals.

ingredients...

1 cup vegetable broth

1 cup uncooked instant couscous

3 tablespoons vegetable oil

2 tablespoons white vinegar

2 tablespoons lemon juice

1 teaspoon garlic powder

¼ cup fresh parsley, minced

¼ cup fresh basil, minced

1 15-oz (425-g) can chickpeas

4 plum tomatoes, diced

1 medium cucumber, diced

get cooking...

1 In a small saucepan, bring vegetable broth to a boil. While on the heat, stir in couscous. Immediately cover pot, turn off stove, and remove saucepan from heat so liquid is absorbed into couscous. When all liquid is absorbed, fluff up couscous using a fork. Be careful because the saucepan is hot. Set couscous aside and allow it to cool.

2 Combine oil, vinegar, lemon juice, and garlic powder in a mixing bowl. Gently fold in the parsley and basil.

3 Add chickpeas, tomatoes, and cucumber to the cooled couscous. Mix in oil and vinegar mixture.

4 Cover with plastic wrap and refrigerate. Serve cold.

Chickpeas can be found in traditional recipes around the world. They're also known as garbanzo beans and ceci beans.

"We will often invite over our neighbors and have a potluck meal of leftover Shabbat dinner and Saturday lunch for our *Seudah Shlishit.*"   —Rabbi Ozur Bass

If you do not have vegetable broth, you can use water to make the couscous instead.

ROSH HASHANAH

L'Shanah tovah! Happy New Year! Rosh Hashanah brings families together to celebrate the autumn harvest and a sweet new year with brisket, tzimmes, sweet potato casserole, honey cake, and more!

Rosh Hashanah is the Jewish New Year. It celebrates the anniversary of God creating the world, and looks ahead to making the new year better. This is a time of celebration and reflection.

Along with any good celebration comes good food! Naturally sweet foods like honey, apples, raisins, and carrots are served at Rosh Hashanah, to remind us of the sweet things that lie ahead. Often, Rosh Hashanah feasts begin by dipping apples in honey, and saying a prayer asking God for a wonderful year.

There are many food traditions followed during Rosh Hashanah.

Families cook together for the new year meal.

"Having a big celebratory dinner with friends and family is the best way to remember why it is important to keep our relationships healthy."
—Rabbi Ozur Bass

For instance, challot are often baked in a circular shape, which symbolizes the crown of God. When eaten during the new year celebration, challah is dipped in honey.

Pomegranates and their many seeds (called "arils") are symbols of blessings in the new year. These Mediterranean fruits are in season starting in October, and so dishes containing pomegranate seeds are often eaten at Rosh Hashanah.

Some Jewish communities have the custom of eating different foods and blessing one another with ideas about the food itself. For example, they will eat from the head of a fish and say, "May it be your will that we be like the head (leaders) and not the tail (followers)." Other families eat the head of a fish—or simply place one on the table—to represent the "head" or beginning of the year.

What Rosh Hashanah traditions does your family celebrate?

sweet ginger gefilte fish

Gefilte fish is made from finely chopped fish that has been cooked with onions and carrots. Sweetened by orange juice and honey, this gefilte fish recipe can help you welcome a sweet new year.

ingredients...

1 16-oz (450-g) loaf gefilte fish, defrosted

1 tablespoon fresh ginger, grated

¼ cup soy sauce

¼ cup orange juice

¼ cup honey

1 tablespoon brown sugar

get cooking...

1 Preheat oven to 350°F (180°C).

2 Press fish into a jelly roll pan or round cake pan.

3 Whisk remaining ingredients in bowl and pour on top of fish.

4 Cover with foil and bake for 30 to 35 minutes, until heated through.

5 For a twist, you can cut your finished gefilte fish into fun shapes with cookie cutters!

Be gentle with your gefilte shapes!

Frozen gefilte fish loaves can be foun[d] in kosher grocery store[s] or the kosher section o[f] some large grocery stores. If you can't fin[d] them, jarred gefilte fis[h] will work just fine.

" Gefilte fish is one of the many foods whose recipe shows where a family came from in eastern Europe. Jews from Poland eat their gefilte fish sweet, whereas Lithuanian and Russian Jews eat it with no sugar and more pepper." —Rabbi Ozur Bass

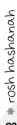

rosh hashanah

This recipe is pareve and can be served with either dairy or meat meals.

Most gefilte fish is made of carp and whitefish.

soda pop brisket

This is a traditional Jewish dish and a real crowd pleaser. Your friends and family will be surprised to learn that the secret ingredient is cola!

ingredients...

1 medium onion, sliced into rings

3- to 4-pound (1.3- to 1.8-kg) flat
  brisket, trimmed

2 cloves of garlic, minced

2 tablespoons yellow mustard

1 tablespoon Worcestershire sauce

1 tablespoon olive oil

1 cup soda, cola flavored (not diet)

parsley for garnish (optional)

Let meat sit for about 10 minutes before you cut it.

get cooking...

1 Preheat oven to 350°F (180°C).

2 Line baking sheet with aluminum foil. Place half of onion slices on baking sheet, and place brisket, fat side up, on top of onions.

3 In small bowl or measuring cup, stir together garlic, mustard, Worcestershire sauce, olivo oil, and soda.

4 Pour mixture over top of brisket and place remaining onion slices on top. Cover with foil.

Cover the whole brisket.

5 Bake for 2 hours, or until the meat reaches an internal temperature of 175°F (80°C).

Pour slowly!

rosh hashanah

34

This recipe is meat. For a Kosher meal, serve only with other meat or pareve foods.

To serve brisket, slice it thinly across the grain.

"The word *tzimmes* is one of those great Yiddish words that has come to mean many different things. It can be used to mean trouble, or a whole lot of something, or a big deal, as in 'Don't make such a big tzimmes over all of this!' "   —Rabbi Ozur Bass

Some people cook a piece of beef in tzimmes to impart a meaty flavor.

sweet carrot tzimmes

Tzimmes (pronounced *SIM-iss*) sounds like how it is prepared: simmered! The longer you cook it, the more like a thick sauce it will become. You can serve it chunky, like ours, or blend it smooth. Every family has their own special way of preparing tzimmes.

get cooking...

1 Combine all ingredients in a saucepan, making sure that the carrots and fruit are covered in liquid.

2 Bring to a boil. Allow mixture to boil for 10 minutes.

3 Reduce heat and allow mixture to simmer, uncovered, for 25 to 35 minutes or until the liquid evaporates and the tzimmes thickens.

ingredients...

1½ pounds (680 g) carrots, sliced into coins

½ cup dried cranberries

½ cup dried apricots, diced

¼ cup golden raisins

¼ cup raisins

½ teaspoon salt

½ teaspoon cinnamon

1 11-oz (325-ml) can apricot nectar

1 cup water

This recipe is pareve, and may be served with meat or dairy foods.

Although it is served at almost every holiday, tzimmes is very common at Rosh Hashanah because it helps everyone start the new year on a sweet note. It is also served at Passover because it is a great topping for matzoh!

rosh hashanah

harvest rice with pomegranate seeds

The beautiful seeds of a pomegranate are called "arils." They look like shiny red jewels in this holiday rice that celebrates the rich harvest at the beginning of a new year.

ingredients...

2 tablespoons olive oil

½ cup onion, chopped

½ cup celery, chopped

1 cup apple, chopped

¼ cup dried cherries

¼ cup pecans, chopped

1 6- to 8-oz (170- to 225-g) package
    quick-cook rice pilaf mix, regular or
    vegetable flavor

½ cup pomegranate arils

get cooking...

1 Heat oil in a medium-sized sauté pan over medium-high heat.

2 Add onion, celery, and apple, and cook until soft and translucent, stirring frequently. Reduce heat to medium, and add cherries and pecans.

3 Set mixture aside on plate.

4 Using the same pan, prepare rice according to package directions.

5 To remove arils, have an adult cut the crown off of a pomegranate, and break the fruit into segments. Holding segments over a bowl, use fingers or a spoon to scoop out seeds.

The arils are easy to scoop out.

6 Add arils and the fruit-and-vegetable mixture to cooked rice, stirring to combine.

For a Kosher meal, serve with either meat or dairy foods, as this recipe is pareve.

If you can't find fresh pomegranates, you can use frozen arils, which are available year-round

rosh hashanah

38

"Pomegranates, with their many seeds, are a traditional Rosh Hashanah fruit. They represent wishes for a year filled with many wonderful new beginnings. In Hebrew the word for *pomegranate* is 'Rimon,' which means 'crown.' We eat the *Rimon* to crown the head of the Jewish year."   –Rabbi Ozur Bass

sweet potato casserole

With a crisp, candylike topping, this vegetable dish is an extra sweet way to welcome the new year. You can use baked, boiled, or canned sweet potatoes.

ingredients...

3 cups cooked sweet potatoes, mashed

½ cup brown sugar

½ cup butter, melted

½ cup milk

2 eggs

1 teaspoon vanilla extract

For the topping:

¾ cup brown sugar

⅓ cup all-purpose flour

⅓ cup butter, melted

1 cup pecans, roughly chopped

get cooking...

1 Preheat oven to 350°F (180°C).

2 In mixing bowl, combine mashed sweet potatoes with brown sugar, melted butter, milk, eggs, and vanilla. Break up any chunks of sweet potato with your spoon. Mixture should be totally smooth.

3 In a separate bowl, use fingers to combine brown sugar, flour, melted butter, and pecans for the topping. Set aside.

4 Spoon sweet potato mixture into oven-safe dish, and sprinkle pecan mixture evenly on top.

5 Bake for 30 to 35 minutes, until sweet potatoes are warmed through and the topping has formed a crust.

"My family loves to serve this with marshmallows instead of pecans. After preparing the sweet potatoes and warming them through, top with marshmallows and put under the broiler just long enough for the marshmallows to brown."
—Rabbi Ozur Bass

To prepare mashed sweet potatoes, scrub potatoes well and microwave for 6 to 8 minutes or until potatoes are soft throughout. Sweet potatoes can also be boiled for 20 to 24 minutes or until soft. Canned sweet potatoes work beautifully, as well.

rosh hashanah

40

This recipe is dairy. For a kosher meal, serve only with other dairy or pareve foods.

Sprinkle on a little cayenne for a spicy twist!

Top your honey lemon cake with a light sprinkling of powdered sugar.

honey lemon cake

"Every Jewish cook I know has a different version of honey cake. It wouldn't be Rosh Hashanah without this dessert! I like to have a slice of honey cake with cream cheese on it for breakfast before going to services for Rosh Hashanah."
—Rabbi Ozur Bass

Don't wait for Rosh Hashanah to make this delicious cake. You can bake this moist, spicy dessert any time.

get cooking...

1 Preheat oven to 350°F (180°C). Oil and flour a 9 x 13–inch (23 x 33–cm) baking pan or a bundt pan (as shown).

2 Combine sugar, honey, vegetable oil, eggs, lemon zest, and juice. Stir well.

3 In another bowl, combine flour, baking powder, baking soda, salt, and cinnamon. Add this mixture slowly to honey mixture, combining well. Stir in the water.

4 Pour into prepared baking pan and bake for 35 to 40 minutes.

ingredients...

½ cup sugar

1 cup honey

½ cup vegetable oil

3 eggs

2 teaspoons grated lemon zest

¼ cup lemon juice

3 cups all-purpose flour

3 teaspoons baking powder

1 teaspoon baking soda

½ teaspoon salt

1 teaspoon cinnamon

¼ cup water

To test a cake for doneness, insert a wooden toothpick into center of cake. It should come out clean when done.

Get all of that batter in there!

This recipe is pareve and may be served with either dairy or meat meals.

YOM KIPPUR

Families fast during Yom Kippur, and attend services at synagogue. When the fast is over, everyone comes together for delicious bagels, egg dishes, kugel, and more.

Second to Shabbat, Yom Kippur is the holiest day of the Jewish year. During the ten days before Yom Kippur, Jewish people think about their behavior over the past year. They apologize to other people for anything they have done wrong. On Yom Kippur itself, they apologize to God and try to figure out how to to avoid the same mistakes over the next year.

During Yom Kippur, people fast, which means they do not eat or drink anything from sunset until sunset the next day. The fast is a way to focus people's minds on who they would like to become rather than simpler things like what they're going to eat. Of course hungry fasters often think about *when* they'll eat again! In fact, some synagogues pass around small boxes that contain cinnamon and cloves. These are called *B'samim* boxes. People sniff the spices, which helps ease their hunger during services.

The long day of prayer and fasting ends when the shofar—a ram's horn—is blown. At the sound of the shofar, everyone's serious mood is broken and there is a sense of joy that comes over the community. People get together at one another's homes to break their day-long fast. Some synagogues have potluck break-the-fast meals so that the whole community

"Some people say *Tzom Kal*, or 'have an easy fast' at Yom Kippur. I like to say 'Have a meaningful fast.'"   –Rabbi Ozur Bass

can share this time together.

Because Yom Kippur is a holy day and no food can be cooked, food is prepared before the holiday begins. Eating lighter foods like eggs, kugel, and pastries is traditional (and is easier on an empty stomach than heavy foods). Breaking the fast is a welcome celebration at the end of a serious holiday.

Light foods, such as bagels and cream cheese, are often eaten to break the fast.

bagels with cream cheese

Turn your kitchen into a bagel shop by making hot, fresh, chewy bagels, complete with your own homemade flavored cream cheeses!

get cooking...

1 Pour warm water into large mixing bowl, then add yeast and stir until dissolved.

2 Add malt, flour, and salt, and mix until dough forms. Knead for 10 minutes, until dough is no longer sticky.

3 Use fingers to oil the inside of the bowl lightly. Place dough back in bowl and set aside for 1 hour to rise.

4 Divide risen dough into 8 equal pieces and form into balls. Cover with plastic wrap and set aside for 30 minutes.

5 To boil the bagels, add water, malt, and brown sugar to a large saucepan. Bring to a boil.

6 Preheat oven to 450°F (230°C). Line two baking sheets with parchment paper.

7 Uncover dough balls. Poke a hole about 2 inches (5 cm) in diameter in middle of dough ball to form bagel. Have an adult place them in the boiling water and cook for 1 minute on each side.

8 Remove bagels from water with slotted spoon and place on baking sheet. Leave room between bagels. Bake for 15 minutes or until bagels are a deep golden color, then turn over and bake for 5 to 7 more minutes until other side is golden.

ingredients...

1½ cups warm water

1 tablespoon instant yeast

1 tablespoon malted milk powder

4½ cups bread flour

2 teaspoons salt

2 teaspoons vegetable oil

For boiling bagels:

2 quarts water

1 tablespoon malted milk powder

1 tablespoon brown sugar

Flavored Cream Cheeses

To make your very own flavored cream cheese spreads, simply add the following ingredients to 4 oz (112 g) of softened cream cheese:

Honey Nut Spread
2 tablespoons walnuts, finely chopped

1 tablespoon honey

1 tablespoon brown sugar

Strawberry Spread
¼ cup strawberries, finely chopped

1 tablespoon confectioner's sugar

Garden Vegetable Spread
3 tablespoons carrot, finely minced

2 tablespoons broccoli, finely chopped

1 tablespoon red onion, finely minced

Cinnamon Raisin Spread
3 tablespoons raisins, finely chopped

1 tablespoon brown sugar

½ teaspoon cinnamon

Homemade bagels are the best!

To add poppy or sesame seeds, carefully press one side of bagel into a dish of seeds just before baking.

This recipe is pareve, and may be served with either dairy or meat.

smoked salmon frittata

This creamy egg dish tastes like an omelet and is easy to make. Make two or three to serve all your break-the-fast party guests.

ingredients...

6 eggs, beaten

½ cup sour cream

1 teaspoon dried dill

2 tablespoons butter

½ cup smoked salmon, chopped

¼ cup onion, finely chopped

¼ cup cream cheese, cut
   into small pieces

This recipe is dairy. For a Kosher meal, serve only with other dairy or pareve foods.

get cooking...

1 Preheat oven broiler.

2 Whisk together eggs, sour cream, and dill in bowl.

3 Melt butter in 12-inch (30-cm) oven-safe sauté pan over medium heat. Add salmon and onion, and cook for 2 to 3 minutes.

4 Pour egg mixture into pan and drop pieces of cream cheese into eggs. Cook for about 5 minutes or until eggs become firm.

5 Place pan under broiler for 3 to 4 minutes, until frittata is lightly browned and puffed.

This recipe can be made a day in advance and stored in the refrigerator. Reheat before serving by placing under broiler for about 2 minutes, or until warmed through.

"Many people serve bagels with cream cheese and lox at a break fast. This recipe is a clever way to combine all those tastes together in one dish!"   -Rabbi Ozur Bass

Be sure to use a pot holder when removing pan from oven. The handle will be very, very hot!

"Kugel is one of the most popular and well-known Jewish foods. When it has dried fruit in it, it is called *Yerushalmi*, which means 'from Jerusalem.'" -Rabbi Ozur Bass

This recipe is dairy. For a kosher meal, serve only with other dairy or pareve foods.

Al dente means "to the tooth," which means to cook the pasta until firm.

basic any-which-way kugel

Kugel is a baked egg-and-noodle dish that can be sweet or savory. Everyone has his or her favorite ingredients. With this recipe, you can make one delicious kugel or custom-make mini kugels to suit everyone's tastes!

serves 12

get cooking...

1 Preheat the oven to 350°F (180°C). Lightly grease a 9-inch (23-cm) square pan.

2 Bring a saucepan of water to a boil. Cook the noodles according to package instructions until they are al dente, then drain.

3 In a large bowl, stir together butter, cream cheese, sour cream, eggs, sugar, vanilla, and cinnamon. Add apple cider and milk, stirring to combine. Gently stir in noodles.

4 If you're adding mix-ins, do that now (see sidebar).

5 Transfer noodle mixture to baking pan.

6 In a small bowl, combine cornflake crumbs, butter, sugar, brown sugar, vanilla, and cinnamon. Spread topping over noodle mixture.

7 Bake for about 50 minutes or until kugel is bubbly and golden.

8 Let cool for 10 minutes.

ingredients...

For noodle mixture:

1 8-oz (225-g) package of broad egg noodles

½ cup butter, softened

1 8-oz (225-g) package of cream cheese, softened

1 cup sour cream

4 eggs, slightly beaten

½ cup sugar

1½ teaspoons vanilla extract

1 teaspoon cinnamon

1 cup apple cider

½ cup milk

For basic topping:

1½ cups cornflake crumbs

½ cup butter, softened

¼ cup sugar

¼ cup brown sugar

1 teaspoon vanilla extract

1 teaspoon cinnamon

Make customized mini kugels!

Use the same measurements as the regular recipe, except reduce your liquids to:

¼ cup apple cider

3 tablespoons milk

Lightly grease small oven-proof dishes or disposable foil mini pie pans.

Follow steps 1 through 3. Then:

4. Add 1 tablespoon of mix-ins, such as crushed pineapple, maraschino cherries, mini chocolate chips, preserves or jam, maple syrup, shredded apple, raisins, dried fruit, almond slivers, or pecans.

5. Top with cornflake-crumb mixture or more of your mix-ins.

6. Place containers on a baking sheet and put in the oven. Bake for about 12 minutes or until kugels are bubbly and golden.

mandel bread

Sometimes called mondel bread or *Mandelbrot*, this cookie is very much like Italian biscotti. It is baked twice to make it very crunchy.

"Be sure to make enough mandel bread so that there is some left for breakfast the next day. It's great warm from the toaster with butter on top."
-Rabbi Ozur Bass

ingredients...

3 eggs

¾ cup sugar

2 teaspoons vanilla

¾ cup vegetable oil

3½ cups all-purpose flour

2 teaspoons baking powder

¼ teaspoon cinnamon

½ cup almond slivers

For the topping:

¼ cup sugar

2 teaspoons cinnamon

get cooking...

1 Preheat oven to 350°F (180°C).

2 Beat eggs and sugar in medium mixing bowl until light and fluffy. Add vanilla and oil. Sift flour, baking powder, and cinnamon into wet mixture. Stir until combined. Gently stir in almonds.

3 Separate dough into two equal portions. Shape each portion into a rectangle about 5 inches x 10 inches (12.5 cm x 25 cm), and 1-inch (2.5-cm) thick. Place them on an ungreased baking sheet.

4 Combine remaining sugar and cinnamon in a small bowl. Sprinkle over dough rectangles. You can top with almond slivers, if you like.

5 Measuring with a ruler, mark the dough at 1-inch (2.5-cm) intervals. This will create guides for cutting the cookies after baking.

An adult can mark the dough with a knife.

6 Bake for 20 minutes until golden and firm to the touch. Remove from oven. Using a large spatula, move cookie rectangles to cutting board. An adult should carefully slice through the marks, creating long, 1-inch (2.5-cm)–wide cookies. Then place cookies, cut side down, back on warm baking sheet and return to oven.

7 Bake cookies again until they are golden and toasted, up to 10 minutes.

Mandel means "almond" in German.

yom kippur

52

This recipe is pareve. Mandel bread can be eaten with dairy or meat foods.

You can substitute ½ cup of chocolate chips for almonds, if you like.

SUKKOT

Bundled up in their sukkah, Jewish families celebrate the abundance of autumn foods. Sukkot brings hearty pumpkin soup, stuffed cabbage, stuffed apples, and happy, stuffed bellies!

Sukkot celebrates the fall harvest and connects us to the Earth. One of the symbols during this holiday is the symbol of the four species, called the

Baked apples are a favorite Sukkot treat!

lulav and *etrog.* The *lulav* is made of three plants—palm, willow, and myrtle branches. An *etrog* is a fruit that looks and smells like a large lemon. When Jewish people wave these four species, they are asking God to help provide enough rain so that the crops can grow and there will be enough food for the year.

The Hebrew word *sukkot* means "many booths." The Jewish tradition teaches that a sukkah is a booth or tent in which our Israelite ancestors lived as they wandered in the desert after leaving Egypt. During Sukkot, families build similar booths in their

"We try to replace our home with our sukkah during Sukkot. We bring out our best dishes and have elaborate meals in our sukkah. And as long as the weather is good, we spend the night in the sukkah, too!" —Rabbi Ozur Bass

yards, and decorate them with drawings, paper chains, strings of popcorn, and fruits and vegetables.

There are many traditions that are followed during Sukkot. For instance, the roof of a sukkah must be made of plants that have been cut down. And there must be just the right amount of coverage: You want shade to protect from the sun, but you also want to make sure that a person sitting in the sukkah can see the stars at night. The best part of having a sukkah is relaxing in it and visiting with friends.

Eating in your sukkah is fun, too. Meals usually include seasonal fruits and vegetables, and should be easy to eat outside. Foods like *holishkes* (cabbage rolls) are especially festive, because they are like little cornucopias, stuffed with plenty.

Pomegranates are a symbol of plenty.

pumpkin soup

serves 4

Pumpkin soup is a terrific dish to enjoy in your sukkah, and it will keep you warm on a chilly day. Add a spinach salad filled with fruits and nuts to make it a meal. Enjoy an assortment of quick breads like cranberry, cinnamon raisin, and banana nut with your soup.

ingredients...

3 tablespoons butter

1 medium onion, finely chopped

1 clove garlic, finely chopped

1 tablespoon brown sugar

1 cup potato, peeled and shredded

1 cup apple, peeled and shredded

1 14½-oz (430-ml) can vegetable broth

½ cup water

½ teaspoon salt

¼ teaspoon ground black pepper

1 15-oz (425-g) can cooked canned unsweetened pumpkin (not pie filling)

1 12-oz (350-ml) can evaporated milk

⅛ teaspoon ground cinnamon

⅛ teaspoon ground nutmeg

get cooking...

1 Melt butter in large saucepan over medium heat.

2 Add onion, garlic, and brown sugar to saucepan and cook until soft, about 4 minutes.

3 Add potato and apple, and cook until tender, about 1 to 2 minutes.

4 Add broth, water, salt, and pepper.

5 Turn heat to medium-high and bring mixture to a boil, stirring occasionally.

6 Reduce heat and cook for 15 minutes on low, stirring occasionally.

7 Stir in pumpkin, evaporated milk, cinnamon, and nutmeg.

8 After a few minutes, taste soup. If soup is too thick, add ¼ cup water. If it's too thin, add a ¼ cup more evaporated milk. Cook for 5 more minutes on low.

This recipe is dairy. For a kosher meal, serve only with other dairy or pareve foods.

sukkot

56

"A good hearty soup is definitely a plus on a cold fall night. It's fun to invite people over and form a line to pass along the food from the kitchen to the sukkah."

–Rabbi Ozur Bass

Chicken broth can be used in place of vegetable broth; however, the soup would not be kosher.

Cabbage rolls can be made in advance and refrigerated for a day before they are baked.

holishkes (cabbage rolls)

This cabbage roll, or stuffed cabbage, is like a miniature meatloaf wrapped in a cabbage leaf. It's extra delicious when drenched in a tangy sweet-and-sour sauce.

serves 6

get cooking...

1 Preheat oven to 350°F (180°C).

2 Combine rice, egg, water, onion, garlic, and beef in mixing bowl.

3 Separate the mixture into 12 portions. Scoop each portion into middle of a wilted cabbage leaf, roll, and tuck ends under. Line up the rolls in your pan, seam side down.

4 Combine crushed tomatoes, tomato sauce, lemon juice, brown sugar, and Worcestershire sauce in small bowl. Pour mixture over cabbage rolls.

5 Cover dish with foil and bake for 60 minutes.

ingredients...

1 cup cooked rice

1 egg, beaten

½ cup water

½ cup onion, minced

1 clove garlic, minced

1 pound (450 g) ground beef

12 cabbage leaves, wilted

For the sauce:

1 28-oz (800-g) can crushed tomatoes

1 8-oz (225-g) can tomato sauce

2 tablespoons lemon juice

2 tablespoons brown sugar

1 tablespoon Worcestershire sauce

"Stuffed cabbage always reminds me of sleeping in a sleeping bag. It's a perfect symbolic meal to eat when we spend the night in our sleeping bags in the sukkah!"
—Rabbi Ozur Bass

To wilt cabbage leaves, place a whole head of cabbage in the freezer the night before you make the recipe. Remove the cabbage 3 hours before you need it. The leaves will peel off easily.

For a kosher meal, serve only with other meat or pareve foods.

baked stuffed apples

Sukkot is all about enjoying the bounty of autumn. What better way to celebrate than to go apple picking with your friends and family, and then make a delicious dessert out of your very own harvest?

ingredients...

6 apples, cored

½ cup quick-cook oats

¾ cup brown sugar

2 tablespoons lemon juice

1 tablespoon maple syrup

2 teaspoons cinnamon

6 tablespoons butter

1 pint vanilla ice cream (optional)

get cooking...

1 Preheat oven to 400°F (200°C). Place cored apples in baking dish.

2 In a small bowl, combine oats, brown sugar, lemon juice, maple syrup, cinnamon, and butter. Pack mixture into apples.

3 Bake for 18 to 22 minutes or until apples are soft.

4 Place apples in individual bowls and top each with a scoop of ice cream.

When baking with apples, select apples with firm flesh, such as Rome Beauty, Cortland, and Granny Smith.

Be careful! Apples and filling are hot!

This recipe is dairy. For a Kosher meal, use margarine instead of butter and leave out the ice cream, or serve only with dairy or pareve foods.

HANUKKAH

Families gather around the warm glow of menorah candles during this winter holiday. Delicious fried latkes, doughnuts, and savory dumplings warm everyone's belly, while spending time with family and giving gifts warm everyone's heart!

Hanukkah, or the Festival of Lights, is an eight-day celebration that reminds us of the importance of faith and hope.

In ancient times, a Syrian ruler named Antiochus controlled Israel and did not want anyone to practice Judaism. However, a Jewish leader named Mattathias and his sons, including Judah Maccabee, led a successful revolt against Antiochus. Throughout his life, Judah Maccabee and his brothers continued to fight against Antiochus, eventually winning power and taking back the Temple in Jerusalem. The holiday of Hanukkah recalls the miracle of this military victory against impossible odds. It also celebrates the idea of lighting the lights of God even in the darkest of nights. We remember this by lighting the menorah for the eight nights of Hanukkah.

Jewish tradition teaches that when the Temple was recaptured and was to be rededicated to the Jews of Israel, only one day's worth of oil was found to light the lamps.

Miraculously, the oil lasted eight days.

"There is a wonderful tradition in honor of the heroism of Judith: women should not do any work while the menorah lights are burning."
– Rabbi Ozur Bass

Because oil is an important part of the Hanukkah story, food cooked in oil is part of Hanukkah celebrations. Latkes, doughnuts, and Israeli *sofganiyot* are all cooked in oil.

Besides food, there are other wonderful Hanukkah traditions. Each night of the holiday, Jews around the world light another one of the eight candles on the menorah. The menorah is often kept in a window so that the miracles of Hanukkah are announced to the world.

While the latkes are frying and the menorah is lighting the night, families love to play dreidel, which is a game of

Fried *ponchik* are a sweet treat!

chance. The reward is a stack of chocolate coins called gelt (and bragging rights, of course).

While many people love sweet applesauce with their latkes, some prefer savory sour cream with chives. Why not try both?

potato latkes with applesauce

serves 6

Potato pancakes, or latkes, are perhaps the most recognizable Jewish food. Carrying on the Hanukkah tradition of frying foods in oil, latkes are crispy and delicious.

potato latkes:

1. Shred potatoes with a grater. Watch your fingers!

2. Put potatoes and onion on paper towels and squeeze out the liquid.

3. Put dried potatoes and onion in medium bowl, then add egg, flour, and salt. Combine well.

4. Heat half of canola oil in skillet until very hot, then scoop mounds of potato mixture (about 2 tablespoons each) into pan. Do not crowd pan.

5. Press mounds down with spatula to flatten. Reduce heat and cook until bottoms are golden, about 5 minutes. Flip latkes and cook until golden on other side, then remove cooked latkes to a paper towel to drain. Repeat, using remaining canola oil as needed.

6. Serve immediately, or transfer to an oven-safe dish and keep in a warm (250°F or 120°C) oven until ready to serve.

applesauce:

1. Stir together all ingredients in a medium saucepan.

2. Cover saucepan and cook over medium heat for 15 to 20 minutes, or until apples are soft. (This will depend on the type of apples you use.) Remove from heat and allow mixture to cool.

3. Using a potato masher, mash mixture until your applesauce is as chunky or smooth as you like.

"As the latkes are frying, everyone gathers in the kitchen and tells stories, plays dreidel, and gives presents to celebrate the joy of bringing the light of the menorah into a dark time of year."
—Rabbi Ozur Bass

ingredients...

For the latkes:

1 pound (450 g) potatoes, peeled

½ cup onion, finely chopped

1 large egg, beaten

2 tablespoons all-purpose flour

½ teaspoon salt

½ cup canola oil

For the applesauce:

4 apples, peeled, cored, and diced

¾ cup water

1 tablespoon brown sugar

½ teaspoon ground cinnamon

This recipe is pareve, and may be served with meat or dairy meals.

savory cheese sofganiyot

An unusual twist on the classic Israeli *sofganiyot* (pronounced *SUF-gan-yot*), our version of this recipe has a cheese filling that recalls the story of Judith's bravery as she fed rich cheeses to Holofernes.

get cooking...

1 In a small bowl, mix together softened cream cheese, cheddar cheese, and parsley.

2 Separate biscuits and flatten each one so diameter is about 4 inches (10 cm). Place about a tablespoon of the cheese mixture on a biscuit. Place another biscuit on top and pinch edges together so cheese is fully enclosed. Repeat until you have 5 *sofganiyot*.

3 Heat the oil in a saucepan to 350°F (180°C). While waiting for oil to heat, line a baking sheet with paper towels.

4 When oil is ready, have an adult use a slotted spoon to lower *sofganiyot* into oil. Cook for 2 to 3 minutes on each side, until the dough is cooked through and goldon brown on both cidoc.

5 Remove *sofganiyot* from oil with slotted spoon and place on baking sheet. While still hot, sprinkle with salt.

ingredients...

3 oz (85 g) cream cheese, softened

1 cup mild cheddar cheese, grated

1 teaspoon dried parsley

1 (10 count) package of pre-made refrigerated biscuits

24 oz (710 ml) canola oil (for frying)

2 teaspoons salt

Note: you can find pre-made biscuits in the refrigerated section of most supermarkets.

This recipe is dairy. For a kosher meal, serve only with other dairy or pareve foods.

Sofganiyot is traditionally stuffed with jelly. This is a savory version.

"Hanukkah in Israel is usually cold and rainy. There is nothing better to warm your insides than getting a fresh, steaming-hot *sofganiyot!*"
—Rabbi Ozur Bass

raspberry ponchik

serves
5

Polish *ponchik* are fried doughnuts stuffed with jelly. Eastern European Jews brought these with them as they moved to Israel. This quick and easy recipe allows anyone to celebrate Hanukkah with homemade jelly doughnuts.

get cooking...

1 Separate biscuits and flatten them so diameter is about 4 inches (10 cm).

2 Place about a teaspoon of jelly or jam in the center of each biscuit. Bring the edges together to form a ball. Pinch it closed at the top to seal in the filling.

Don't overload the *ponchik*.

3 When all 10 *ponchik* are ready, pour the oil in a saucepan and bring to 350°F (180°C). While waiting for oil to reach temperature, pour sugar and cinnamon onto a plate.

4 When oil is ready, have an adult use a slotted spoon to lower *ponchik* into oil. Cook for about 2 minutes on each side, until the dough is cooked through and golden brown.

5 Remove from oil with slotted spoon and place on plate with cinnamon sugar. Gently roll the *ponchik* to coat. Be careful, *ponchik* will be hot!

ingredients...

1 (10 count) package of pre-made refrigerated biscuits

24 oz (710 ml) canola oil (for frying)

¼ cup raspberry jelly or jam

¼ cup sugar

2 teaspoons cinnamon

Note: you can use any flavor of your favorite jelly, jam, or preserve.

This recipe is dairy. To plan a kosher meal, serve only with other dairy or pareve foods.

Ponchik are the eastern European version of Israeli sofganiyot.

"A great trick to remove some of the oil from the cooked *ponchik* is to put the cinnamon and sugar in a paper bag. When the *ponchik* are done, toss them in the bag and gently shake. The *ponchik* will get coated in cinnamon sugar, and the bag will absorb some of the oil."
—Rabbi Ozur Bass

TU B'SHEVAT

Wheat, barley, figs, and dates play a leading role in Tu B'Shevat meals. If the weather's nice enough, plan a picnic to celebrate the trees in your yard or favorite park. If it's still too cold, have an indoor picnic, complete with blanket, basket, and friends!

Tu B'Shevat is a unique festival that celebrates the birthdays of trees. It occurs at the beginning of spring in Israel, just as trees begin to bloom, and is celebrated by enjoying the outdoors and planting trees. In other parts of the world, however, Tu B'Shevat takes place while it is still too cold to plant trees. Still, the holiday reminds us to remember the land of Israel and that spring is on its way.

If it's too cold to plant a tree where you live, you can celebrate Tu B'Shevat by planting herb seeds in a paper cup and sitting them on a windowsill to grow. If you plant parsley, you can use

Cooking with friends makes every meal special.

"In Hebrew school when I was growing up, our teachers always gave us *bukser* to eat. I never really wanted to try it. Only when I got older did I learn that *bukser* was a dried carob pod. I love to crunch on them now!" —Rabbi Ozur Bass

your harvest a few months later at your Pesach seder.

If planting isn't your thing, another way to celebrate is by giving a plant to someone you love.

Eating fresh fruits is also an important part of this holiday. Some people plan a special meal—like a Pesach seder—that features wheat, barley, grapes, figs, pomegranates, olives, and dates. These foods are called the "seven species," and are important crops in Israel. Tu B'Shevat is our way to celebrate them. Rabbis teach that even when we aren't in Israel, just the act of eating any of

these foods is a way to remember and praise the land of Israel.

Another food that is in season during Tu B'Shevat is carob. It grows in a pod and tastes a bit like chocolate. Carob pods are sometimes dried themselves, and then eaten as well. Dried carob pods are called *bukser*, and are sort of dry and very crunchy.

No matter the fresh fruits or grains that you cook with for Tu B'Shevat, honoring nature and one another is the real spirit of this holiday.

fig spread and tu b'shevat granola

Figs and walnuts taste delicious with cream cheese. Together with granola they make an excellent snack to enjoy while sitting under a tree during Tu B'Shevat. Try the spread on baguette and apple slices.

ingredients...

For the granola:

4 cups oatmeal (not quick oats)

½ cup canola oil

¾ cup brown sugar

2 tablespoons honey

2 tablespoons maple syrup

1½ teaspoons cinnamon

1 teaspoon vanilla extract

½ cup raisins (optional)

¼ cup almonds, slivered (optional)

For the fig spread:

1 cup dried figs, stems removed

⅓ cup walnuts

8 oz (225 g) cream cheese

¼ teaspoon salt

tu b'shevat granola:

1 Preheat oven to 350°F (180°C).

2 Combine oatmeal, canola oil, brown sugar, honey, maple syrup, cinnamon, and vanilla in bowl. Break up any clumps of brown sugar.

3 Pour mixture onto baking sheet. Bake in oven for about 20 minutes, stirring every 5 minutes. Be careful not to burn it.

4 After the mixture is baked, add raisins and almonds (if using). Then pour onto wax paper to cool. Serve warm or at room temperature.

fig spread:

1 Chop figs in food processor until fine. Add walnuts and pulse until walnuts are coarsely chopped. Add cream cheese and salt and process until combined.

2 Put mixture in small bowl. Cover with plastic wrap and chill in refrigerator for 1 hour before serving.

Fig spread is dairy and may be served with other dairy or pareve dishes.

"After the granola mixture bakes, you can add anything you want. Dried cherries, puffed rice cereal, toasted coconut, or chocolate chips are all delicious options." —Rabbi Ozur Bass

Granola is pareve and may be eaten with dairy or meat dishes.

Granola tastes great sprinkled on yogurt.

You can use 3 fresh figs in place of dried figs.

Decorate the cake with frosting or candy leaves, or use real hazelnuts.

hazelnut tree birthday cake

At Tu B'Shevat we learn about the symbolism of hazelnuts. They have edible insides that represent holiness, and outer shells that serves as protection. Since Tu B'Shevat celebrates the birthdays of trees, a birthday cake makes the day even more fun.

get cooking...

1. Preheat oven to 350°F (180°C). Line jelly roll pan with parchment paper.

2. Combine cake mix, eggs, water, and oil and beat until smooth. Pour batter into pan.

3. Bake for about 15 minutes or until done. Let cool for 5 minutes.

4. Turn cake out onto a dish towel. Peel off baked-on parchment paper.

5. While still warm, carefully roll towel and cake lengthwise. Set aside. Allow rolled cake to cool for 30 minutes.

Let the towel help you roll the cake.

6. In another bowl, combine frosting and hazelnut-flavored spread using wooden spoon.

7. Unroll cooled cake log and spread inside of roll with 1½ cups of frosting. Reroll, but without the towel this time.

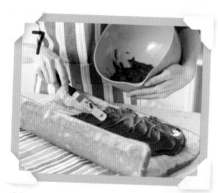

Use a spreader or butter knife.

8. Use remaining frosting to cover outside of cake. You can use a fork to make frosting look like tree bark.

If cake breaks while rolling, cover cracks with frosting.

ingredients...

For the cake:

18.25-oz (517-g) box vanilla cake mix

4 eggs

½ cup water

⅓ cup vegetable oil

For the filling and frosting:

2 12- to 16-oz (340- to 450-g) tubs of chocolate frosting

1 cup hazelnut-flavored spread

Note: you can decorate your cake any way you like. Try sprinkles or multi-colored icing.

This recipe is dairy. For a kosher meal, serve only with other dairy or pareve foods.

PURIM

Purim brings friends, feasts, and fanciful costumes together! Get dressed up and host your own Purim festival. Enjoy hamantaschen, kreplach, lentil salad, delicious deli sandwiches, and more as you celebrate the bravery of Esther.

Kreplach are like little dumplings.

Purim honors the brave and beautiful Esther and her Uncle Mordechai. Long ago they protected the Jewish people living in Persia from the evil Haman, who hoped to destroy them. It is a holiday that is both serious and silly, and is all about turning normal customs upside down.

On Purim, the Book of Esther, or the *Megillat* Esther (also known as the Megillah), is read out loud from a scroll. The story tells how King Achashverosh, a Persian, chose Esther, a Jew, to be his wife. As the new Queen of Persia, Esther hid her religious beliefs, fearing for her safety. But when Achashverosh's

"The reading of the *Megillat Esther* is done with a lot of audience participation. We are told to erase the name of Haman so every time his name is read in the story, we make lots of noise to drown out the sound of his name." —Rabbi Ozur Bass

general, Haman, called for the deaths of all Jewish people in Persia, Esther bravely asked her husband the king to spare the lives of her people. With the help of her Uncle Mordechai, Esther turned a scary time for the Jewish people into a time of great celebration.

There are many different foods that are served on Purim, including delicious hamantaschen, which means "pockets of poppyseeds" in German. In Israel they are called "*oznei* Haman,"

or "Haman's ears."

Some people eat vegetarian feasts in honor of Esther, as it is said that Esther ate only seeds and nuts when she was living in the palace to make sure she followed the rules of kashrut.

Along with the delicious food come fun and festive Purim customs. People wear costumes and masks to the reading of the *Megillat* Esther. What costumes do you wear for Purim?

AchashVerosh's sandwich crown

This sandwich looks like a king's crown, and will feed a crowd. Everyone will get into the festive spirit of Purim!

get cooking...

1 Preheat oven to 350°F (180°C).

2 Roll dough into a snake 2 feet (60 cm) long and about 3 inches (7.5 cm) in diameter.

3 Place on greased baking sheet, forming a circle and pressing ends together. Brush bread with oil and sprinkle with sesame seeds.

4 Bake for 25 to 30 minutes, until golden brown.

5 Allow bread to cool, then have an adult slice the ring horizontally.

Ask an adult to slice the bread.

6 Layer lettuce, turkey, pastrami, tomatoes, and onions on bottom half of loaf.

Layer on as much as you want!

7 Spread mayonnaise and mustard on other half of loaf, and place on top.

8 To finish your crown sandwich, you can put a grape tomato and olive on each toothpick. Stick them into the loaf to resemble gems and jewels on a crown.

This recipe is meat. For a Kosher meal, serve only with other meat and pareve foods.

ingredients...

24 oz (680 g) bread dough

2 tablespoons vegetable oil

1 tablespoon sesame seeds

1 cup lettuce, shredded, or 10 leaves

½ pound (225 g) deli turkey

½ pound (225 g) deli pastrami

½ cup tomato, sliced

¼ cup red onion, thinly sliced

3 tablespoons mayonnaise

3 tablespoons yellow mustard

For serving:

10 toothpicks

10 grape tomatoes and/or 10 olives

"On Purim afternoon, there is the tradition of sharing a large festive meal, called a *Seudah* (pronounced *seh-oo-DAH*). The meal begins with people making jokes and creating funny versions of some of the traditional prayers said at more serious holiday meals."
—Rabbi Ozur Bass

You can use ready-made refrigerated bread loaves, defrosted store-bought dough, or challah dough.

"The Persian Jewish community celebrates Purim with big parties. One of my friends, whose parents are Iranian, gets together with many other Persian Jewish women. They each make their own version of sesame-seed candy and have taste tests."

—Rabbi Ozur Bass

Be careful! Sometimes small rocks can be mixed in with raw lentils.

Persian lentil salad

This recipe includes traditional Persian ingredients like mint, parsley, and lime juice. And because lentils are seeds (not beans), they represent the seeds that Esther ate to keep kosher while she lived at the palace.

ingredients...

½ cup dry lentils

2 cups water

1 teaspoon salt

1 cup chickpeas

1 cup green bell pepper, diced

1 cup red bell pepper, diced

1 cup yellow bell pepper, diced

1 tablespoon jalapeno pepper, minced

¼ cup green onion, chopped

¼ cup mint, chopped

¼ cup parsley, chopped

2 tablespoons lime juice

2 tablespoons olive oil

get cooking...

1 Cook lentils by bringing lentils, water, and salt to a boil. Reduce heat to medium and cook for 25 minutes or until lentils are tender. Drain and rinse with cold water.

2 Toss together cooked lentils and all other ingredients in a bowl. Serve warm or chilled.

This recipe is pareve. For a kosher meal, serve with either dairy or meat foods.

You can use canned lentils for this recipe:

Drain and rinse 1 15-oz (425-g) can of lentils and reduce cooking time to 15 to 20 minutes.

purim

turkey kreplach

Kreplach are a traditional Jewish food any time, not just on Purim. Like the suspense of the Purim story, the contents of a kreplach remain a mystery until you bite into it! This recipe features a turkey filling, but you can use whatever meat or veggies you like.

get cooking...

1 Preheat oven to 375°F (190°C).

2 Combine all ingredients in a bowl except wrappers and oil.

3 Cut wonton wrappers in half using knife or pizza cutter. Wrappers should then be rectangles.

4 Place a teaspoon of mixture on wrapper and fold twice to form a triangle. On the final fold, moisten the edge of the wrapper with water to seal the dough.

5 Brush baking sheets with vegetable oil and place kreplach on them. Brush tops of kreplach with oil. Bake for 13 to 15 minutes. Kreplach should be crunchy and golden brown.

Kreplach are very similar to Italian ravioli or Chinese wontons.

Fold the corner over to make a triangle.

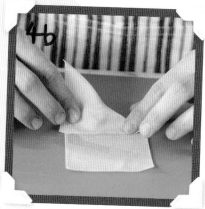

Fold the triangle across the wrapper for the second fold.

ingredients...

1 pound (450 g) ground turkey, cooked

12 oz (340 g) spinach, cooked and chopped

1 egg

¾ cup bread crumbs

½ teaspoon garlic powder

1 teaspoon Italian spice mix (garlic, basil, and oregano)

3 tablespoons vegetable oil

1 package square egg roll or wonton wrappers

Note: Egg roll or wonton wrappers can be found in the produce section of most grocery stores.

This recipe is meat. For a kosher meal, serve only with other meat or pareve foods.

"Kreplach are a delicious addition to any good soup. Sometimes I take kreplach that I have frozen and put them in my Shabbat chicken soup."

—Rabbi Ozur Bass

Kreplach can also be cooked by boiling in broth or deep frying in oil.

hamantaschen

Hamantaschen are reminders of when Persian Jews were saved from Haman's cruelty. These cookies resemble the tri-cornered hat that evil Haman wore.

makes 60 cookies

ingredients...

1½ cups butter, softened

1 cup sugar

2 eggs, beaten

3 tablespoons orange juice

½ teaspoon vanilla extract

½ teaspoon salt

2 teaspoons baking powder

5 cups all-purpose flour

½ cup apricot jam or preserves

½ cup raspberry jam or preserves

Note: a 3-inch (7.5-cm) round cookie cutter will work best, but if you don't have one then you can use a drinking glass of the same size.

Allow some jam to show throug[h]

get cooking...

1 Beat butter and sugar together.

2 Combine eggs, orange juice, and vanilla in small bowl. Add to butter mixture and combine. Add salt and baking powder, then add flour 1 cup at a time until dough forms.

3 Refrigerate dough for at least 1 hour.

4 Preheat oven to 350°F (180°C). Line baking sheets with parchment paper.

5 Roll out dough until it is ¼ inch (½ cm) thick. Cut out circles using a cookie cutter or a glass, and place on parchment.

6 Put a scant teaspoon of preserves in center of each circle. Pinch sides of circles together to create a triangle. Place formed cookies in freezer for 10 minutes.

Try not to overload with jam.

7 Remove from freezer and bake for 10 to 12 minutes. Cookies should be slightly browned.

"Every year my sisters and I helped our mother make hamantaschen. We sang and laughed and had so much fun as we rolled and cut and filled and pinched. I know the cookies tasted better because we were smiling when we made them."

—Rabbi Ozur Bass

RUTHE

his recipe is dairy.
For a Kosher meal,
serve only with
other dairy or
pareve foods.

Prune preserves are traditional, but
you can use whatever flavor you like.

PESACH

Pesach brings families together to the seder table in celebration of their history and traditions. It is a time to remember the struggles of the Israelites, and to eat and enjoy matzoh, haroset, meringues, and other treats from the Old World.

Pesach, or Passover, celebrates the trials and triumphs of the Israelite people in Egypt.

Pharaoh kept the Israelites as slaves, and treated them cruelly for many years. When he finally decided to let the Israelites follow Moses out of Egypt, the Israelites left in a hurry because they feared that Pharaoh would change his mind. He did change his mind, and sent his army after them. So the Israelites fled into the desert.

Seder plate

Because they left Egypt so quickly, the Israelites did not have time to let their bread dough rise before baking it. So instead of having leavened bread, they had flat matzoh. To remember the escape of Israelite ancestors, many Jews do not eat leavened foods during Pesach. Some families completely remove anything that contains flour or leavening agents (called "chametz") from their homes during Pesach.

"The Torah teaches that the first seder was held the night before the Israelites left Egypt. They ate Passover lamb and talked about the miracles that were happening all around them."

—Rabbi Ozur Bass

During the first two nights of Pesach, a seder is held, at which the Haggadah is read aloud. *Haggadah* means "the telling," and it tells the story of the Israelites' flight from Egypt.

Everything on the seder table is used to help tell the story, especially the items placed on the special seder plate. The symbolic foods on the seder plate are: a roasted shank bone, a roasted egg, horseradish, romaine lettuce (or parsley), celery, and haroset.

After the Haggadah is read, families celebrate with a delicious, festive meal. Many of the dishes traditionally served hearken back to ancient times, and are based on the foods available to the Israelites as they continued their journey through the desert.

Meringue cookies are perfect for Pesach.

haroset

Much of the seder is about the bitterness and sorrow of life in Egypt under Pharaoh. While haroset (pronounced *ha-ROH-set*) looks like the mortar that the Israelites used to build Egyptian cities, it tastes sweet to celebrate being freed from Egypt. Here are two different ways to prepare it: Ashkenazic (which is not cooked) and Sephardic (which is).

Ashkenazic

ingredients...

For the Ashkenazic apple haroset:

6 apples, peeled, cored, and chopped

1 cup walnuts, finely chopped

½ teaspoon ground cinnamon

1 teaspoon sugar

1 tablespoon honey

⅓ cup grape juice

For the Sephardic haroset:

1 cup dried figs

1 cup dried dates, pitted

¾ cup raisins

¼ cup honey

¼ cup water

½ teaspoon cinnamon

¼ cup orange marmalade

½ cup walnuts, finely chopped

ashkenazic apple haroset:

1 Put all ingredients in bowl and mix, crushing apples slightly with spoon.

sephardic haroset:

1 Place all ingredients in saucepan over medium heat. Cook for 5 to 7 minutes or until marmalade melts and fruits are warmed through. Serve immediately.

Both of these recipes are pareve, and can be served with meat, dairy, or other pareve foods.

"Every Jewish community around the world has its own tradition of how to make haroset. Some are sweet, others are more tart or even spicy."   —Rabbi Ozur Bass

Sephardic

You can add strips of orange peel to your haroset, for more flavor.

citrus salmon en papillote

Eating fish is not that common on Passover, but it can be a nice change from the heavier foods that are traditionally served at the seder.

get cooking...

1 Preheat oven to 400°F (200°C). In a small bowl, mix olive oil, tarragon, garlic, orange peel, lemon peel, brown sugar, and orange juice.

2 Cut 4 squares of parchment paper, each 12 x 12 inches (30 x 30 cm). Place sliced onions in the center of each sheet of parchment.

3 Place a piece of salmon on each bed of onions. Spread each piece of salmon with orange peel mixture, then place an orange and lemon slice on top of each fillet.

Wash your hands after touching raw fish.

4 Pull all sides of parchment paper up to form a bundle. Tie with string so parchment paper looks like a small sack.

Tie the bundles tightly.

5 Place packets on baking sheet and bake for 17 to 20 minutes.

6 Ask an adult to cut open the packets (they'll be hot and steamy), and help put each salmon stack on a plate.

ingredients...

2 tablespoons olive oil

1 teaspoon fresh tarragon, minced

2 cloves garlic, minced

1 teaspoon orange peel

1 teaspoon lemon peel

1 teaspoon brown sugar

1 tablespoon orange juice

1 red onion, sliced into thin rings

4 4-oz (112-g) salmon fillets

4 orange slices

4 lemon slices

Note: Other citrus fruits, such as lime and grapefruit will also work well.

"There many different traditions, laws, and customs about food on Passover. Many of the customs depend on how the food was processed or prepared in different Jewish communities all over Europe, Africa, or Asia."
–Rabbi Ozur Bass

This recipe is pareve, so it may be served with either dairy or meat foods.

Steam will get trapped in the packet, and that's what cooks the salmon.

"Sephardic Jews and Jews from Northern Africa have big celebrations called 'Mimouna' as Passover is ending. They open their doors and serve mint tea and many wonderful foods to all the guests who can fit in their homes."   —Rabbi Ozur Bass

serves 8

savory mina

This Sephardic meat pie features ground beef, mashed potato, onions, and spices simmered in a hearty gravy and then baked in matzoh crust.

get cooking...

1 Preheat oven to 350°F (180°C).

2 Put beef, potato, onion, salt, pepper, cinnamon, allspice, and water in skillet. Simmer over medium heat for 30 minutes.

3 While meat mixture cooks, soak 4 matzoh sheets in warm water until they are very soft—almost mushy.

4 Squeeze moisture out of the wet matzoh using paper towels. Press matzoh onto bottom and sides of a 9-inch (23-cm) pie pan.

5 Brush matzoh with 1 tablespoon of vegetable oil and place in oven for 2 to 3 minutes.

ingredients...

1 pound (450 g) ground beef

1 large potato, baked and mashed

½ cup onion, minced

½ teaspoon salt

½ teaspoon ground black pepper

½ teaspoon ground cinnamon

½ teaspoon ground allspice

1 cup water

8 matzoh sheets

1 to 2 cups warm water

2 tablespoons vegetable oil

6 After meat is finished cooking, spoon into matzoh crust.

7 Soak remaining matzoh in warm water until soft. Place pieces of softened matzoh on top of meat mixture to form an outer crust. When finished, brush with remaining vegetable oil and then bake for 20 minutes.

This recipe is meat. For a kosher meal, serve only with other meat or pareve dishes.

Sephardic Jews are descended from Jews in Spain, Portugal, and Turkey.

pesach ✳

93

froggy meringue cookies

Meringue cookies are often served at Passover because they do not use any flour or leavening agents. We've put a fun twist on ours: Instead of plain white meringues we're making frogs!

get cooking...

1 Preheat oven to 200°F (95°C). Line baking sheets with parchment paper.

2 Separate eggs by carefully cracking each egg into a bowl and then gently scooping out the yolk.

2a

Be careful not to break the yolk.

2b

Keep the yolks for another recipe.

3 Put egg whites in bowl. Use electric mixer to beat eggs until they are light and foamy.

4 Add sugar a little bit at a time. Eventually the mixture will become shiny and peaks will stand up when the beaters are removed. (Turn them off first!)

5 Put ½ cup of meringue into a pastry bag or sandwich bag and set aside.

6 Add vanilla and food coloring to rest of meringue mixture, and gently stir until color is even.

7 Drop a tablespoon of green meringue onto parchment paper for the frog's head. Then use pastry bag or plastic bag to add two white meringue dots. Push chocolate chips into dots to form eyeballs.

7

Make the eyes large or small!

ingredients...

4 egg whites

2½ cups confectioners' (powdered) sugar

½ teaspoon vanilla extract

3 drops green food coloring

2 oz (56 g) mini chocolate chips

Note: If you do not have a pastry bag, you can snip the corner off of a plastic sandwich bag and use that instead. (Fill the bag before you snip!)

Not into frogs? Omit food coloring and chocolate chips. By omitting chocolate chips, this recipe becomes pareve, not dairy.

"I love this recipe because we always have toy frogs all over our seder table. The frogs were one of 10 terrible plagues in Egypt that God sent to convince Pharaoh to let the Israelites out of slavery." -Rabbi Ozur Bass

This recipe is dairy. For a kosher meal, serve only with other dairy or pareve foods.

Use a glass or metal bowl to help your meringue stiffen properly.

matzoh brei

serves 1

Matzoh brei (pronounced *MAHT-zoh BRY*) is a fun-to-eat breakfast. It's a lot like traditional French toast, only it's made with matzoh instead of bread.

ingredients...

1 sheet of matzoh
2 tablespoons hot water
1 egg
1 tablespoon butter or canola oil
cinnamon and sugar for topping

get cooking...

1 Break matzoh into small pieces and put in bowl with hot water.

2 In another bowl, beat the egg with a fork.

3 Melt butter or heat oil in frying pan over medium heat.

4 Pour egg over matzoh, then pour into hot pan.

5 Let mixture become golden brown. Flip and cook the other side to golden brown.

6 Sprinkle with cinnamon and sugar and serve immediately.

"We wait all year to eat matzoh brei! We like it for an easy lunch or dinner. After the heavy meals of the seder, it is good to eat lighter foods for the rest of the week of Passover."
–Rabbi Ozur Bass

This recipe is dairy. For a kosher meal, serve only with other dairy or pareve foods.

Matzoh brei can be made savory by adding onions, peppers, or mushrooms to the matzoh-and-egg mixture.

YOM HA'ATZMAUT

The flavors of Israel are celebrated on Israeli Independence Day. People gather at springtime barbecues to dance and sing *HaTikvah*, and eat hummus, falafel, baba ghanoush, *shakshouka* and more!

Yom Ha'Atzmaut is Israeli Independence Day. This day marks the birth of the modern State of Israel.

Yom Ha'Atzmaut is all about pride in Israel and celebrating with friends. It is also a day to feast on traditional Israeli foods, and to take in the beauty of the land by spending time outside. In Israel, many people enjoy barbecues and parties, where there is plenty of Israeli folk dancing and singing.

For Jewish people elswhere, observing Yom Ha'Atzmaut is a way to show support for the country of Israel. It is very much like Fourth-of-July festivities in the United States.

Why is celebrating Israel important? Because Israel is the homeland of the Jewish people. Although there are Jewish communities all around the world, a dedication to the land of Israel

Israeli flags fly high on Yom Ha'Atzmaut.

"You can make your barbecue extra festive with lots of blue and white decorations."

—Rabbi Ozur Bass

has held Jewish people together throughout time.

For almost two thousand years Jews lived without a land of their own. So when Israel finally became a modern state for the Jewish people—in 1948—it was as if a great miracle had happened. Because of this, Yom Ha'Atzmaut is not just a political holiday, but a religious holiday, too.

The rejoicing and celebrating of Israeli Independence Day is a welcome time in spring, because people often gather at outdoor picnics and barbecues. It is especially welcome because it comes after solemn holidays, including Yom Ha'Shoah, which is a day to remember all of the people who perished in the Holocaust.

No matter where you live, celebrating Yom Ha'Atzmaut is easy. The fresh spring fruits and vegetables on the menu can be found everywhere. And most supermarkets have Israeli products in their international foods section.

So get your pots and pans ready, it's time to cook and celebrate!

Israeli salad

Simple foods can be delicious. This refreshing salad perks up every meal. It is great alongside eggs at breakfast, stuffed in a pita with falafel at lunch, or paired with roasted lamb at dinner.

ingredients...

2 cups cucumber, peeled, seeded, and diced

2 cups tomatoes, seeded, and diced

½ cup onion, fincely minced

3 tablespoons olive oil

2 tablespoons lemon juice

½ teaspoon salt

½ teaspoon *za'taar* (optional)

get cooking...

1 Combine all ingredients in a bowl and serve cold.

Za'taar is a strong Middle Eastern spice that tastes a little like oregano. It is actually a mixture of spices, much like curry. And also like curry, every spice seller in Israel has his or her own secret recipe for the mixture of spices in za'taar.

This recipe is pareve and can be served with dairy or meat recipes.

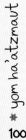

yom ha'atzmaut

100

"When I am in Israel, one of my favorite breakfasts is Israeli salad mixed with fresh yogurt and za'taar."

–Rabbi Ozur Bass

Israeli salad has many varieties. Experiment by adding different fresh spices like mint, parsley or dill.

baked falafel patties and hummus

serves 4-6

Falafel and hummus are popular and traditional foods in Israel. Almost every street corner has a falafel shop just bursting with the flavors of the Middle East. Invite friends who have been to Israel to your Yom Ha'Atzmaut feast. Ask them about the sights, sounds, smells, and tastes of their journey.

ingredients...

For the falafel:

1 15-oz (425-g) can chickpeas, drained

½ cup onion, grated

½ cup parsley, finely minced

2 cloves garlic, finely minced

1 egg

2 tablespoons olive oil

2 teaspoons hot sauce (optional)

1 teaspoon lemon juice

1 teaspoon baking powder

1 teaspoon cumin

1 teaspoon coriander

½ teaspoon salt

1 cup bread crumbs

For the hummus:

1 15-oz (425-g) can chickpeas, drained

¼ cup sesame tahini

3 tablespoons lemon juice

1 clove garlic, crushed

½ teaspoon cumin

2 teaspoons olive oil

falafel patties:

1 Preheat oven to 400°F (200°C).

2 Mash chickpeas in large bowl. Add onion, parsley, and garlic.

3 In a separate bowl, mix egg, olive oil, hot sauce, lemon juice, baking powder, cumin, coriander, and salt. Add to chickpea mixture and stir.

4 Add bread crumbs, using your hands to combine. If mixture is sticky, add more bread crumbs. If mixture is too dry to form patties, add more olive oil.

5 Form into 20 patties, each about 2 inches (5 cm) in diameter.

6 Place patties on lightly oiled baking sheet and bake for 15 minutes. Flip patties and bake for 15 more minutes.

hummus:

1 Place all ingredients except olive oil in blender or food processor, and blend until smooth.

2 If hummus is thicker than you like, stir in some olive oil.

3 Place hummus in bowl and serve with a drizzle of olive oil on top.

Falafel can also be deep fried.

Heat 1 cup vegetable oil in a large, heavy skillet over medium-high heat. Have an adult fry patties for 1 to 2 minutes per side or until golden brown.

"A good falafel seller in Israel makes quite a show when putting the falafel into the pita. Like a pizza maker, he will toss the balls into the air with his tongs and catch them in the pita!" —Rabbi Ozur Bass

These recipes are pareve and can be served with dairy or meat meals.

A warm pita stuffed with delicious falafel, hummus, and Israeli salad is a healthy and tasty lunch.

If you like spicy food, you can add some chopped jalapeños, too.

shakshouka

Meaning "all mixed up" in Hebrew, *shakshouka* is a traditional Sephardic breakfast. The eggs poach in the tomatoey sauce, and it's all served out of the same pan.

ingredients...

2 tablespoons olive oil

2 cloves garlic, crushed

½ cup onion, chopped

2 cups tomatoes, cubed

1 cup green peppers, chopped

1 cup red peppers, chopped

4 eggs

⅛ teaspoon red chili flakes (optional)

This recipe is pareve, and can be served with dairy or meat foods.

get cooking...

1 Heat oil in a nonstick frying pan over medium-high heat, then add garlic and onion. Cook until tender, 4 to 5 minutes.

2 Add tomatoes and peppers. After a few minutes, turn heat down to medium. Allow mixture to simmer for 20 minutes.

3 Create 4 wells in the tomato mixture, each about the size of an egg.

4 Carefully crack an egg into small bowl. Pour into well. Repeat until you have 4 eggs cooking. Place lid on pan and turn heat to low. Cook until eggs are as firm as you like. Sprinkle chili flakes over *shakshouka* before serving.

"In a traditional kosher home, eggs can be used only if they have no spots on the yolks. We crack the egg carefully into a glass, inspect it, and then put it into the bowl. Cracking and checking the eggs is a great way to include younger children." -Rabbi Ozur Bass

yom ha'atzmaut ✳

baba ghanoush

A taste of the Middle East, this is a healthy snack to eat anytime with pita, crackers, and cut-up vegetables.

get cooking...

1 Preheat oven to 400°F (200°C). Wash the eggplant and prick its skin several times with a fork. Place on a baking sheet and roast in oven for 45 minutes. Remove from oven and let cool.

2 Once cool, scrape roasted eggplant (seeds and all) from its skin into bowl.

A spoon works great for this.

3 Put eggplant, lemon juice, tahini, olive oil, garlic, and salt into food processor. Process until the mixture becomes smooth.

4 Sprinkle with paprika and serve.

ingredients...

1 medium eggplant

¼ cup lemon juice

¼ cup sesame tahini

2 tablespoons olive oil

2 cloves garlic, fincely minced

¼ teaspoon salt

¼ teaspoon paprika

Note: Tahini can be found in natural food stores or the Middle Eastern foods section of large grocery stores.

Tahini is easy to make from scratch.

Put 1 cup of sesame seeds in the food processor with ⅓ cup of vegetable oil. Process until seeds are broken down and mixture is smooth.

This recipe is pareve, and can be served with either dairy or meat foods.

"Eggplants are found in cuisine from all over the Mediterranean region, especially in many Italian Jewish recipes."

-Rabbi Ozur Bass

LAG B'OMER

Hot summer days and breezy summer nights are the perfect venue for Lag B'Omer celebrations. Enjoy the day with kebabs, fresh salads, and icy-cold, refreshing pomegranate lemonade!

Pomegranate-seed ice cubes are a nice touch!

Lag B'Omer is the thirty-third day of the counting of the omer. The omer are the 49 days between Pesach and Shavuot.

The word *omer* means "offering." During the 49 days of the omer ancient Jewish people would celebrate the first crop—the barley crop—being harvested. In ancient Israel they would cut measures of barley for each of the 49 days and bring them to Temple as an offering to God.

Today, the Jewish people still count these days in anticipation of Shavuot, which honors the gift of the Torah from God.

"Lag is not really a word. It is a combination of the Hebrew letters that form the number 33. It stands for the thirty-third day of the counting of the omer." —Rabbi Ozur Bass

The counting of the omer is a serious time, and many people believe that certain activities and celebrations, like weddings and parties—even getting a haircut—are forbidden during this time.

However, the thirty-third day of the count—Lag B'Omer—is for rejoicing. Many weddings occur on this day, as well as school festivals, parties, picnics, and bonfires. Athletic events and archery competitions are also associated with Lag B'Omer, in recognition of a brief military victory in ancient Israel.

This holiday falls in early summer, which makes the parties and picnics that much more fun. Warm, summer days and nights make sporting events and big parties extra special. With summer parties come summer foods. Celebrate Lag B'Omer with fresh summer fruits and vegetables, and dishes that are perfect for barbecues and picnics.

tabbouleh

Refreshing but zesty, this cracked-wheat salad is great to eat at barbecues, or for a quick lunch on Shabbat. Use crisp romaine lettuce leaves as spoons to eat your tabbouleh.

get cooking...

1 Have an adult pour boiling water over bulgur wheat and cover the bowl with plastic wrap. Set aside for 1 hour. Drain and let cool.

2 In same bowl, mix together all ingredients except lettuce.

3 Serve your room-temperature (or chilled) salad on lettuce leaves.

This recipe is pareve and can be served with dairy or meat dishes.

ingredients...

½ cup boiling water

¼ cup bulgur wheat

2½ cups tomatoes, seeded and diced

½ cup scallions, sliced

1 cup cucumber, seeded and diced

1 cup fresh parsley, chopped

¼ cup fresh mint, chopped

2 tablespoons lemon juice

2 tablespoons olive oil

2 teaspoons salt

⅛ teaspoon allspice

8 leaves Romaine lettuce

Bulgur wheat tastes nutty.

"Tabbouleh is often served as a side salad. I like mine on a hot summer day with a lot of extra lemon." —Rabbi Ozur Bass

Lag b'omer

Tabbouleh can be spelled many ways, such as taboule, tabboleh, tabouleh, and tabuli.

lamb and vegetable shish kebabs

Tender meat and juicy vegetables are made even more flavorful after being grilled over an open flame for a true taste of the Middle East.

ingredients...

For the marinade:

2 cloves garlic, crushed

3 tablespoons lemon juice

¼ cup canola oil

¼ cup fresh parsley, chopped

1 teaspoon coriander

1 teaspoon cumin

For the kebabs:

1 pound (450 g) lamb fillet, cut into 20 1-inch (2.5-cm) cubes

1 green pepper, cut into 12 chunks

12 cherry tomatoes

Note: you can use metal or bamboo skewers for this recipe.

pomegranate lemonade

Taste Israel's sunshine in your glass. This is more tart and tangy than plain lemonade.

ingredients

6 lemons

5 cups cold water

1 cup pomegranate juice

1 cup sugar

1. Juice lemons. (Be sure to pick out all the seeds.)

2. Combine lemon juice, water, pomegranate juice, and sugar in pitcher. Stir well. Serve chilled.

get cooking...

1 Whisk together marinade ingredients. Pour over lamb chunks and refrigerate for at least 2 hours.

2 Assemble kabobs by alternating meat chunks and vegetables on skewers.

3 Have an adult place skewers on heated grill. Cook for 5 minutes and flip over, then cook until done, about 5 more minutes.

This recipe is meat. To plan a kosher meal, serve only with other meat or pareve foods.

You can also broil the kebabs.

Lag b'omer

113

watermelon salad

Juicy watermelon, succulent tomatoes, crunchy celery, and tasty onion come together in a refreshing salad that is perfect for barbecues. Hollow out the watermelon halves carefully and you can use them as serving bowls.

ingredients...

¼ cup red wine vinegar

2 teaspoons sugar

2 cups watermelon, seeded and diced

1 cup tomatoes, seeded and diced

¼ cup celery, diced

¼ cup red onion, minced

This recipe is pareve and may be served with meat or dairy for a kosher meal.

get cooking...

1 In a bowl, combine red wine vinegar and sugar.

2 Add all other ingredients to bowl and toss to coat with liquid. Serve chilled.

Be creative! Use cookie cutters to cut out watermelon shapes to garnish your salad. Or make an ice bowl in which to serve your salad. Be careful, though—ice bowls don't last very long at picnics!

Watermelon is a great source of vitamins A and C

lag b'omer

114

"Watermelons are abundant in Israel during the summer months. Because of this, they're always part of an Israeli picnic, especially one celebrating Lag B'Omer."

-Rabbi Ozur Bass

SHAVUOT

Delicious dairy foods are traditional on Shavuot. Friends and family gather to celebrate the presentation of the Torah, and then spend hours in discussion and debate. Refresh with creamy cheesecake, blintzes, and stuffed French toast.

The word *Shavuot* means "weeks" in Hebrew. This holiday occurs at the conclusion to the seven-week counting of the omer. These seven weeks correspond to when the first barley crop was harvested in ancient times. The end of the omer is Shavuot, which marks the beginning of the main harvest season. Shavuot also commemorates God's giving the Torah to the Jewish people. The Torah is the central text of the Jewish people, and is the foundation of Jewish identity and law. It is a sacred text, and so Jewish people rejoice on Shavuot.

There are many customs attached to Jewish holidays, and on Shavuot, there is a custom to eat dairy foods. No one really knows where this custom comes from, and people give many different reasons.

One idea is that when the Israelites received the Torah, God reminded them of the promise to lead them to "a land of milk and honey." As a reminder of this promise, the first meal eaten on Shavuot features dairy foods, such as

> "In ancient times the first fruits of the season, called *bikkurim*, were brought to the Temple in Jerusalem as an offering to God."
>
> —Rabbi Ozur Bass

cheesecake, blintzes, and ice cream.

Shavuot falls in springtime, so decorating with spring flowers, and eating fresh seasonal fruits is also a tradition.

The most interesting Shavuot tradition is to stay up all night with friends and family, studying the Torah. There are always lively discussions and debates about history and culture, and wonderful memories are made. This is called a *Tikun Leil Shavuot.*

Will you stay up all night next Shavuot? If you do, be sure to bring some of these delicious treats to your party!

Top your French toast with powdered sugar.

stuffed French toast

Everyone will be delighted by the taste of red, ripe strawberries bursting from this French toast filling. Strawberries are a sweet part of the spring harvest!

get cooking...

1 Whisk eggs, milk, vanilla, and cinnamon together in a shallow bowl. Set aside.

2 Divide strawberry cream cheese among four slices of bread and spread evenly to the edges. Place remaining 4 slices on top to make 4 sandwiches.

3 Heat 1 tablespoon of butter in frying pan over medium heat.

4 Dip one sandwich in the egg mixture and coat it entirely on both sides. Place in pan and cook until golden. Flip and cook until other side is golden. Repeat with remaining butter and sandwiches.

5 When cooked sandwiches have cooled a bit, use cookie cutters to make French toast shapes!

ingredients...

2 eggs

⅔ cup milk

1 teaspoon vanilla extract

½ teaspoon cinnamon

About 4 oz (112 g) strawberry cream cheese, at room temperature (see page 46 for recipe)

8 slices of bread (challah works great!)

4 tablespoons butter

Note: use any flavor cream cheese you like.

This recipe is dairy. For a Kosher meal, serve only with other dairy or pareve foods.

"When I was young, my family used to go strawberry picking every year and we always came home with very full bellies and baskets. To me, the summer still can't start without spending time with my family in the strawberry fields!"
–Rabbi Ozur Bass

5a

Watch out for hot cream cheese!

5b

Use any shapes you want!

French toast tastes great with maple syrup and powdered sugar.

If you like your French toast eggy and rich, allow bread to absorb more mixture.

"No one really knows why we eat dairy on Shavuot. My favorite reason is because we say that the Torah is like milk and honey in our mouths. Just like milk helps us grow and keeps our bodies strong, the Torah helps our minds and souls grow and keeps our communities and families strong."   -Rabbi Ozur Bass

Blintzes are delicious topped with a dollop of sour cream or whipped cream.

blueberry blintzes

Blintzes are pancake-like crepes filled with creamy sweet cheeses. When smothered in blueberry sauce, there is no tastier way to celebrate Shavuot.

get cooking...

1 Preheat oven to 350°F (180°C).

2 Combine all blintz ingredients in bowl except crepes. Spread ¼ cup of mixture down middle of each crepe. Roll crepe and tuck ends in, burrito-style. Place blintzes seam-side down in 8-inch (20-cm) square baking dish.

3 Bake for 10 to 12 minutes or until warmed through.

Fold the sides in as you roll.

4 Combine blueberries, sugar, and cornstarch in small bowl. Microwave for 2 minutes and stir. Microwave for 2 more minutes and stir again, then pour over baked blintzes and serve.

ingredients...

For the blintzes:

1 cup small-curd cottage cheese

1 cup cream cheese, softened

½ cup powdered sugar

1 teaspoon vanilla extract

8 crepes, 8 inches (20 cm) in diameter

Note: Premade crepes can be found in the refrigerated case in the produce section of most grocery stores.

For the blueberry topping:

2 cups frozen blueberries

1 tablespoon sugar

1 teaspoon cornstarch

This recipe is dairy. For a kosher meal, serve only with other dairy or pareve foods.

shavuot

121

classic cheesecake

serves
12

This cheesecake is so good that your family will ask you to make it for every holiday! You can experiment by adding mix-ins like chopped-up cookies or candy bars.

get cooking...

1 Preheat oven to 350°F (180°C). Grease a 9-inch (23-cm) springform pan thoroughly. Be sure to get the bottom edges of the pan.

2 In small bowl, mix crushed cookies and melted butter together until the mixture looks like wet sand. Spoon into bottom of springform pan and press down to form crust.

3 In medium bowl, mix cream cheese and sugar until just combined. Add milk and vanilla, stirring gently. Then, gradually add beaten eggs.

4 Mix in sour cream and flour. If adding mix-ins, stir in gently.

5 Pour mixture into springform pan. Tap pan on countertop to remove air bubbles.

6 Bake for 60 minutes. Do not open the oven door at all, as cheesecake can crack.

7 After 60 minutes, turn oven off, even if cheesecake seems loose in the middle. Leave cheesecake to cool in oven with the door closed for 4 to 5 hours.

8 Refrigerate until served.

ingredients...

For the crust:

25 vanilla wafer cookies, crushed

4 tablespoons butter, melted

For the cheesecake:

2 pounds (900 g) cream cheese, at room temperature

1½ cups sugar

¾ cup milk

1 tablespoon vanilla extract

4 eggs, beaten

1 cup sour cream

3 tablespoons all-purpose flour

Optional:

½ cup mix-ins (such as chocolate chips, crushed cookies, crushed candy bars, broken-up brownies, fudge, peanut butter, or anything else you like)

"On Shavuot there is a tradition to stay up all night with people in the community learning and sharing thoughts about the Torah. Cheesecake is one of the most popular desserts on Shavuot because of the tradition to eat dairy. But I like it because the sugar helps me stay up late!"
—Rabbi Ozur Bass

Ingredients should always be at room temperature when you start.

shavuot

122

This recipe is dairy. For a kosher meal, serve only with other dairy or pareve foods.

To crush cookies, place them in a sealed plastic bag and crush away!

To make this kosher for Passover, simply omit the flour and the cookie crust.

NOTES:

Jot down any notes, thoughts, or ideas that you have about any of the recipes in the book. When you make the recipes again, be sure to check back here to see your comments. This will help you add your personal flair to each dish!

....
....
....
....
....
....
....
....
....
....
....
....
....
....

NOTES:

INDEX

acknowledgments

Author's note:
Thanks to all who tried my recipes and washed my dishes. Special thanks to all my kids at the Charles E. Smith Jewish Day School, who taught me as much as I taught them. Very special thanks to Brian Bloomfield: *Ani L'Dodi V'Dodi Li.* Additional thanks to DK for believing in the value of teaching kids to cook, and for producing such beautiful books to that end. www.teachkidstocook.com

Publisher's note:
DK Publishing would like to thank the many people who made this book so delicious: Angela Coppola and assistants Ghazalle Badiozamani and Alfredo Fernandez; Susan Vajaranant and assistants Noura AlSalem, Matt Burdi, Rebecca Jurkevich, and Tracy Keshani; Josefina Munroe; Tamami Mihara; Liza Kaplan; Eugene Brophy; and Lorraine McCafferty. And especially our models: Andrew Cook, William Cook, Sydney Elizabeth, Allie Roth, David Roth, Daniel Schwabinger, Jake Schwabinger, Rowena Spector, Saskia Spector, Atalya Sternoff, Mia Sternoff, and Lauren Tomaselli.

Thank you to the Kaplan family, and Peggy and Mickey Knox for generously lending their knowledge and Judaica.

A very special thanks goes to the Charles Schiller Studio. www.studio-a-nyc.com

Photo credits:
Page 98: Israeli flag, Getty Images

Author Jill Colella Bloomfield is the founder of Picky Eaters, a kids' cooking consulting company. Along with creating materials for corporations about kids' cooking, she enjoys giving hands-on cooking lessons for kids aged two to teen. A devoted foodie, Jill loves adventures, such as touring farms and visiting food factories. Jill lives in St. Paul, Minnesota, and loves exploring the farmer's markets there.

Consultant Janet Ozur Bass is a Conservative Rabbi who teaches middle schoolers in Maryland. She loves cooking, reading, traveling, and hosting tons of people for every Jewish holiday and occassion she can think of. She has even been known to invent a few just to have an excuse to open her home. Janet is married to a cantor, and they are the proud parents of three terrific children.

Have fun while you cook!